Issues in Contemporary Christian Thought

Issues in Contemporary Christian Thought

A Fortress Introduction

Duane Olson

Fortress Press
Minneapolis

ISSUES IN CONTEMPORARY CHRISTIAN THOUGHT
A Fortress Introduction

Cover image: Descent from the Cross © Banque d'Images, ADAGP / Art Resource, NY
© 2010 Raymond Poulet / Artists Rights Society (ARS), New York / ADAGP, Paris
Cover design: Ivy Palmer Skrade
Book design: PerfecType, Nashville, TN

Library of Congress Cataloging-in-Publication Data
Olson, Duane.
  Issues in contemporary Christian thought : a Fortress introduction / Duane Olson.
    p. cm.
  ISBN 978-0-8006-9665-8 (alk. paper)
  1. Philosophy, Christian. 2. Christianity and culture. I. Title.
  BR100.O47 2011
  230.01--dc22
                                2010044870

Manufactured in the U.S.A.

Contents

Part Three: Christianity and Cultural Transformations

Preface

The thesis of this book is that the developments of modernity are decisive for contemporary Christian self-understanding. In this context, the
meaning of modernity is kept intentionally broad. In its deepest historical reach, it includes the large-scale social and political transformations
that emerged from the Enlightenment period, such as the development
of the modern nation-state and the promotion of democratic political
ideals. It includes the Enlightenment's valorization of the freedom of the
individual, a freedom that includes independent choice in religious matters. It includes the emergence of a secular culture in the West with its
art, music, literature, movies, media, and communal forms. It includes
the demands that have emerged in the past century or two to make real
the promise of liberty for all by overcoming the oppressions manifest
in colonialism, racism, sexism, and heterosexism. Most importantly, it
includes the emergence of independent critical fields of inquiry in the
natural, social, and human sciences, as well as these sciences' major findings throughout the past several centuries.

All these elements and more are what is meant by "modernity" or
"the modern context." While Christianity certainly had a decisive role
to play in birthing this context, it also has had to respond to it. How
can or will the doctrine of creation be made compatible with the physicist's theory about the emergence and history of the material universe
and with the biologist's explanation for the cause of the variety of living
species on earth? How is the Bible to be understood as God's Word, or
Jesus as God's son, given the historian's ideas about how the Bible was
constructed and the Christian community formed? What should be the
role of women in church and society given women's demonstrations of
equal value and ability and their critique of a church that has denied
them opportunity while providing religious justification for this denial?
What about the role of gays and lesbians in church and society? Can
Christianity be of service in restoring the natural environment, or does
it simply promote an orientation that is environmentally destructive?
These are the kinds of questions to which Christianity needs to respond
in the modern context. While some of these questions are newer than

others, none of them are being asked for the first time in the twenty-first century. They have engaged the minds and hearts of countless numbers of professional theologians and faithful laypeople over the past decades, and, in some cases, centuries. Christianity and Christians live in the modern context, even while they wrestle with and ask how the ancient faith they have inherited and to which they are committed is compatible with and should express itself in this context.

The intention of the book, which comes out of this Christian wrestling with modernity, is to give a limited expression to Christian responses to modernity on an introductory level. There are several important elements about the text's approach to this that require explanation. First, the text makes an effort to clarify in the most basic way what modernity itself involves and why it raises certain challenges or questions for Christianity. With this, the book shows how the contemporary context for interpreting Christian meaning is unique from the ancient context in which Christianity emerged, from medieval Christian civilization, and from the period of the Protestant Reformation. Many questions that are potent today simply were not relevant and therefore were not asked in these prior contexts. Establishing and understanding the context from which some distinctively modern questions for Christianity have emerged is part of the task of this text.

Second, as an introduction, this text seeks to present general patterns of the Christian response to modernity as well as some admittedly limited but more in-depth responses of individual theologians. Because the territory to be covered is vast and because there is no systematic way of deriving a necessary set of responses to modernity, in every case there is room for criticism of the patterns of thought and the theologians selected. Openness to such criticism is the risk taken by writing this text. Concern about this risk is mitigated at least somewhat by the acknowledgment that the text makes no claim at comprehensiveness and in the hope that the ideas presented will motivate deeper penetration and engagement with the vast and creative field on which a narrow beam of light has shined.

Third, in covering Christian responses to modernity, the text covers both traditional theological territory and issues that are more strictly cultural. In other words, the text tries to show how intellectual developments in modernity have elicited a variety of responses in Christianity regarding its understanding of creation, the Bible, God, Christ, and human destiny. It also tries to show how multiculturalism, the women's movement, gay rights, and environmental concerns have in their own ways yielded a set of creative responses.

Finally, a word about the use of language in the text needs to be clarified. In this preface and at times in the text, the terms *modernity* or *modern context* are used to refer broadly to the contemporary period. In certain contexts today, these terms no doubt seem outdated. In much of academia, at least, the more common term for the contemporary period is *postmodern*, a term that has been in vogue for several decades. The fact I do not use this term does not imply a rejection of the idea connected to its coinage—namely, that the contemporary context has changed in significant ways from the context of the Enlightenment period. It does not imply a rejection of the insights of postmodernity and its critique of Enlightenment rationality. As I understand it, among other things, postmodernity has stressed the limits of knowledge and been skeptical about universals, often promoting a pluralism of views. In important ways, it has sought to penetrate claims to knowledge to find the power relations, which, in its understanding, are effective in and often determinative of those claims. These insights are valuable and are taken up in a multiplicity of ways in the text. Having said this, however, the term *postmodern* is for the most part avoided in the text for several reasons. For one, in my judgment, the meaning of the term remains unsettled and contested. Beyond the general insights listed above, which can be and often are interpreted in dramatically different ways, the term is often connected to a single kind of contemporary thought embodied in deconstruction. I want to avoid the confusion that would be involved in regarding this single perspective as the only or even predominant contemporary perspective. Further, in displaying the context for contemporary theology, the text often focuses on general patterns of thought and broad historical and scientific conclusions, many of which emerged and eventually became normative over the past several centuries. In examining Christian theological responses, the text often reaches back deeply into the twentieth century and pursues with seriousness some of the directions of thought that emerged between that century's world wars. Given the attempted reach of the text, it is simply not productive to continually bump against the question of just what approaches, conclusions, and insights of what thinkers are modern and what are postmodern. It is to avoid the requirement of hammering out this distinction again and again in the presentation that the term *modern* is used with as broad a meaning as possible, while what are considered typically postmodern ideas are at times freely adopted.

The text itself contains nine chapters. The first five concern modern ideas and aspects of traditional Christian theology, while the last four address cultural issues and Christian life and thought. The first two chapters are intended as a unit and should be understood together. All of the remaining chapters can be read, understood, and taught independently.

When I first came to McKendree University, where I have taught for eleven years as a full-time professor, I was assigned a course called Introduction to Christianity. It is a general education undergraduate course and is typically populated with mostly first- and second-year students. The question I faced in preparing to teach this course was the same one faced by teachers of many other general education courses: Since you only have one course in which to teach a vast area, on what will you focus? Certainly a respectable answer to this question for a course called Introduction to Christianity is to do a historical survey of Christianity. One can establish the Old Testament context from which Christianity emerges, read and study parts of the New Testament, speak about transformations toward orthodoxy in the Patristic period, trace the establishment of Christian civilizations in East and West in the Middle Ages, describe the fracturing of Western Christianity in the Protestant Reformation, and cover the ongoing emergence of Protestant groups in the post-Reformation context. In fact, this is the pattern I followed when I began teaching the course.

While I do not want in any way to diminish the value of learning church history, I became dissatisfied with this approach in this course. As is typical in a modern university, my courses regularly had more women in them than men. I wondered whether these young women knew that this ancient faith about which I was speaking had been re-thought in profound ways by contemporary feminists. Many of my students were science majors, or they were required to take science classes as part of general education. I wondered if they knew about the profound dialogue between science and the Christian faith through the past few centuries. Many of my students were learning critical methodologies for analyzing and interpreting texts in other classes. I wondered if they knew about the generations of ongoing critical scholarship that has been applied to the Bible and whether they had thought about what this might mean for Christianity today. These kinds of questions led me to reshape the class to focus on Christianity in a broad sense and modernity. Out of this reshaping, this text was born.

Over the past several years, I used rudimentary forms of the chapters of this text in my classes, along with other material. In 2009, I was awarded a sabbatical by McKendree University and used that opportunity to write the bulk of this text.

There are many people to thank. I am grateful to McKendree University for providing the sabbatical that led to the writing of this text and for supporting me in the process of its publication. Thanks to my colleagues at McKendree, with whom I am constantly kept in a stimulating and engaging dialogue about a host of issues that deepen and broaden me as a scholar and as a person. Thanks to Michael West and the fine people at Fortress Press whose questions, suggestions, and editing improved this text in multiple ways. Thanks to my research assistant, Michael Anderson, for his careful and critical reading of the text and for helping put together the glossary. The text is better because of his work. Thanks to the students in my Introduction to Christianity class over the years. Virtually all varieties of American Christianity, as well as forms of international Christianity, have been represented in these classes. Many of these students are ardent believers, many are skeptics, and many are reeling from all things Christian. There have been representatives of other world religions, along with confirmed atheists and agnostics. I have learned much about the culture and about the dynamics of contemporary Christianity from engagement with this diversity.

Special thanks must go to the religion majors and minors whom I have had the privilege to teach over the past eleven years at McKendree University. It has been a rare and special treat to be able to have the same students in five, six, or seven different courses. You keep coming back! What more could a teacher want over the years than to be able to sit in seminar after seminar with intelligent, interested, and engaged students and discuss new texts and ideas. In all cases, my goal was to impart some wisdom. In all cases, I ended up receiving more knowledge and insight than I had to give.

Finally, thanks to my daughters, Jody and Robin. You have always given me reason upon reason to feel satisfaction with the present and optimism about the future. And to my wife, Brenda: simple words of thanks fail. I do not know how you do it. You continually have more insight, more ideas, more energy, more understanding, and more good plans than I ever anticipate. I am happy to be part of it.

Part One

Understanding Contemporary Christian Thought

Chapter 1

Setting the Stage: Christianity and the Developments of Modernity

Imagine you lived in Western Europe in 1600. Many elements of your life would be dramatically different. Materially, the majority of people at that time were servants or dependents of aristocratic landowners. Chances are, you would be in that class. Politically, you would live in a monarchy, since there were no democracies. Europe was split into Roman Catholicism in the south and Protestant factions in the north. There was no freedom of religion, only intolerant established religions, so which brand of Christianity you supported would most likely depend on where you were born.

Most significant for the ideas examined in this chapter, whether you were Protestant or Roman Catholic, you would have affirmed certain basic presuppositions about the world, since they were affirmed by all Christian groups of the time. These ideas constituted part of the worldview of people in 1600. A worldview is the set of background presuppositions about reality that is held by the people of an era. These presuppositions are regarded as self-evident, and they remain for the most part unquestioned by the majority of people.

Basic to the worldview of people in 1600 was the affirmation that the universe was created by God according to the story in Genesis 1. In that story, the universe was made in seven days. Human beings were created on the sixth day, and genealogies in the Bible run from the creation of the first man and woman to Abraham and other characters in the Bible. Various biblical scholars attempted to add up those genealogies and determine when the earth was created. The most notable attempt was made by an Irish bishop named James Ussher (1581–1656). Through careful biblical and historical research, he determined that the earth was created in 4004 B.C.E. This date was widely accepted in the English-speaking world, being added as commentary in the versions of numerous Bibles. Thus, the universe was seen as very young.

Not only was the universe thought to be young, but following the biblical story, the universe was considered to be small and shaped with the earth at its center. This made sense experientially, since from the perspective of the earth's inhabitants, the sun and stars seem to move around the earth. It also made sense religiously, since the creation story and biblical history make it clear that the creation and destiny of human beings are the central purpose of creation. Logically, then, humans should be in the spatial center of the universe.

As the Genesis story continues, human beings are created from the dust of the earth by a special act of God. All humankind descends from a common pair named Adam and Eve. This pair had been placed in a paradisial garden, but because of their disobedience to God, they were kicked out. God altered reality as punishment for their disobedience. Sin, hardship, and physical death were brought into the world for the first time. For European Christians in 1600, the ultimate explanation for why we suffer, why we must die, and why we do wrong was rooted in the primal sin of our ancestors.

Not only was the story of the creation and fall of humanity into sin accepted as literally true in 1600, but so was the entirety of the biblical account. There was no official doctrinal formulation of the literal truth of all parts of the Bible, nor was there a serious concern to prove the literal truth of the Bible. Instead, it was taken for granted. In the biblical story, God is a dramatic actor on the stage of human history. God calls Abraham and sets his people apart for a special relationship and special destiny. God speaks to Moses from a burning bush and miraculously leads the children of Israel out of slavery in Egypt, gives them a divinely ordained law, miraculously sustains them when they wander in the wilderness, and miraculously leads them to conquer the promised land. When the Israelites disobey, God raises up another nation to destroy them, but God brings them back from exile in order to do the greatest thing of all: to come in the flesh to redeem God's people in Jesus' death and resurrection. Because the Jews, who were originally chosen to be God's people, rejected Jesus, God rejected them and established his people as the Christian church. Whether you were Protestant or Catholic, you regarded yourself as standing in the legacy of that unique realization of God's will in the world.

Clearly, many people in Western civilization today take issue with parts or all of this worldview. The Genesis story is widely disregarded as giving a scientific account of the process of creation or the cause of evil, suffering, and death. Our vast universe is understood to be billions of years old, and convincing evidence has been given that life on the planet evolved over the course of hundreds of millions of years through natural selection. Furthermore, a new way of viewing biblical history has developed and become normative in academic scholarship on the Bible. Academic scholars think the biblical history was written in layers by a community whose beliefs developed over a long period of time. The community continually looked back on its history and reshaped it, giving different interpretations of that history in light of present events and beliefs. Moreover, scholars understand the biblical writers as having been influenced by the worldview of their time not only in scientific matters, but also in ethical, social, and political matters. From the contemporary perspective, much of what the biblical writers present as normative presupposes an alien worldview.

The story of the contemporary worldview's emergence from the common presuppositions of 1600 is the story of the development of modern thought. While it may seem odd to begin a book on contemporary Christianity with a look at the developments of modern thought, it is important to do so because understanding its emergence and the questions it brings helps to understand contemporary Christianity. While in many ways Christianity spawned modern thought, it has also been compelled to respond to significant questions raised by modern thought. This chapter explains in broad outline the meaning of the emergence of modern thought for Christianity. The following chapter provides a framework that articulates some of the main Christian responses to the developments of modernity.

The Enlightenment and the Development of Critical and Autonomous Reason

The historical movement most responsible for the development of modern thought is the Enlightenment. The Enlightenment was a movement of thought among the intelligentsia in Western Europe and the American colonies that began in the seventeenth century and reached its zenith in the eighteenth. Some of its most notable representatives were Diderot, Voltaire, and Rousseau in France; Reimarus, Lessing, and Kant in the German states; Bacon, Locke, and Hume in Great Britain; and Jefferson, Madison, Franklin, and Paine in the American colonies.

While the Enlightenment was a diverse movement, its most characteristic feature was the elevation of human reason. The elevation of human reason refers to the affirmation of the capacity of the human mind to discover what is good and what is true by reflecting on reality on its own, or independent of reliance on external authorities. This includes the affirmation of the capacity of the human mind to discover what is good and true without relying on revealed authorities such as the Bible or church teaching. Immanuel Kant said the motto of the Enlightenment was "Dare to know! 'Have the courage to use your own understanding.'" He said the Enlightenment represented the "emergence from . . . the inability to use one's own understanding without another's guidance."[1] The Enlightenment sought to transcend the condition in which humans did not make full use of their reason but submitted to external authorities to know what was true and good.

This elevation of reason put it above the position it had been granted in previous Christian history. In classical Christian theology, while human reason was thought to be warped by sin, it was believed to have been made by God and it had an important role to play in Christian reflection. Many great thinkers of the Middle Ages used reason either to explain certain Christian beliefs or to show that certain Christian beliefs could be proven true. However, reason was always limited or circumscribed by a commitment to revelation. Revelation was understood as God's act of communication to human beings. The record of that communication is the Christian Bible. In interpreting the Bible, the church had developed doctrines including the belief that God is a Trinity and Jesus is an incarnation of God. These doctrines were accepted as true and taken to be beyond the pale of criticism by human reason. The Bible and the church doctrines derived from it were authorities. They represented divine truth, and human reason was subject to them. With the elevation of human reason in the Enlightenment, many Enlightenment thinkers reversed this relationship for the first time since Christianity became dominant in Western history in the fourth century. Instead of accepting the Bible and church doctrines as unquestioned authorities, they subjected these authorities to human reason. The power they found in human reason transcended even revelation.

For Enlightenment thinkers, the appeal of human reason lay in its universality. Everyone has reason; therefore, whatever is discovered by reason is accessible and provable by all. While matters of taste, such as a preference for chocolate or vanilla ice cream, may be private, all that reason discovers about the universe and its operation, about proper human behavior, about what lies beyond the universe is open to proof or disproof and therefore to universal assent by all. What was needed was simply an unbiased way of looking at the data. Enlightenment thinkers were convinced that such an unbiased perspective is possible, and that philosophical reflection and the developing sciences in every field could examine their data in rigorous, methodical, and unbiased ways to establish universal knowledge.

Because reason was directed to what is universally true, it offered hope of transcending the particularities of religion based on revelation. Roman Catholics, Protestant groups, Jews, and Muslims all claimed they had the true revelation or interpretation of that revelation vis-à-vis each other. If reason simply had to submit to revelation, there was no way of adjudicating their conflicting claims. Many Enlightenment thinkers thought reason should supersede revelation, or at least purify it, and thereby reduce the claims of revelation to an essential core that could be affirmed by reason and was common to all religions.[2] The very need for revelation implies a human incapacity that many Enlightenment thinkers were unwilling to admit. They thought if God had to reveal things to human beings in history and act in history to save people, then God had not made human minds and wills very well in the first place. This was an inadequacy they were unwilling to claim either of God or of the human mind and will.[3]

With their demand that religion be universal and reasonable, some Enlightenment thinkers created a rival religion to Christianity called Deism.[4] This was the first non-Christian religion to emerge on Christian soil since the triumph of Christianity over the paganism of the Roman Empire in the fourth century. Many parts of Deism were rooted in and compatible with Christian beliefs of the time. For example, Deists believed the order of the world proves that a good and rational Creator made it, and they thought the rationality and goodness of the Creator were revealed more and more as human beings uncovered the laws by which the universe operates. With the Christian thinking of the time, they affirmed that God gave people an immortal soul and a conscience to know the difference between right and wrong. They tended to be more optimistic than classical Christianity about human capacities. Deists believed people have free will and are able to do what is right, and they thought rewards and punishments would follow in the afterlife based on people's actions in this life.

What was notably absent from Deism was any belief in miraculous divine intervention in the world, and this is where it veered most sharply from standard Christian views. Such divine action was deemed unnecessary because God had made human beings properly in the first place. Belief in divine intervention was considered superstitious. The universe was conceived as a great machine, and the emerging natural sciences discovered rational laws by which the universe operates that were thought to be immutable. Belief in divine intervention was placed on the same level as belief in fairies or trolls, or the belief that a black cat brings bad luck. Accepting it meant resorting to an illogical explanation for events instead of relying on a rational explanation.

Not everything Enlightenment thinkers said and did had lasting significance. While influential, the religion of Deism never achieved great popularity among the masses of people, and it largely faded from the scene in the nineteenth century. Today, Enlightenment thinkers are roundly criticized for being overly confident about the objective and universal scope of reason. A vast new intellectual movement has risen that calls itself "postmodern." While this is a diverse movement, two common themes of postmodernity are the limitations of reason and the affirmation that the thinking subject is always embedded in a particular time and place with presuppositions that the subject can never fully escape. The presuppositions of the knower always affect the reflective process in such a way that humans can never see reality in a purely objective and universally rational way. These are vital and significant insights that are taken seriously by scores of contemporary thinkers, even while individual thinkers interpret the precise meaning of these insights in different ways. In general, the very use of the term "post-modern" implies that the modern period, which is primarily identified with the Enlightenment, is over. Despite this understanding, however, it is important not to overlook the contributions of the Enlightenment. The Enlightenmenteffectively changed the character of intellectual reflection in the West. The work of Enlightenment thinkers initiated an enduring pattern of thinking that remains significant today even for postmodern thinkers who point out the limitations of Enlightenment thought.

Two important aspects to the enduring pattern of thinking inherited from the Enlightenment are the critical and the autonomous sides of reason. Critical reason refers to reason's power to critique religious authorities or sacred objects rather than simply submit to them. Reason today, as it functions in Western academic contexts, for example, does not presuppose it must submit to the teachings of church, synagogue, or mosque. Except in some private religious schools, academic instructors do not sign a religious creed assenting to a certain set of beliefs, thereby giving the assurance that what they find in their research and say to students will not conflict with those beliefs. The lack of such submission means that reason wields a potentially critical power in relation to religious beliefs. Scholars are free to criticize religious ideas on the basis of independent research and reflection in their fields. This does not mean all academic scholars reject religion, and in fact, this is far from the case. It does mean, however, that they are free to reject it or to criticize, adapt, and rethink religious ideas as they deem appropriate, instead of simply submitting to traditional religious convictions. Not only in academia, but in news outlets, the popular media, and the culture more broadly, one finds the expression of the free critical power of reason in relation to religion.

Autonomous reason refers to the power of reason to construct new ideas on its own. Autonomy means "self-law," so autonomous reason is reason that discovers truths by itself and functions by its own laws, or its own critique of itself, instead of submitting to authorities. This aspect of reason inherited from the Enlightenment is responsible for creating the independent sciences as we know them today—the natural, social, and human sciences. Over the past few centuries, these scientific fields have broken free from submission to religious authorities, and secular academia functions on its own. Physicists and biologists, for example, do not first submit to the truth of the biblical account of creation before analyzing their data. Instead, they independently analyze their data, following a tradition of such independent analysis in their fields in which they generate and test hypotheses about the data regardless of whether their hypotheses accord with the biblical account or not. The proper method to analyze the data and the correct hypotheses to account for the data are matters of consensus and ongoing debate, but decisions about method and content are to be made by rational reflection and not by assent to a revealed authority. The quoting of biblical verses as proof texts about the origin of the universe has no weight in a scientific discussion that analyzes the data on the basis of autonomous reason.[5]

When reason is both autonomous and critical, it may come into conflict with the Bible and church teaching. Autonomous reason discovers new truths about reality. On the basis of these new truths, critical reason may critique a biblical account or a doctrine of the church, or argue it is to be understood in a new way. This is the situation of reflection in academia and the broader culture today, and it is an inheritance of the elevation of reason and critique of authority introduced in the Enlightenment. It explains the breakdown of the monolithic worldview held in 1600, described at the beginning of this chapter.

ADDITIONAL INFORMATION

Galileo, Scientific Method, and Church Authority

Galileo Galilei (1564–1642) was one of the rare scientific geniuses of Western history. His work was so novel and brilliant that not only what he discovered but also the method he used to make his discoveries changed the course of future scientific inquiry. Galileo is widely credited for inaugurating the modern scientific method in which hypotheses using mathematical calculations are combined in an interactive way with rigorous experiments and observations in order to come to verifiable conclusions. Using this method, he made extraordinary advances in the human understanding of the nature of motion.

Galileo also explored the movement of heavenly bodies. He built on and transformed previous theories about the place of the earth in relationship to the sun. Famously, combining theory with observation, he became convinced that the earth spins, and the earth and the other planets move around the sun, rather than the sun and planets moving around the earth. He made his view known publicly, only to have the Inquisition of the Roman Catholic Church denounce the position as contrary to what was then regarded as known physics and the teaching of the Bible. This did not stop Galileo from eventually publishing his views, for which he was brought to trial before the Inquisition in 1633, condemned, forced to recant his views, and held under house arrest for the remainder of his life.

Galileo was no materialistic atheist, a position that would become acceptable in Western history only centuries later. By all accounts, he was a pious Christian believer and ardent lover of the church. Like other scientists of the early modern period, he understood his scientific work in theological terms as disclosing truths about the wondrous universe God made, and as an expression whose purpose was to give glory to God. He was, however, working at a time in which the natural sciences had not yet emerged from religious control. They had not yet become autonomous, something that would happen only after his time as the result of the influence of the Enlightenment. In Galileo's time, not only were the sciences under religious control, but the religious authorities read the Bible literally and thought at least certain truths of the natural sciences could be derived from that reading. Such truths had divine sanction and were not to be contradicted.

In his letters and writings, Galileo himself tried to argue for another position. He claimed the Bible and science have different goals. The Bible teaches about salvation, while science teaches about how the universe operates. Consequently, there should be no interference or conflict between what each one affirms. If there appears to be conflict, he argued, the Bible should not be taken literally. Scripture could still be regarded as true if it were interpreted in a metaphorical fashion. Galileo did not take the posture of critical reason and argue that the limitations of the biblical writers mean some affirmations of the Bible are not to be regarded as true. Instead, he affirmed that if it is interpreted correctly, the Bible can still be understood as true. Critical reason in relation to the Bible would emerge only later in Western history, also as a result of Enlightenment influence.

Despite his time and place in history and the tragic way he was treated by the church, Galileo inaugurated new ways of thinking about the relationship between Christian faith and the emerging natural sciences. His work stands at the beginning of a debate about the relationship between Christianity and the natural sciences that continues strongly into the present day.[6]

Historical Criticism of the Bible

In the seventeenth and eighteenth centuries, many Christians were oblivious to or unconcerned with the transformations of thinking that were characteristic of the Enlightenment. Other Christians were aware of these transformations and either resisted them, thinking they threatened Christianity, or embraced them, thinking they were an outgrowth of Christianity and could be shown to be compatible with it. Whatever the individual responses in the period of the Enlightenment, the impact of the emergence of modern thought on Christianity has only deepened over time, and it is no longer a serious option for Christians to ignore it.

This section delves more deeply into the questions modern thought has raised for Christianity by looking at an important development in modernity called historical criticism or higher criticism of the Bible.

Tracing the development and major findings of historical criticism vividly shows the impact of autonomous and critical reason on Christianity. It also exposes significant questions regarding the formulation of traditional Christian doctrines. Prominent among the questions raised is the nature of the relationship between faith and history, a question that the remainder of this chapter will engage in a significant way.

Historical criticism is a summary term for a view of the Bible that affirms the cultural conditioning and limitations, as well as the individual creativity, of the biblical authors. Historical criticism flourished particularly in Germany in the eighteenth and nineteenth centuries, and in the twentieth century, it became part of mainstream academic scholarship on the Bible everywhere in the West. It is the standard scholarly approach to the Bible in academia today, as reflected in the fact that it is used in all mainstream introductory academic textbooks on the biblical literature.[7] While historical criticism examines the Bible with a critical eye and traces the human element involved in the construction of the Bible, this does not mean it is incompatible with the affirmation that the Bible is divine revelation. Historical criticism has been embraced by many Christian denominations, and hosts of leading historical critics are also Christian believers. What historical criticism does, however, is raise questions about how Christians can and should understand the Bible as divine revelation. Examining what historical criticism is and looking at some of its major findings show how this is the case.

The Two Main Hypotheses of Historical Criticism

As autonomous reason made key discoveries in the natural sciences in the nineteenth century, these discoveries pointed to the scientific limitations of the biblical authors. The fact that the earth is not the center of the universe was well established by the nineteenth century, but it was in the nineteenth century that it was postulated through studying the stratigraphy of the earth and fossil records that the earth was much older than the six thousand years affirmed by the biblical account. In 1859, Charles Darwin built on the idea of an ancient earth in his groundbreaking work *The Origin of Species*. He argued that all complex life-forms, including human beings, evolved from less complex forms by natural selection over vast reaches of time. While there was initial controversy about Darwin's theory in the scientific community, evolution through natural selection became accepted fairly quickly as the normative large-scale explanatory paradigm for understanding diversity in biological phenomena, and it remains so today.

These scientific findings compelled many Christians to face, for the first time, the idea that in the biblical stories of creation and fall in Genesis 1–3, God was not supernaturally imparting information about the beginnings of the universe to an author who could not possibly have been there to witness the events. Instead, the author or authors were creatively retelling stories that expressed beliefs the ancient Israelites held about God, creation, and the origin of evil. Quite naturally, these stories presupposed the scientific worldview of the ancient Israelites, who did not know about the discoveries of Copernicus or Darwin. Autonomous reason in the natural sciences, along with critical reason's interrogation of the biblical literature, showed the scientific limitations of the biblical authors. They held to the science of a bygone era that modern people could no longer accept.

Historical critics affirmed more than just scientific limitations of the biblical authors. Analyzing the Bible with the same critical tools they used to analyze other historical documents, critics argued the biblical authors were conditioned and limited broadly by their culture. While they worked creatively within those limitations, the biblical authors were limited historically, ethically, and theologically.

Using critical reason, historical critics asked penetrating questions about the historical texts of the Bible: What did the writers know? How did they know it? When did they write? As a concrete example, consider the story of God's calling of Abram in Gen. 12:1-9 (Abram's name is later changed to Abraham). In these verses, God makes tremendous promises to Abram that a great nation will come from him, that all people of the earth will be blessed by him, and that his children will inherit the land that came to be known as Israel. Critical reason naturally asks how the writer knew this happened. Was the writer there with Abram when God spoke to him, so the writer heard God's voice as well? Did Abram tell someone, who told someone, who told the writer?

This critical questioning of the text led historical critics to certain basic hypotheses about the construction of the historical sections of the Bible. Two main hypotheses form the framework for the analysis of the text by contemporary historical critics. The first one is that there is a gap between the historical events recorded in the Bible and the writing down of those events by the biblical writers. In the case of the New Testament Gospels, the length of time was several decades, but in the case of the narratives in the Hebrew Bible, it was often hundreds of years. There is evidence of this gap throughout the biblical narratives. In fact, in the story of the calling of Abram in Gen. 12:1-9, the author lets the reader know he or she is telling of an event in the past when the author says, "*At that time* the Canaanites were in the land" (12:6, italics added). The author is saying that back when the calling of Abram occurred, the Canaanites were in the land. This implies the Canaanites are not in the land when the author is writing. Since the Israelites followed the Canaanites into the land, the author must be writing when the Israel-ites are there. When you trace the history implied by this affirmation, it means the author is writing a story about events purported to have hap-pened at least five hundred and probably closer to eight hundred years before the time of the author.

Between the event and the writing down of the event, the commu-nity that finally wrote the Bible transmitted a memory of the event at first by word of mouth. This is commonly called "oral tradition" by historical critics. Generations of people told and retold the events of the past and in this way kept a memory of their history alive. Eventually, some of this material was written down in diverse sources that the biblical writers used in combination with oral tradition to write their narratives.

The uncovering of this process implies that the biblical authors were historically conditioned and limited. They had sparse historical informa-tion that had been passed on through the generations in complex and very human ways. The information they received and used was subject to the vagaries of all such human transmission.

The second hypothesis of historical critics is that the community and the biblical authors transformed the events of the past primarily out of a theological interest. The believing community, whether it was the ancient Israelites or the early believers in Jesus, was not strictly con-cerned with detailing accurate history. The community was concerned with understanding what it thought God was doing in history. Based on what the community understood God to be doing in the present, the community and, subsequently, the biblical authors themselves changed the details of past events and even created entire stories of events.

Consider again the story of God calling Abram and giving promises to him in Genesis 12. Most historical critics think this story has only a faint historical core. On the whole, it is the creation of the Israelites, who were already a nation in the land of Israel and who looked back upon their coming into the land as the activity of God. The Israelites thought God put them in the land and made them a great nation. This was their theological conviction. They also remembered Abraham as their most distant ancestor, as a kind of founding father of the Israelites as a people. They created the story of God's calling and giving these specific promises to Abraham to stress their conviction that being who they were, where they were, was God's will. It was the unfolding of a plan that God had for them all along. In this interpretation, the story does not so much explain what happened to Abraham as it exposes the later Israelites' theological convictions.

The hypothesis that the biblical writers changed and created stories primarily out of a theological interest implies that the biblical writers were in some sense limited and conditioned by their time theologically. They sought to interpret God's actions in their history, but they had no absolute transcendent standpoint from which to make this interpretation. Neither Abraham, nor Moses, nor the biblical historians had directly imparted supernatural knowledge about the past. Nor did they have such knowledge about the future. Instead, the historians who wrote the biblical text all sought to understand God's actions in the past, and they projected the future in different ways in light of this understanding.

Combining the two hypotheses of historical criticism yields the main approach of historical critics to the biblical narrative as a whole. To historical critics, the biblical narrative consists of a fusion of events from the past and theological interpretations that change and transform those events. Historical critics argue about how much of the text narrates actual history and how much of it involves the transformation of events by theological interpretation, but this argument takes place from within the supposition that the text includes both elements.

Theological Questions and Challenges Raised by Historical Criticism

Historical criticism of the Bible emerges from the development of critical and autonomous reason and has become part of the contemporary worldview of many Westerners. Its emergence has raised a number of important theological questions and challenges. Two of the major challenges are examined in this section. These challenges are new in Christian history in the sense that Christians who lived before the rise of historical criticism did not have to face them in the same way or with the same power as those who live with the legacy of historical criticism.

The first and perhaps most obvious challenge historical criticism brings to theology is that it calls into question the absolute veracity of the biblical narrative. Put bluntly, historical critics claim things did not always happen in the way things are said to have happened in the Bible. There is an overlay of creative interpretation and transformation of events by the believing community that transmitted the memory of those events and by the biblical writers who creatively wrote down those interpretations. Given this interpretation of the biblical text, what does it mean for Christian doctrines that are based on historical events and, in particular, for doctrines based on miraculous events? The Bible often records divine intervention in the form of miracles, and a standard understanding of those doctrines claims the miracles actually occurred. Consider, for example, not only the miracles Jesus is purported to have done during his lifetime, which many Christians throughout history have claimed give testimony to his divine status, but also the miracles that happened to him, including the virgin birth, his bodily resurrection from the dead, and his ascension into heaven. Historical criticism at least raises the question of whether they actually happened. Are they based on real historical memory, or are they the creative theological interpretations of early believers in Jesus?

Some historical critics argue for the latter, not only for the miracles related to Jesus, but for all the miracles recorded in the Bible. They claim there is a significant difference in thinking between the ancient biblical writers and modern people. Since the ancient authors wrote before the development of the natural and social sciences, they often gave a supernatural cause to events they did not understand but to which contemporary people would give a natural cause.[8] Being ancient people, the biblical writers had a worldview that affirmed the reality of direct divine intervention in history, while people today can no longer affirm such a worldview and need to have alternative explanations or interpretations of what the biblical writers understood and presented as miraculous divine intervention.

Other historical critics disagree and claim the ancient biblical writers' understanding of the universe was not that far from the contemporary understanding. While there may be exaggeration at times in the biblical text, and all recorded miracles may not have occurred, or did not occur precisely as the text claims, this does not mean no miracles occurred. In any case, however, this debate about the veracity of miracles and what it implies for the understanding of Christian doctrines is a new debate that has emerged as historical criticism has become the normative approach to the Bible. In 1600, a Christian scholar who questioned whether the miracles recorded in the Bible actually occurred would have been labeled a dangerous heretic. Today, it is commonplace for Christian scholars to question whether recorded miracles happened and to take a stand on the issue one way or the other.

The second major theological challenge raised by historical criticism is its affirmation that the biblical text does not have a completely unified point of view. For historical criticism, the biblical text developed over time as the authors of the text and the community from which the Bible came engaged in a continuous interpretation of events. Sometimes biblical authors of the same period interpreted events differently or in ways that stood in tension with one another. Sometimes, as events changed, the theological interpretations of the community changed, and the community adapted and rewrote its history. While old interpretations were often expunged, at times they were allowed to remain in the text, and a new understanding of what God was doing that stood in tension with an old one was placed alongside the old. The biblical text contains multiple interpretations and layers of interpretation built upon one another, many of which stand in some level of tension or conflict with one another.

The fact that the biblical text has layers of interpretation in tension with one another is a challenge for theology because traditionally Christian doctrines were thought to be derivable from the single voice of the Bible. Since the Bible was divinely inspired, the doctrines were thought to be equally inspired, expressing biblical truth in concise and abstract form. If the biblical writers did not have a single voice but the text presents a range of theological options, which of the options within this range is true?

This last question can be developed with two major examples. A long-standing argument in Christian theology claims that one proof of the fact that Jesus is the Messiah is that hundreds of years before Jesus came, Old Testament prophets predicted a Messiah would come and do precisely what Jesus did.[9] This argument, showing the connection between Old Testament prophecy and New Testament fulfillment by Jesus, is used to prove that the events of the incarnation, death, and resurrection of Jesus must be part of a divine plan. Historical critics have shown, however, that the Old Testament has a variety of perspectives about the future. It does not uniformly point to the coming of a Messiah, nor does it present in undeniable detail that the Messiah will do what Jesus did. Among other things, this approach affirms that a Jewish interpretation—one that denies Jesus is the Messiah—can be based on a legitimate reading of the Old Testament. If the Old Testament does not uniformly and unambiguously point in one direction, what does this mean for the Christian affirmation that Jesus is God's Messiah?

ADDITIONAL INFORMATION

The Suffering Servant of Isaiah

One of the most renowned passages in the Hebrew Bible for the Christian interpretation of Jesus as fulfilling God's plan as the Messiah is the passage about a "suffering servant" in Isa. 52:13—53:12. This passage describes a servant of the Jewish God, Yahweh. The servant goes through tremendous suffering without complaint. This suffering is at the hands of others and is clearly a matter of injustice. The servant is brought to death. Surprisingly, however, this suffering and death is interpreted as part of Yahweh's plan (53:10-12). The servant suffers unjustly as an offering for the sins of others in the same way that an animal brought to the temple as a sin offering suffers for the sins of those who brought it. Because of the servant's willingness to suffer as part of God's plan, God will exalt and raise the servant to a high status.

The early Christian community clearly used this passage—along with many others, of course—to understand the meaning of Jesus' death and resurrection. In Acts 8:32-35, the disciple Philip affirms that a quote from Isaiah 53 refers to Jesus.

It is easy to see how this passage could be applied to Jesus by Christians. Most academic scholars today, however, think that in its context, the passage refers to the nation of Israel in its exile. The suffering of the servant described in the passage is in the past tense. Only the anticipated exaltation is in the future tense. Scholars think this passage was written by an unknown prophet around 540 B.C.E., a time when it looked as if the defeated Israel, which had undergone suffering and exile to a foreign land, was going to be set free and allowed to return to its homeland. The unknown prophet, using poetic metaphor, spoke of the nation of Israel as Yahweh's servant and described the nation's suffering and exile as if it were a death. Surprisingly, this was seen as part of Yahweh's plan. The nation suffered for others, and other nations would realize this when Israel was freed from captivity and allowed to return to its homeland in glory.

If this passage in context refers to the nation of Israel, it complicates the simple Christian interpretation that claims a prophet from hundreds of years in the past miraculously predicted in detail what would happen in the future when Jesus came. It does not necessarily deny Christians the opportunity to apply this passage to Jesus. Christians can still claim that a passage that meant one thing in the Old Testament context can express ideas or meanings that help explain what God is doing in the new and different context of Jesus' life, death, and resurrection. In fact, many Christians today embrace this interpretation. However, this is a more complex and nuanced interpretation than the claim that detailed knowledge was miraculously given by God to a prophet who wrote about events that were to happen hundreds of years later. In this more nuanced view, one must admit that other possibilities for interpretation of this passage are also present.

Another example is the New Testament authors' understanding of Jesus. Since the time Christianity affirmed in its major creeds that Jesus was an incarnation of God, both fully God and fully human, it has been assumed that the New Testament unambiguously affirms this position. However, historical critics have shown this assumption is not so easy to make. When one examines the individual authors of the New Testament in their own right, it appears they did not all understand Jesus to have been an incarnation of God who was both fully God and fully human. Some writers thought of Jesus as a human being who was full of God's Spirit and who was adopted by God, performed God's will, and was exalted by God for his faithfulness.[10] What does it mean for contemporary theology if the New Testament writers had more than one view of Jesus?

This chapter has attempted to show that the kinds of insights and questions that arise with the development of modern thought are important for contemporary Christian self-understanding. While many Christians find the insights and questions of modernity threatening, others have found them exhilarating, and they have spawned a creative outpouring of theological reflection in the contemporary period. The next four chapters cover some of this creative outpouring. Chapter 2 presents a framework situating major theological positions in relation to the developments of modern thought. Chapters 3, 4, and 5 each deal with the development of classical theological themes before examining the way some contemporary theologians have understood and at times transformed those themes, given the insights of modern thought.

Chapter 2

Surveying the Field: Options in Contemporary Christian Thought

This chapter presents a broad framework with a typology whose purpose is to explain some of the variety in contemporary Christian theology. The typology establishes categories that make distinctions between truly divergent theological positions while also embracing many individual theologians and believers under a common type.

Every typology must be established by some principle, and the main principle used in this typology is the relationship between faith and history. The reason for choosing this idea is that it is a significant factor for theology, given the developments of modern thought described in the previous chapter. Admittedly, there are other possible ways of organizing the field of theology today, and if other criteria were used, theologians and groups of believers would be arranged differently. This raises an important point: although there are significant differences among the types presented here, representatives of the different types may still hold much in common. All representatives of all types believe life-transforming power is present and available to Christians because of what God has done in Jesus Christ, even though they may interpret the meaning of that belief differently.

Furthermore, while the categories used in this chapter are meant to clarify differences among Christian believers and theologians, these categories are not exhaustive, and they are not straitjackets. They do not say all there is to say about different theologians' insights and creativity, and it is certainly possible for individuals to combine aspects of two or more of the types presented here.

The examination of each type involves analyzing its claims regarding the historical reliability of the biblical narrative, including the creation and fall stories of Genesis 1–3 and the important Christian doctrines of the virgin birth, incarnation, bodily resurrection, ascension, and second coming of Jesus. The examination also covers the question of how the various claims with regard to these issues could be justified.

Biblical Literalism

One important response to the developments of modernity discussed in the previous chapter, including the development of historical criticism of the Bible, is to call those developments into question and affirm biblical literalism. In general, biblical literalists refute modernity, elevating the literal truth of the Bible and a traditional understanding of many Christian doctrines. They do this over against what they regard as the so-called truths of the modern world.

Biblical literalists have a profound reverence for the Bible. It is a sacred authority, the word of God. Their attitude of reverence for the whole Bible keeps them from taking a critical stand in relation to it. Instead of criticizing the Bible on any level, biblical literalists claim human reason should subject itself to the truth of the Bible.

For biblical literalists, the Bible is true because it is directly inspired by God. Although fallible humans wrote the Bible, biblical literalists affirm God worked supernaturally, inspiring the biblical writers and assuring that what they wrote down was what God wanted. For many biblical literalists, the first theological doctrine they affirm is that the Bible is inerrant (meaning without error) or infallible. Theologians who take this perspective have developed sophisticated ways of expressing what biblical inerrancy or infallibility means, given the great variety of literature in the biblical text. Important to such meaning is the affirmation of the historical accuracy and theological unity of the Bible.[1]

Biblical literalists recognize that the message of the biblical writers was originally directed to people who were living in different historical and cultural situations than our own. Because of this, the biblical authors wrote in the language of the time (Hebrew or Greek), using all of the idioms of that language, and often presupposed familiar historical and cultural knowledge of their audience. Owing to these linguistic, historical, and cultural factors, many biblical literalists affirm the importance of studying the original languages of the Bible and learning as much as can be learned about biblical history and culture. The difference between biblical literalists and those who accept historical criticism, however, is that while literalists recognize the biblical writers spoke *to* a culture, they deny the biblical writers were limited or conditioned *by* their culture in what they wrote. To literalists, the biblical writers transcended their cultural limitations in writing God's word that is transcendent of all cultural limitations. This transcendence is a miracle, since ordinary humans are always limited and conditioned by their culture.

In speaking God's word above the conditioning of their culture, biblical literalists affirm that the biblical writers agree on their message. From Genesis to Revelation, the Bible is thought to have a single, unified message. The New Testament writers agree with each other, and they correctly interpret the Old Testament, which uniformly points to the New. Since biblical literalists think the Bible has a unified message, many interpret different parts of the Bible in light of each other, a method that makes sense if you believe the authors are ultimately presenting a single message from God without any levels of disagreement. Although biblical literalists create different kinds of theology from the Bible, they think these different theologies are due to the limitations and errors of biblical interpreters, not due to multiple perspectives within the text itself.

On matters of science, many biblical literalists continue to accept the story in Genesis 1 of creation in seven literal days. However, some regard the scientific evidence for an old earth as so overwhelming they think the biblical author was being intentionally metaphorical when writing of a seven-day creation. These literalists think the "days" referred to in Genesis are actually metaphors for vast periods of time. The acceptance of an old earth, however, does not imply the acceptance of the theory of evolution of species through natural selection. Instead, these literalists affirm that while the earth is old and may have ancient life-forms on it, God created the distinct species of life whenever and wherever these exist. This is especially the case for human beings, who are regarded as having been made by a special act of God according to the story in Genesis 2–3. In general, biblical literalists affirm there was a literal garden of Eden and a literal Adam and Eve. Adam and Eve are the literal parents of the entire human race, and they initiated the human fall into sin with its consequences.

ADDITIONAL INFORMATION

Teaching Evolution in the Public Schools

In 1925, John Scopes, a high school biology teacher in Dayton, Tennessee, was found guilty of teaching the theory that "man was descended from a lower order of animals."[2] Scopes had openly violated what was then a new Tennessee law against teaching evolution in the public schools. Scopes was encouraged to come forward and admit this violation by the American Civil Liberties Union, which wanted to expose the issue and force a trial about it. Two of the nation's leading lawyers, Clarence Darrow and William Jennings Bryan, took up the case, and the trial that led to the charge against Scopes was a national sensation.

On the whole, the trial was not about whether Scopes violated the law, since Scopes freely admitted he did, and the defense was not concerned with denying he did. Instead, the defense made the trial about the legitimacy of the law against teaching evolution. At the time, certain Christian groups were mounting campaigns against the teaching of evolution in public schools and waging battles to outlaw it. They argued that public schools should teach belief in divine creation as expressed in the biblical book of Genesis instead of belief in evolution. They had succeeded in getting the new law against teaching evolution passed in Tennessee. These anti-evolution forces found their hero in the prosecuting attorney, William Jennings Bryan, who was a national figure, having run for president several times. Bryan was a leader in the broader anti-evolution movement, and he agreed to take up this case although he had not practiced law for some time.

Scopes was represented by the renowned attorney Clarence Darrow. Darrow tried to use the spotlight of this case to argue for the importance of progressive scientific learning in public schools, learning that invariably should include the teaching of evolution. In the process, Darrow attempted to show the intellectual backwardness and ignorance of those in the anti-evolution movement who held to a literalist reading of the Bible. In a dramatic moment, he actually called Bryan to the stand and questioned him not just about belief in a literal reading of the first few chapters of Genesis, but about belief in a literal reading of all kinds of biblical passages. Most analysts of the case regard this as a moment of victory for Darrow, who effectively presented Bryan as confused and out of touch.

The outcome of the trial was that Scopes was found guilty and fined $100, although the verdict was later overturned on a legal technicality. What the trial meant culturally, then and now, continues to be analyzed. At least in one important layer of analysis, the anti-evolution forces suffered a serious setback as a result of the trial, because they were presented in much of the national media as backward and ignorant.

In the decades after the trial, the theory of evolution gained even greater acceptance in the scientific community. At the same time, in certain locales, there remained attempts to outlaw or circumscribe the teaching of evolution in the public schools. Legal cases from the 1960s forward bear witness to the clash that was bound to come from these conflicting tendencies.

Key among these more contemporary cases is one from 1987, *Edwards v. Aguillard,* a case that went all the way to the U.S. Supreme Court. The case had to do with a Louisiana law that required the description of what was called "creation science" alongside the teaching of evolution. Creation science purports to give scientific evidence for the view that the universe was created by God in accordance with the description of the book of Genesis.

The U.S. Supreme Court struck down the Louisiana law as violating the First Amendment to the Constitution, which says there should be no establishment of religion by the government. In the ruling, the Supreme Court essentially said creation science is not science, but religious belief parading as science. Publicly funded institutions such as public schools cannot make laws that promote particular religious beliefs, which is what the Louisiana law in fact did.[3]

The decades since the *Edwards* ruling have seen more rounds of activity in the evolution-creation debate. In particular, since the 1990s, some Christians who are either biblical literalists or sympathetic to the position of biblical literalism have promoted a theory called "intelligent design" in the public sphere. Unlike the more traditional view of creation science, it affirms belief in an old earth. It also claims there can be small evolutionary adaptations within species or organisms. What it denies is macro-evolution, or the idea that species themselves evolved from lower life-forms through natural selection. Proponents of intelligent design have proposed arguments claiming that individual species are irreducibly complex, so they could not have evolved. Living organisms are a complex interworking of parts. They give evidence of a whole having come together as the result of some external design, rather than by the piecemeal process implied by evolution.

Most scientists who support evolution have regarded intelligent design theory as unworthy of a response, although some have made efforts in that regard. Proponents of intelligent design have mounted some limited challenges to the exclusive teaching of evolution in a few states. In an important decision in 2005, a federal district court struck down a requirement of the Dover, Pennsylvania school board that intelligent design be promoted in science classes. The court claimed this requirement promoted religion and intelligent design was not legitimate science.[4]

The issue of teaching evolution in the public schools remains contentious because the American public is deeply divided over the acceptance of the theory of evolution. According to a Pew Forum poll from 2005, 44 percent of Americans believe "humans and other living things have evolved over time." By contrast, 42 percent think "humans and other living things have existed in their present form since the beginning of time."[5]

On matters of history, biblical literalists think the biblical writers narrated events accurately or as they actually occurred. Among other things, this means biblical literalists believe all of the miracles reported in the Bible happened as they are reported. In traditional fashion, biblical literalists think the miracles show that God truly is behind the sweep of history recorded in the Bible. The events from God's calling of Abram to the formation of the Christian church occur because of divine intervention in history. For biblical literalists, this shows that God is in control of history. It shows that the salvation recorded in the biblical message is from God, and the Christian church is the unique fulfillment of God's will in the world today.

On theological matters, since biblical literalists believe in the miraculous history recorded in the Bible, they affirm doctrines based on these miracles and interpret them literally. Some important beliefs of biblical literalists are the virgin birth of Jesus, the literal incarnation of God in Jesus, the substitutionary atonement provided by Jesus' death on the cross, and the physical resurrection, physical ascension, and physical return of Jesus.

Biblical literalists vary greatly in what doctrines they emphasize and just how they understand those doctrines. Some stress the importance of the physical return of Jesus and regard it as imminent. They think certain prophetic books of the Bible, especially Daniel in the Old Testament and Revelation in the New Testament, give supernatural information about the future in a kind of secret code, and many explanations are given to try to unlock this code. A common interpretation has to do with God instantly taking all believers from the earth to heaven at some secret time in the near future. After this follows a period of chaos and evil. This is ended when Jesus returns to defeat the powers of evil and reign for a time on earth. Finally, this is followed by the last judgment of all people, where the faithless are thrown into the lake of fire and the faithful are given eternal life in paradise.

Evidence for Truth

Biblical literalists often emphasize that Christian doctrines, including the doctrine of the inerrancy or infallibility of the Bible, must be taken by faith. In this context, faith means cognitive assent to the truth of a proposition. They may claim the Holy Spirit works in a person either to give the person this faith or not. Those who experience the inner working of the Holy Spirit are led to affirm the basic truths held by biblical literalists. Those who deny those truths either have not experienced the Spirit's presence in their lives or have become closed to it.

Critics of biblical literalism point out that this is a problematic epistemological position because it is unfalsifiable, or closed to critical reflection.[6] No evidence of any kind can prove it is wrong, since it does not rest on data that can be scrutinized by anyone, but on the claim of the hidden supernatural working of the Spirit on a person's mind and will.

Despite the common emphasis on doctrines being known by faith through the inner working of the Holy Spirit, many biblical literalists also apply the use of reason to seek some level of proof for what they believe. Thus, for example, in scientific matters, many biblical literalists try to show how a literal reading of the creation account and the story of Noah's flood can make sense of the fossil record and biological phenomena. In historical matters, many biblical literalists attempt to harmonize discrepancies among the biblical authors both in the authors' reporting of history and in their theology. It is important for a position that claims the Bible has no errors to show that the biblical text contains no internal tensions or conflicts in its account of history or theology.

Biblical literalists may engage in rational argument with historical critics about the construction of the biblical text. Many try to show there is not a significant gap between the events recorded in the text and the writing of the text. This makes it more likely that the text would be historically accurate. They also try to show that the biblical authors were concerned to display accurate history in what they wrote and did not engage in theological elaboration or transformation of stories. In the end, however, there is a limit to what can be argued about these issues by biblical literalists, since an infallible text written by fallible humans could only occur by a miracle.

Engaging in rational debate to prove the Bible's literal truth can be problematic for biblical literalists, because the possibility always exists that they would lose an argument or that another position that does not support biblical literalism would prove to be stronger than the position of biblical literalism. The paradox faced by biblical literalists is that if they argue everything should simply be accepted by faith, their position seems to be secure, but it is also groundless in the sense that it is not based on anything that can be rationally argued. Lacking any rational basis for their position, biblical literalists could not hope to convince others of it. Conversely, if they engage in rational debate, they run the risk of losing security because they must open themselves to the evidence, and the evidence may prove them wrong. This is a serious challenge to biblical literalism because, as shown in the previous chapter, on so many issues there is an intellectual consensus today about the evidence that conflicts with the position of biblical literalism.

In general, biblical literalists give no place to the critical or autonomous modes of thinking that have developed since the Enlightenment. Biblical literalists' thinking begins with submission to the authority of the Bible, which is not criticized. The operation of human reason is limited to proving what faith accepts. Reason is not acknowledged to have the power to turn back on the content of faith and analyze it critically. Autonomous reason does not function, because no discrepancies are acknowledged between the findings of reason in the autonomous sciences and the biblical account. If it appears there are such discrepancies, biblical literalists say the autonomous sciences must be wrong.

The rejection of critical and autonomous thinking by biblical literalists represents a premodern way of thinking. Their way of being premodern has a distinctive twist, however, because unlike the premodern people who lived before the Enlightenment, biblical literalists today must formulate and articulate their positions consciously against the developments and challenges of modernity. Whereas premodern people could be called naive literalists because they were unaware of the challenges of modernity to come, biblical literalists today are perhaps more accurately called conscious literalists. They need to hold their positions consciously against the challenges of modernity.

Because of their stand against developments of modern thought, biblical literalists are criticized by more liberal Christians who seek greater openness to those developments. More liberal Christians regard as unacceptable the rejection of developments in the autonomous natural and historical sciences, claiming there is simply too much evidence for them. To reject them would be to contradict the discoveries of human reason and thereby fall into destructive conflicts between faith and reason. They regard reason as one of God's gifts to humans that God expects humans to use, and they seek to come to terms with the discoveries of the autonomous sciences even though this means denying biblical literalism. Instead of limiting reason only to prove what biblical literalism accepts by faith, more liberal Christians accept that critical reason and the discoveries of the autonomous sciences must have a place. They seek a synthesis between faith and historical criticism that may require rethinking certain traditional beliefs.

Biblical Literalists in the United States

There are biblical literalists in all Christian denominations. In the United States, they have the greatest concentration in a broad and significant movement called Evangelical Protestantism, although it should be emphasized that not all Evangelical Protestants are biblical literalists. Evangelical Protestants in predominantly white churches make up approximately 26 percent of the U.S. population.[7] Most of these Evangelical Protestant groups began in the United States, rather than being traditions that originated in the sixteenth-century Protestant Reformation. They tend to emphasize the autonomy of the local congregation and minimize the importance of a national church structure. They place a high value on a conversion experience and on living a transformed life as a result of this experience, a life that is often defined by a conservative personal and social ethic. They include most Baptist groups, including the Southern Baptist Convention, which is the largest Protestant denomination in the United States. They also include Pentecostal churches, such as the Assemblies of God; Holiness churches, including the Church of the Nazarene; Restorationist churches, including the Church of Christ; and a host of independent or loosely affiliated churches.

Many historically black churches promote an emphasis on biblical literalism. Approximately 7 percent of the U.S. population is associated with a historically black church.[8] Most of these groups began in the United States when African Americans emerged from the period of slavery and formed independent churches. Most are characterized by a charismatic worship style with enthusiastic singing and dramatic preaching and testifying. They tend to have a distinctive emphasis on social justice. They include Baptist groups, such as the National Baptist Convention; Pentecostal churches, among them the Church of God in Christ; and churches in the Wesleyan tradition, such as the African Methodist Episcopal Church.

Roman Catholic literalists are distinctive, because they add a literal belief in the traditions of the church to the idea of biblical literalism. They affirm that the Roman Church, under the guidance of the Holy Spirit and the successor chosen by Jesus to lead the church in the person of the pope, has developed authoritative teachings to be believed by all the faithful. These teachings include many things, and the importance as well as the authority of any individual teaching are often open to debate. In the modern period, three teachings in particular have been explicitly raised to the level of infallibility. They are a belief in the infallibility of the pope when he speaks ex cathedra (from his position as the official leader of the church regarding its doctrine), the immaculate conception of Mary, and the bodily assumption of Mary to heaven. Roman Catholic literalists accept them literally.

Theological Literalism

The position of theological literalism consists of those who accept historical criticism yet, overall, seek to maintain many traditional interpretations of Christian beliefs. This means they often have much in common with biblical literalists in their interpretation of theological doctrines. However, their acceptance of historical criticism leads to disagreements with biblical literalists on other issues and gives their faith a different character, one that is more embracing of the kinds of challenges and questions articulated earlier that arise with the emergence of modernity.

In accepting historical criticism and acknowledging the cultural limitations of the biblical authors, theological literalists reject a direct view of the inspiration of the Bible. They believe the Bible is the word of God, but it is a complex word. Revelation from God occurs in history to the believing community of Jews and Christians. The believing community that experiences and receives this revelation is a conditioned and time-bound entity. In important ways, the community is determined by the cultural beliefs of a certain time and place, and members of the community interpret the revelation in significant measure according to their limited cultural understanding. This means the biblical text contains a revelation from God that is housed in a particular cultural form. The

Bible contains both a timeless word from God and time-bound cultural elements from the people who received that word. To understand and use the Bible correctly, one must be prepared to criticize the time-bound cultural elements in the Bible while also abstracting its timeless message and translating its meaning into our own new and different context.

Theological literalists affirm that the biblical writers had scientific limitations. The biblical writers held an ancient scientific worldview, and theological literalists think the explanations of contemporary sciences on many matters are too compelling to ignore. This means, for theological literalists, that the story of the seven-day creation in Genesis 1 should not be read literally. Contemporary science tells us the process by which the earth was formed and all living species came to be. In particular, theological literalists affirm that the theory of evolution through natural selection is the best biological explanation for the origin of all life-forms.

Theological literalists think the process of evolution was not a mindless material process, but a process directed or intended by God. They offer different explanations of the way in which God directs or intends the evolutionary process. For example, some say that since it appears there are indeterminate factors in the evolutionary process, God works in an unseen way in those undetermined places to direct the process. Others say an intention is built into the evolutionary process from the beginning toward the development of self-consciousness that emerges through a complex process of progress, regress, and further progress. In any case, theological literalists are committed to the idea that there is no necessary conflict between biological evolution and their faith.

Even though it does not accurately describe the process of creation, the biblical story of creation in Genesis 1 is still valuable for theological literalists because of the theological truths that can be abstracted from it. For example, the story affirms that there is an ontological difference between God and the universe, that everything depends on God, that God is responsible for the order of the universe, and that created life is essentially good.

Theological literalists do not believe in a literal garden of Eden or a literal Adam and Eve. There was no original paradise from which human beings fell in an initial act of disobedience by humanity's first parents, incurring as punishment physical death, suffering, and the propensity toward evil. This implies that physical suffering and death are built into the universe from the beginning. They require some kind of explanation other than humanity's initial sin. Theodicy, which is the attempt to explain the compatibility between an all-good and all-powerful God and the existence of suffering and evil, has come to the fore in a new way in the modern period through the deliteralization of the garden of Eden story. Theological literalists still value the garden of Eden story as describing the disrupted character of human existence in a powerful way, even though they do not think it tells literally how this disrupted character came to be.

Theological literalists accept the basic hypotheses of historical critics about the construction of the historical portions of the Bible. They think complete historical accuracy should not be expected from ancient writers who often wrote centuries after the events they recorded on the basis of information handed down by oral tradition and sparse written traditions. They acknowledge that the believing community and the biblical authors often changed stories or even created stories primarily out of a theological interest. There is much legend, folklore, and exaggeration in the biblical narratives. They agree that each generation of believers interpreted what they saw God doing in their own time in ways that both built on and conflicted with past interpretations. Thus, various interpretations stand in some level of tension with one another in the Old and New Testaments.

While affirming the main tenets of historical criticism, theological literalists also affirm that God acted as a direct and indirect causal agent in the history of Israel and the formation of the Christian church. Theological literalists think there is a basic framework, or overall pattern, in the biblical story that accurately describes God's activity and from which the Christian church has derived true theological affirmations.

The main connection, then, between biblical literalists and theological literalists is the common affirmation that God acts directly as a causal agent in human history and that the biblical story contains a record of this activity. Whereas biblical literalists say every biblical account and interpretation of this activity is accurate, theological literalists see exaggeration in the accounts and conflicts between them but nevertheless affirm a main pattern in the biblical account that is subsequently interpreted correctly by the church and is true. The fact that each generation of biblical authors only realized in a fragmentary way what God was doing in their own time is owing to the theological conditioning and limitations of the biblical authors. However, Christians today stand at the conclusion of the process by which the church has been able to discern the main outline of God's actions in history and has formulated an adequate theology based on it.

Since theological literalists accept the idea of literal divine intervention, they believe that at least certain key miracles in the biblical account are historical. They may disagree over a miracle like the virgin birth of Jesus—some thinking it actually occurred, and some thinking it is a created story making a theological point about the specialness of Jesus. In general, however, they are willing to affirm the miraculous character of key events like the exodus in the Old Testament and the physical resurrection of Jesus in the New Testament—although, regarding the latter event, they may claim they cannot really understand what it involved. They accept that the church is correct in its assessment of Jesus as having both a divine and human nature. While remaining a human being, Jesus is a literal incarnation of God. They may affirm a literal second coming of Jesus, but many do not. For those who do, there is no intense imminent expectation of the event. For those who do not, God's work in history is thought to be carried on through the action of the church in the world. The church has received the Holy Spirit and should bring this Spirit to the world rather than anticipating the physical return of Jesus to bring order to the world. Eventually, God will draw all creation into the kingdom of God, but this will occur at the end of time and is something humans are not really able to understand from their current limited vantage point. They believe in an afterlife, but many today do not stress the idea of eternal damnation of unbelievers, because they think this contradicts God's loving nature.

Theological literalists are willing to affirm that the New Testament authors had different views about Jesus and that some did not believe Jesus was a literal incarnation of God. Since Jesus was fully human, they regard those parts of the Bible as valuable, even though they are limited. While theological literalists recognize diverse streams of interpretation about Jesus in the early Christian community, they argue that the correct stream is the one that affirms that Jesus is a divine incarnation. The church affirmed the truth of this stream in its ecumenical councils, and theological literalists think the church was led by the Holy Spirit to make that affirmation.

Similarly, theological literalists grant that the New Testament represents only one way of reading the Old Testament. For example, there are a variety of perspectives in the Old Testament about what the Messiah will be like. Theological literalists agree they do not all point to the events of Jesus' life, much less to the idea of Jesus' divinity. Nevertheless, theological literalists affirm that the interpretation of the Old Testament that connects with the claim that Jesus is the Messiah is a true interpretation. The events of Jesus' life allow the New Testament writers and the early church to see the past in a new and true light. The fact that this new interpretation does not fit with everything in the Old Testament is owing to the theological limitations of the Old Testament writers.

Faith and Reason

Theological literalists give a role to critical reason in their acceptance of historical criticism of the Bible, and they acknowledge the importance of autonomous reason by affirming the need to rethink some traditional beliefs in light of contemporary knowledge. They take a wide range of positions, however, on the question of what or how much of their faith is provable by reason. Because theological literalists think the biblical text is not always historically accurate but contains exaggerations and theological transformations, some theological literalists say reason cannot discover the actual history behind the text, so any beliefs based on this history must necessarily transcend reason. While reason is kept from knowing this history, faith produced by the inner working of the Holy Spirit believes in the miraculous character of the main outline of the biblical story. Others disagree and say the truth of significant miraculous events recorded in the Bible is a matter of rational debate. These events can be proven or at least shown to be rationally plausible.

An example of the diverse points of view on the relationship of faith and reason with regard to biblical miracles is seen in the contrasting positions taken on this issue by two important twentieth-century Protestant theologians who broadly represent this theological type, Karl Barth and Wolfhart Pannenberg. Barth argues that reason has no independent role in relation to the truths of revelation. The truths of revelation simply have to be accepted by faith, which Barth understands as something created by God in the believer upon hearing the word of God that convinces the believer of the truth of Christian affirmations.[9] Pannenberg argues that the plausibility of Christian doctrines that are rooted in historical events, such as the resurrection of Jesus, must be open to rational proof or disproof.[10] Both individuals are creative thinkers, and their theologies are developed in significant ways beyond this single question and the brief outline of a theological type I have presented. In general, much creative thought is done by theological literalists in terms of applying the meaning of Christianity to the world today that goes beyond the single issue of faith and history, the primary issue considered here in establishing these theological types.

Theological Literalists in the United States

Theological literalists are no doubt found in all denominations. While many evangelical Christians fit into this type, the greatest concentration of theological literalists is in Roman Catholicism and mainline Protestant denominations. Roman Catholics make up approximately 24 percent of the U.S. population, while mainline Protestants make up approximately 18 percent of the population.[11] Mainline Protestant groups are groups with a long presence in the United States, many of them having their origin in the Protestant Reformation of the sixteenth century. They generally have a strong national church structure. Because they emphasize openness to culture and contemporary ideas, mainline churches often include a variety of theological perspectives. They tend not to draw sharp lines about what someone must believe and how someone must understand it to be a part of the church. The main denominations are Presbyterian Church (U.S.A.), United Methodist Church, United Church of Christ, Episcopal Church, Evangelical Lutheran Church in America, American Baptist Church, and Disciples of Christ.

Roman Catholics have a long tradition of what is called "natural theology." This approach to theology affirms the power of human reason to discover some theological truths independent of revelation. In principle, this makes Roman Catholic thinking open to autonomous reason. Despite this, for a long time, the Roman Catholic Church in the modern period resisted ideas that stemmed from the Enlightenment, including historical criticism of the Bible, because so many of these ideas were associated with critical reason. It was not until well into the twentieth century that the Roman church officially opened itself to historical criticism of the Bible and a more open pattern of reflection that seeks a synthesis between Christian belief and contemporary thought. Vatican II, a church council that met in 1962–1965, was a decisive step in this process of opening the church to modern thought.

Theological Reinterpreters

Theological reinterpreters represent the most liberal wing of contemporary Christian thought. They critique theological literalists as not taking contemporary thought seriously enough and making the necessary reinterpretation of traditional Christian doctrines on that basis. They see a need to make a more serious reformulation of traditional Christian ideas to make Christianity relevant to modern people. An important idea that theological reinterpreters critique and biblical and theological literalists accept is the idea of direct or literal divine intervention in history.

Reinterpreters think the idea that God intervenes in history as a direct causal agent in violation of natural laws is an unacceptable idea to modern people. This critique presupposes there is a significant difference between the ancient worldview accepted by the biblical writers and the worldview accepted by contemporary people. Reinterpreters accept historical criticism with its affirmation that the biblical writers were limited and conditioned by their culture in certain ways. They argue that belief in literal divine intervention is one of the cultural limitations of the biblical authors and does not need to be accepted by Christians today.

Instead of believing in divine intervention as a direct and literal phenomenon, reinterpreters say what ancient people called divine intervention was really a certain kind of religious experience. Reinterpreters believe in religious experience as a genuine encounter with God that is transformative and potentially life-changing. They do not deny God exists, which would make them atheists. They do not say God is inaccessible, which would make them deists. They believe God's power and God's reality are present to humans. A transforming encounter with God can and often does occur in religious experiences. It occurred in the foundational events of Christianity, and it continues to occur in the ongoing life of those who embrace Christianity.

Theological reinterpreters commonly call the worldview that accepts literal divine intervention "mythological."[12] A myth is a story about God, the Gods, or spiritual beings like angels and demons, and their interaction with humans. All ancient cultures produced myths, and for the most part, everyone in those cultures took them literally. A literal view of the New Testament myth presupposes that the universe consists of three tiers. God and other semi-divine beings like angels are in the top tier above the earth in heaven. The devil and other supernatural forces of evil are in the bottom tier under the earth. Humans are in the middle tier on the earth between these agents of good and evil. In a mythological worldview, much of life on earth is explained by the intervention of these supernatural agents from above or below the earth.

In the New Testament myth, Jesus is understood as the incarnation of a preexistent divine being who does battle with satanic forces while on earth, finally defeating them in his death and resurrection. After rising from the dead, he returns to God, ascending upward, while sending his Spirit to be with his followers on earth. All of this is a mythological story that should not be taken literally. Yet reinterpreters do not think the story should be thrown out. It is vital to keep the story and proclaim it, because it bears witness to a genuine religious experience, and it brings forth such an experience in its hearers when it is proclaimed. However, the meaning of the story needs to be reinterpreted into nonmythological or nonliteral terms for modern people to accept it. Because modern people can no longer believe in the three-tiered mythological universe and direct supernatural intervention from above or below, the meaning of the story must be abstracted from the ancient cosmology in which it was housed in order to make the word of God found in the Bible a living reality for people today.

Reinterpreters give different reasons for why people today can no longer believe in a mythological universe. On a basic level, they point to the fact that people know today that God is not literally above the earth and the devil beneath it. Contemporary people have a fundamentally different cosmology or view of the universe than the biblical writers, who apparently thought God was literally up in the sky and the devil literally down in the earth.

Reinterpreters claim that, along with having a different cosmology, modern people look for a different way of explaining events than the way of the biblical writers. People today seek universal explanations for things based on the uniform character of reality from moment to moment. What happens in the world at any second is the result of the totality of causes from the previous second. To explain the state of things at one moment requires a universal description of reality, a description whereby the state of things at that moment is caused by the character of reality that everyone experiences or to which everyone has access in the previous moment. Divine intervention is an invalid explanation because it breaks the explanatory causal sequence by recourse to a particular cause outside the realm of universal experience.[13]

This does not mean reinterpreters believe in purely natural or material causes to explain all phenomena. Again, if they did, they would be either materialistic atheists or deists, and they are neither. Reinterpreters believe people experience God and are transformed by this encounter. Religious experience is a genuine cause. But religious experience is universal. The transforming divine presence is at least potentially available to everyone. Christian experience is a particular type of religious experience, or a particular way of accessing the universal divine presence. Reinterpreters think they can explain Christian experience and the transformation it brings to people's lives by an analysis of religious experience, instead of needing to have recourse to a literal interpretation of supernatural activity. Christian experience involves an experience or encounter with God, but this encounter need not be interpreted as God literally intervening in the course of human events in an inexplicable way.

Reinterpreters can be especially critical of an interpretation of Christianity that insists on belief in an interventionist God, or a God understood as a heavenly being who intervenes in history from time to time. In this interpretation, to be a Christian means to believe literally either in every divine intervention recorded in the Bible (biblical literalists) or in the main divine interventions recorded in the Bible (theological literalists) and the theological statements derived from them. For reinterpreters, not only do modern people have difficulty believing in such a God or having such a faith, but it is an inadequate idea of God and of faith.

To think of God as a direct causal agent in history implies that God is a being that exists alongside of the universe. God is out there somewhere, watching what occurs on earth and intervening from time to time. This idea of God is problematic because it applies characteristics of the created universe to God. It presupposes that God is an independent being in space and time watching events on earth transpire and acting as a discrete cause within the series of causes. But space, time, causality, and even personhood are all characteristics of the created universe. As transcendent and ontologically distinct from the universe, God cannot be subject to characteristics of the universe. To think of God correctly means to deny that God is literally in space and time, and also that God is a literal cause or person.

Likewise, if faith is understood as believing in literal divine intervention and the theological ideas derived from it, then faith has merely a cognitive meaning. It means cognitive assent to the truth of certain historical events and doctrinal propositions. Contrary to this, reinterpreters stress that, at its core, faith has an existential meaning. Faith does not mean accepting that certain facts about reality are true, but instead being transformed in some experience or encounter with God. Christianity is one discrete type of encounter with God, and Christian theology consists of articulating what the Christian encounter uniquely involves, but the living core of faith is experience and not cognitive assent to a set of doctrinal statements as facts about reality.[14]

Panentheism and Its Implications

Instead of an interventionist God that exists alongside the universe, reinterpreters propose a different understanding of God and God's relation to the universe that is often called panentheism. Panentheism is a description of reality that is between pantheism and theism, affirming and critiquing elements of both. Pantheism means "God is everything." This does not mean pantheists think God is literally every individual thing in the world, but they think God permeates everything without transcending the world, being finally identical to the whole. Theism literally means "Godism," but the definition of theism that has developed since the Enlightenment and the rise of Deism is that God exists alongside the world and intervenes in it from time to time. While both theists and deists believe God transcends the world and exists alongside it, theists claim God periodically intervenes in the world, while deists deny this claim.

Panentheism means "everything is in God." Panentheists disagree with pantheists that God is identical to the world and affirm with theists that God transcends the world. At the same time, they disagree with theists that God exists as a separate being alongside the world, intervening in it from time to time, and affirm with pantheists that God's presence pervades the world. In panentheism, God both pervades and transcends all finite reality. While God is transcendent, God cannot be reified or turned into another thing alongside the world to which characteristics taken from the world are literally applied. To do this is to reduce the transcendent God to the world or to subject God to the structure of the world. God's transcendence is, most basically, unknowable otherness. It is perhaps best expressed as the depth of the world, but it is a depth that is related to the world. God is the ground of all things and can be known in and through all the things of the world, including the beauty in nature, a work of art, or a system of law produced by human culture. God is not a particular beautiful object like a flower, but a flower is one place where humans experience beauty, and in any experience of beauty, something of the inexhaustible and infinite character of reality is manifest, and that is God.

According to panentheists, since God pervades everything in the world, God can be known in and through all of the things of the world. Everything can mediate God's presence, and in a fundamental sense, religion has to do with experiencing God's presence through finite objects and acts. In the history of religions, almost every conceivable kind of object has been used at some time or other to mediate the divine presence and power. People have looked to sacred stones, trees, animals, rivers, and mountains or to sacred beings imaged much like people, only with greater powers, to experience the divine presence. However, if God transcends the world, then none of the objects that mediate God's presence can literally be God or be confused with God. Instead, they are symbols that represent God. A symbol is a finite object or image that mediates the transcendent divine presence to the religious believer. Both a sacred stone and the image of a loving father in heaven are symbols by which the believer experiences the divine presence.

While theological reinterpreters deny literal divine intervention, they think what is interpreted as literal divine intervention by ancient people is really the experience of the universal divine presence and power known through symbolic objects or events. They seek to understand Christianity not as the one unique place in history where God literally acted, but as an interlocking system of symbols whereby Christians experience the divine presence. Christian doctrines are not to be interpreted literally as describing what God did in discrete causal actions in history, but they are important expressions of symbolic meaning.

This does not mean history is unimportant for theological reinterpreters. History is the place where different ways of experiencing God have been realized. Among the manifold experiences of God in history, certain ones have been taken as normative, and they form the living world religions. Many reinterpreters argue for a development in the long history of religion. They argue for a kind of progressive revelation in which more adequate ways of experiencing and understanding God emerge in the course of human history. Some argue that the Christian religion represents the highest or superlative way of experiencing and understanding God. They set up criteria by which they seek to show that Christianity is the supreme revelation. Other reinterpreters view this as a kind of theological imperialism, and they place Christianity essentially on the same level as the other world religions.[15]

Since they deny literal divine intervention, theological reinterpreters do not believe in the literal virgin birth or the physical resurrection and physical ascension of Jesus to heaven. In critiquing these things that are stated as literal events in the biblical text, reinterpreters rely on the hypothesis of historical criticism that the believing community and the biblical writers elaborated on historical events with a theological interest in accord with the worldview of their time. It is not the literal occurrence of these events but their symbolic meaning to believers that is important to reinterpreters. For example, reinterpreters say that while the resurrection of Jesus is not an actual physical event, it is an important symbol for Christians, because it is the way Christians experience the power of God over sin and suffering in their lives. The resurrection is not true as a literal event, but it is true as a symbol that mediates the divine presence and its healing and restoring power. Likewise, reinterpreters say the ascension of Jesus to heaven is not something that happened literally to Jesus' body. It is a symbolic way of expressing that even though Jesus is not physically present, the Spirit of God, or the divine presence that is experienced through Jesus, is still present in the community of believers.

Reinterpreters do not believe in the literal incarnation of God in the person of Jesus or the idea that God literally descended to take on human flesh in the person Jesus. They say what the doctrine of the incarnation is attempting to express is Jesus' specialness as a symbol of God. God shone through the human person Jesus of Nazareth and the events of his life in a particularly powerful way. Christians continue to experience the presence of God in Jesus and in the story of his life, death, and resurrection. For reinterpreters, it is in this sense that Jesus is divine. Jesus is one with God, because through Jesus, Christians come into relation with God and experience God's transforming power. Through Jesus, Christians are reconciled to God and experience new life. This does not mean Jesus literally had a divine nature, but Jesus is the preeminent symbol of God for Christians.

Theological reinterpreters are critiqued by both biblical literalists and theological literalists as sacrificing too much of the Christian faith to the modern world or modern thinking. Biblical and theological literalists think belief in literal divine intervention and the doctrines built around it is essential to Christianity. They say Christianity loses its historical bearing and meaning when divine intervention is denied and Christianity becomes an ahistorical religion, rather than the unique witness to God's decisive acts for human salvation in history.

The Place of Theological Reinterpreters in the Church

Two significant twentieth-century theologians who shared many of the ideas germane to this theological type are Rudolph Bultmann and Paul Tillich.[16] Both sought to reinterpret the mythological worldview of the New Testament, denying a literal interpretation of supernatural intervention. Tillich engaged in an analysis of universal religious experience in a way Bultmann never did. With this, Tillich followed the path of the nineteenth-century figure Friedrich Schleiermacher, often called the father of modern theology. Schleiermacher understood Christianity as a unique determination of the religious essence he called the "feeling of absolute dependence."[17] As with all creative thinkers, each one's theology has unique emphases and is developed in ways that transcend this basic outline and stand in tension with it at certain points.

Many people in mainline Protestant and Roman Catholic churches hold to some variation of this position. It gives an interesting dynamic to those traditions to have both theological literalists and theological reinterpreters represented in them. Different people in the same pew may understand Christian meanings in different ways.

It is important to stress again that the categories established here are intended to give a broad outline for theological reflection on some key issues, but they should not be understood as either exclusive or comprehensive categories. They are intended as a starting point for grasping some of the range of diversity in Christian belief today. The next three chapters expand on many of the ideas introduced in this chapter. In particular, they examine Christian beliefs regarding God, Christ, and human destiny. Each chapter analyzes the classical formulation of these Christian ideas and then moves to a presentation of the way notable contemporary theologians are thinking through their meaning, given the theological tradition they have inherited and the developments and transformations of modernity.

Part Two

Classical Christian
Thought and Contemporary
Transformations

Chapter 3

God and Cosmology

In national surveys over the past several decades, the number of Americans who say they believe in God has remained quite steady, standing above 90 percent.[1] While God is a common object of belief, philosophers and theologians through the centuries have realized there are fundamental difficulties involved in thinking about God. Among these difficulties are the questions of whether belief in God can be rationally justified, how God's relationship to the universe is to be conceived, and how to make sense of human language for God. These questions have been major challenges in the history of Christian thought, and they have spawned creative and ingenious responses.

This chapter analyzes some of these responses in contemporary Christian theology, the analysis being done in the context of the biblical and historical background from which contemporary theology arises. When the issue is stated in this way, it is clear that the area to be covered is vast, and it is important to recognize at the outset that this chapter and the following chapters on theology make no attempt at a comprehensive account. Rather, they are intended to provide an introduction to some of the main ideas in the biblical and theological tradition and a selective look at ways in which some contemporary Christian theologians are thinking through these ideas in light of various intellectual developments of the modern world. It is hoped this analysis will prove fruitful as an introduction to the vast history of Christian reflection and will stimulate further reflection and ever-deepening ways to think about one's own commitments.

Biblical and Greek Roots of the Christian Idea of God

From its opening pages, the Bible assumes the existence of God rather than seeking to prove God's existence. It is true there are some parts in the Bible that suggest God can be known from creation, but these

remain suggestions or declarations and are never developed into systematic rational proofs. In the Bible as a whole, God's existence is assumed.
In the Hebrew Bible (Christian Old Testament), God is presented
overwhelmingly as a historical agent in covenant relationship with God's
people Israel. In the New Testament, God is understood to be present
in Jesus of Nazareth.

In the defining and formative moment of the Jewish relationship with
God recorded in the Hebrew Bible, God frees God's people from slavery
in Egypt and enters into a covenant relationship with them on Mount
Sinai. God's action in history in this formative event and throughout the
Hebrew Bible is not used by the biblical writers to attempt to prove that
God exists; rather, it is used to show that Israel's God is the true God.
The assumption of the existence of Deity remains in the background
even of the Israelites' recording of God's acts.

In Israel's earliest understanding of God, one that goes back at least
to the early part of the thirteenth century B.C.E., the God with whom the
Jews are in covenant is not assumed to be the only God of the universe.
In the events surrounding the exodus of the Jews from slavery, the Jewish
leader Moses reveals to the Israelite people a clan God named Yahweh.
Other Gods are assumed to exist, something that is made clear in the
first of the Ten Commandments given to the people by Moses, which
says the Jewish people are not to have these other Gods "alongside" or
"before" their God Yahweh (Exod. 20:3). The Jewish people are to be in
an exclusive relationship or covenant with their God Yahweh. The laws
of the first five books of the Hebrew Bible describe the terms of this
covenant, and these include the requirement that the Jewish people not
worship other Gods. However, at least initially, the existence of these
other Gods is not denied, but assumed.

ADDITIONAL INFORMATION

God's Name in the Hebrew Bible

In an intriguing passage, the Hebrew Bible gives evidence that the
Jewish leader Moses, who lived in the thirteenth century B.C.E.,
introduced the distinctive personal name of God to the Israelites. In
chapter 6 of Exodus, God speaks to Moses, telling him to go to Phar-
aoh and insist the Israelites be set free from slavery. In verses 2b-3,

God says, "I am Yahweh. I appeared to Abraham, Isaac, and Jacob as El Shaddai, but by my name 'Yahweh' I did not make myself known to them" (NRSV translation with my addition of Hebrew names).

In the context, Moses has fled Egypt for his life. He journeyed into the desert wilderness after killing an Egyptian soldier and finding out others knew about it (Exod. 2:11-15). While in the wilderness, he met and married the daughter of a priest of the ethnic clan of the Midianites (Exod. 2:16-22). Later, when he frees the Israelites from slavery and reenters the desert wilderness, his family, including his father-in-law, meet him and give praise to Yahweh for what Yahweh has done (Exod. 18:1-12; see also Num. 10:29-32).

Given the connection between Moses' association with the Midianites and the introduction of the name Yahweh to the Israelites, it is possible that Yahweh was the God of the Midianite people. It is also possible that Mount Sinai, where Moses takes the Israelites to receive the law, was the sacred mountain of this desert tribe. It is only during and after the time of Moses that Israelite names appear with a shortened version of Yahweh in them, giving further credence to the idea that Moses introduced this name. The name of Moses' successor, Joshua, means "Yahweh saves" and is a variant of the name Jesus.

At the time the Hebrew Bible was written, the language of Hebrew did not have vowels but was written with consonants only. The name for God introduced by Moses consisted of the four consonants *YHWH*. It is unclear what this name means, although an intriguing passage in Exod. 3:14 connects the name with the verb *to be*. It is also unclear how this name was pronounced, since no vowels were originally connected to it. Conventionally, it is written and pronounced Yahweh (yah-way).

Sometime in the period during which the writing of the Old Testament was drawing to a close, Jewish communities began to regard God's special name as too holy to be spoken aloud. This caused a problem for reading the biblical text, especially reading it out loud in public settings. One had to substitute something for God's name in the text. The common substitute used was "Lord." Approximately three hundred years before the time of Jesus, in a bold move, the Jewish community in Alexandria, Egypt, began translating the Bible from Hebrew to Greek, the language they commonly used. In this translation, every time the word *YHWH* appeared in Hebrew, they translated it as "Lord" in Greek.

The tradition of translating *YHWH* as "Lord" has continued in the vast majority of modern-day translations, including the most popular English translations, the King James Version, the New Revised Standard Version, and the New International Version. Generally, modern translations capitalize the letters of *Lord* to alert the reader that in the original Hebrew, the term is not *Lord* but *YHWH*, God's personal name. Despite the capitalization, referring to God as Lord in place of God's personal name tends to give a more universal sense or meaning to the references of God in the Old Testament. God is universal Lord instead of an individual deity with a personal name. The translation itself reflects a movement away from a clan deity to the universal God of creation and salvation history.

An important theological development evident in the Hebrew Bible is the Israelites' emerging affirmation that their God is the only God of the universe, who made it and who directs all events within it. This shift takes place over the course of hundreds of years and is certainly in place by the time of the exile of the southern kingdom of Judah early in the sixth century B.C.E. The prophets active just before and during the exile, including Jeremiah, Ezekiel, and Second Isaiah, all declare that other nations, including the Babylonians who defeated the Jews and the Persians who allowed the Jews to return to their homeland, act unknowingly at the behest of the Jewish God, who is the one God of the universe. The Jewish understanding of God burst through the idea of a limited clan deity to the idea of a universal God directing all of human history, though in special covenant relationship with the Jews.

The idea of a universal God who is in final charge of all human events continued in Judaism into the time of the New Testament. The Jews regarded the Roman Gods as nothing but empty idols without meaning and power. Their God, who was in special relationship with God's covenant people, was the only God.

In their presentation of God as a historical agent, both the Old and New Testaments make assumptions about who God is without developing a systematic accounting of God's attributes or attempting to undertake a rational explanation of the nature of God's being. Assumptions about God being powerful, loving, and just are all implied in the rich stories of the biblical narrative, but there is never a distancing reflection in relation to the narrative to definitively list God's attributes. Likewise, infusing the biblical narrative is an affirmation of God as creator of the universe whose being is not itself created, but the Bible contains no systematic treatise on the reasons for and nature of uncreated being.

The kind of systematic rational reflection on the narrative that seeks to understand God's attributes and the nature of God's being occurs in the developing history of the Christian tradition in significant measure as a result of the influence of Greek thought. Ancient Greece is the home of Western philosophy, and one of the perennial tasks in the Western philosophical tradition is to think about things in a comprehensive and systematic way. The attempt at rational, orderly, and systematic reflection has had an enduring influence on Christian theology and eventually led to the development of the great theological systems in the Middle Ages.

The influence of Greek thought on Christianity goes deeper than simply encouraging the clarification of implied notions from the Bible. Greek thought also brought content that influenced Christian reflection. Greek thinking in various forms had spread through the Mediterranean region from a period roughly three hundred years before the time of Jesus. It was the thinking of the educated elite in the Roman Empire. Early in its history, when Christianity separated from Judaism, it inevitably encountered Greek ideas, including ideas about God.[2] Over long periods of time, these ideas were refined and selectively fused with ideas from the Bible.

The understanding of God in Greek thought is not singular and unified but complex and nuanced in its developments. Classical Greek thinkers like Plato (429–347 B.C.E.) and Aristotle (384–322 B.C.E.) in their own time and in their own way each burst through their culture's belief in many limited, humanlike Gods. Over the centuries, their ideas were adopted and adapted by disciples who kept their thinking alive and revised it in their own ways.

While classical Greek thinkers differed in their ideas of God, what is common is that they did not focus on God as an actor in human history as the Bible does, but understood God to be the ultimate explanation for the meaningful and rational order that is perceived in the human grasp of reality. Greek thinkers did not primarily understand God as the originating creator of the order that is perceived in the universe. In fact, Plato thought an inferior deity and not the true God created the universe, and Aristotle thought the universe had always existed. Instead, Greek thinkers emphasized the idea that the meaningful order—experienced in knowing, in conceiving of what is good and beautiful, and in seeing things change—is possible only because there is a God who is the ultimate source and final explanation for these things.

In explaining how the mind is able to grasp reality, Plato claimed that things in the universe are but pale representations of universal forms to which the mind has access and that the mind uses to understand reality. In themselves, these forms constitute a realm that is eternal and unchanging, separate from the finite and changing things in the universe.[3] For Plato, true knowledge, or knowledge that is valuable and meaningful, consists not in examining the world of finite changing things, but in contemplating the eternal unchanging forms.

Christian theologians influenced by Plato's ideas affirmed that the forms about which Plato spoke were in the mind of God. God created the universe through the forms, and that is why the universe has the order it does and why and how it represents God, even if imperfectly. Plato's turning away from the finite changing world to find true knowledge in internal contemplation of the eternal and unchanging forms fed a developing stream in Christian theology that stressed withdrawal from the world for the sake of mystical contemplation of God. While this emphasis is in many theologians, it is seen clearly in Augustine (354–430), a theologian influenced by Platonic thought who is decisive for establishing the theological tradition of the Christian West. In one of his early writings, Augustine famously claims, "I desire to know God and the soul. Nothing more? Nothing whatever."[4]

Important aspects of Aristotle's thought were unknown in the Christian world until well into the Middle Ages, but when they were introduced, they were decisive for the developing Christian idea of God. For Aristotle, God was understood as complete fullness toward which everything is drawn in realizing itself. Everything in the universe is becoming or actualizing its limited being. God alone is fully actualized and has nothing to realize. Instead, God is the unmoved fullness that in an ever-present way draws or moves all things to the actualization of their finite and limited being.

The greatest thinker of the High Middle Ages, Thomas Aquinas (1225–1274), synthesized the Aristotelian idea of God with the biblical idea. In Thomas's theology, Aristotle's God, who is the ultimate explanation for the changes that are observed in the universe, is the same God who created the universe, entered into a covenant with the Jews, and became incarnate in Jesus.[5]

In the biblical perspective, God is actor and director in the sweeping drama of history that moves from creation through redemption to final consummation. In the Greek perspective, God is ever-present fullness and the ultimate explanation for the rational order experienced in the human mind and in reality. Augustine and Thomas represent watersheds in the Christian theological tradition, as each in his own way synthesized the God of the Bible and the God of the philosophers to explain the ultimate character of reality and answer ultimate questions about human origins, human history, and final human destiny.

Transformations in Reflection on God during the Enlightenment

The Enlightenment of the seventeenth and eighteenth centuries brought a number of significant transformations in thinking about God in the Christian West. It provides an important background for understanding issues in the contemporary period.

While the Enlightenment had many aspects, above all, it emphasized the elevation of human reason. Two important transformations in thinking about God come from this elevation of human reason.

First, for many Enlightenment thinkers, the elevation of human reason implied a determined quest for a rational explanation rather than a supernatural explanation for all experienced phenomena. Owing to various intellectual transformations, the universe was seen as a great machine. The emerging scientific method of hypothesis, testing, and observation was seen as the way to unlock the secrets of this machine. Rational, causal explanations of events were regarded, at least by some Enlightenment thinkers, as the only valid explanations.

Inevitably, this led some Enlightenment thinkers to criticize the idea of miraculous intervention by God in history. These thinkers rejected the God of the Bible insofar as this God was understood as a historical agent who acts in and directs human history. Instead, they posited a distant God who created the universe and lets it run on its own. Such is the God of Deism, a rational form of Enlightenment religion that arose from Christianity. The deistic God is a rational creator who made a rational and orderly universe. The universe is independent of God, and humans—having been created with reason—are left to unlock the secrets of God's own creativity by applying the scientific method to creation. God also leaves it to humans to bring about moral progress, something many Enlightenment deists regarded as inevitable. Human moral progress was entrusted to humans by God, and it was considered beneath the created human stature or human dignity for God to have to intervene in order to save humans from themselves.[6]

While Deism was an important Enlightenment development, the Enlightenment was not a single unified movement. Some Enlightenment thinkers agreed with the deists that God made a rational creation for humans to discover, but they did not abandon the idea of God's direct intervention in history. Instead, they argued that the divine intervention recorded in the Bible not only occurred but also could be rationally proven. This demonstrates the elevation of reason characteristic of the Enlightenment, as reason is relied upon and applied to areas of the Christian faith in new ways.[7]

The second important transformation in thinking about God brought about by the elevation of reason in the Enlightenment had to do with the question of whether it could be proved that God exists. Some of the great thinkers of the Middle Ages, including Anselm of Canterbury (1033–1109) and Thomas Aquinas, had developed proofs for God's existence. These proofs, however, were developed in a context that was overwhelmingly assured of God's existence. Anselm and Thomas were monks who spent a significant part of each day in communal and private worship and prayer. The proofs they gave were never regarded as necessary or essential for belief in God. They were merely attempts to show that some aspect of what they already believed was rational. This context changed in the Enlightenment.

With the elevation of reason in the Enlightenment came a stress on believing only that which could be proved by reason. Because of this, it became important for many Enlightenment thinkers to give proofs for God's existence. Without such proofs, one could not lay claim to the fact that the foundation of one's beliefs was rational. If the foundation of one's beliefs was not rational, how could anyone be certain his or her beliefs were not mere flights of fancy, and how could anyone expect other people to accept or agree with his or her beliefs? These questions were posed anew with the Enlightenment.

The proof for God's existence that came to greatest prominence in the Age of Enlightenment is commonly called the teleological proof or proof from design. It proceeded from the common worldview of the time, arguing that the universe and individual elements within it are like a machine with all of its parts rationally ordered together. Machines do not just happen by accident but are the products of intelligence. So, according to the teleological proof, the universe must be the product of an intelligence.[8]

Numerous Enlightenment thinkers held that the proofs for God's existence were valid. At the same time, other important thinkers launched critiques of the traditional proofs. Most famous among the critics were David Hume (1711–1776) and Immanuel Kant (1724–1804).[9] Hume was agnostic about the human ability to prove rationally that God exists. Kant criticized the traditional proofs of his day and then proposed a new proof, which was never widely accepted.

ADDITIONAL INFORMATION

The Traditional Proofs for the Existence of God

At least since the publication in 1781 of Immanuel Kant's great work, *Critique of Pure Reason*, it has been common to identify three traditional proofs for God's existence. Profound and sophisticated formulations and critiques of each proof have been developed by philosophers through the centuries. What follows is a very basic articulation of common ways of formulating these proofs, along with an equally basic articulation of standard critiques of each proof. Any good text in the philosophy of religion will provide more detailed information regarding the proofs.

The Ontological Proof for the Existence of God

What is commonly called the ontological proof has roots in the work of Anselm of Canterbury. The proof given here follows Anselm's main argument.[10] This proof differs from the other two proofs in that it begins with an idea of God in the mind and on that basis attempts to prove that God exists. Put into premises and a conclusion, it runs as follows:

1. God is "that than which nothing greater can be conceived."
2. This is a thought in the mind.
3. It is greater to exist in the mind and reality than in the mind alone.

Therefore,

4. Since God is "that than which nothing greater can be conceived," God must exist in reality.

Critics of the proof find problematic the assumption in the proof that one can move through logical argument alone from (a) the existence of an idea in the mind to (b) the reality of that idea outside the mind. Critics often claim that verifying whether something exists outside the mind requires relying on the experience of the world given through the senses.

The Cosmological Proof for the Existence of God

Both the cosmological proof and the teleological proof begin with some observed feature of reality and attempt to show that the ultimate explanation of this feature requires the affirmation of the existence of God. The cosmological proof has a deep history, with important formulations being given in the work of Thomas Aquinas.[11] In a significant way, Thomas's formulations relied on the metaphysics of Aristotle. The formulation given here does not rely on Aristotle's metaphysics but on the idea of contingency. A contingent being is a being that exists but does not have to exist. It relies on something else for its existence. A necessary being is a being that exists through itself and does not rely on anything else for its existence.

1. All individual beings in the universe, and the interlocking series of beings that makes up the universe as a whole, are contingent beings.
2. The existence of only contingent beings is not possible.

Therefore,

3. There must be a necessary being that makes the universe of contingent beings possible.

Critics take a wide variety of postures in relation to this argument. One common approach is to claim that it cannot be assumed that reality as such, or reality that is beyond any possible human experience, must correspond to human ideas of rationality. This means that even if it is assumed that the universe is contingent as a whole, it cannot be known whether there must be a necessary being to explain the contingent universe. From the perspective of the human idea of rationality, it may seem like there should be a necessary being. Still, there is no way of knowing that the human idea of rationality applies to reality as such.

The Teleological Proof for the Existence of God

The teleological proof also has a long and storied history, a version of it being found in the work of Thomas Aquinas. The proof rose to special prominence in the Enlightenment of the seventeenth and eighteenth centuries, a time in which the universe was conceived as a great machine. A popular formulation is found in the work of the Enlightenment thinker William Paley (1743–1805).[12] His formulation is the basis of the following version:

1. A machine is a unity of parts that work together for some purpose.
2. Machines give evidence of having been designed by an intelligence.
3. The universe, in its individual parts and as a whole, is like a machine.

Therefore,

4. The universe gives evidence of having been designed by an intelligence.

This proof is critiqued from many angles. One direction of critique claims that even if the proof works, it does not establish the existence of the God of monotheism. If the universe is designed, it could have been designed by one of many deities, perhaps a weak and inferior one, or it could have been designed by a group of deities. Any flaws in the design of the universe could suggest a weak deity or perhaps a malevolent one. Another line of critique says there could be an internal "natural" reason for the order that is perceived in the universe. The order does not need to come from external design, but could come from some internal principle or principles. Particularly regarding the biological order of the universe, evolution through natural selection could explain the unity of parts present in complex living things.

While the Enlightenment included the reflection of both proponents and critics of the proofs for God's existence, on balance, the critics have been more important historically. For one thing, their critiques are still taken seriously in the contemporary context, and this has been at least part of the reason for a shift in the intellectual climate from the

Enlightenment era to the present. At least for some people in the contemporary period, the failure of the traditional proofs to provide rational evidence for God is part of the justification for adhering to atheism or agnosticism. A secular or purely naturalist point of view has intellectual respectability in the contemporary period. It is not taken to be simply the result of a person's rebellion against God or a moral failure of some sort. Also, while the proofs for God's existence still have their share of proponents who attempt to adapt them to new contexts and new scientific knowledge, taking the critics seriously has meant proponents of the proofs have generally scaled back their claim to certainty with regard to the proofs. Rather than seeing their arguments for God as definitive, proponents in the contemporary period tend to say the proofs can show God's existence either as more likely than not or as not an unreasonable thing to affirm.

Another reason the critics of the proofs were historically important is that their challenge regarding the justification of belief in God spawned new ways of providing this justification that bypassed the traditional proofs. Following the age of the Enlightenment, new and significant approaches to the question of God's existence emerged that regard the traditional proofs as either irrelevant or secondary.

Justifying Belief in God in the Contemporary Period: Karl Barth and Paul Tillich

There is no single method or single answer to the question of how contemporary theologians justify belief in God. Lively discussions continue to exist in the field of philosophy of religion regarding proofs for the existence of God and how successful they are in justifying belief in God. Some of the most interesting formulations of proofs for the existence of God today are variants on the teleological proof that attempt to accommodate the contemporary scientific understanding of the universe. They seek to show that a highly specific order was required for the universe to emerge from the big bang and to contain the conditions that would ultimately make it possible for life to exist and evolve into self-consciousness. For some, such a specificity of order implies the universe must have had a designer.[13]

Two twentieth-century theologians, Karl Barth and Paul Tillich, who were arguably the most important Protestant theologians of the past century, provide alternative ways of affirming belief in God. In their own ways, both men sidestep the traditional proofs for God's existence that were so important to Enlightenment thinkers. However, Barth and Tillich differ significantly in the way each one sidesteps the proofs.

Limits of Rational Thought: Barth

Karl Barth (1886–1968) is notable for claiming humans cannot know God or prove God exists through their rational faculties. He rejected all the traditional arguments for the existence of God and claimed there is no place in the structure of the human being where there is contact between the transcendent God and finite humans. In their natural state, humans are completely cut off from God.[14]

There were theological reasons behind Barth's claim that humans are completely cut off from God. Most notably, he wanted to affirm the principle of God's freedom in relation to humans. For Barth, God's freedom means God must be completely outside human knowledge and control. As such, it is completely up to God to decide whether God would make God's self known to humans in a divine revelation. The fact God would choose to do this shows the extent of God's graciousness to lowly humanity.

For Barth, it is in the account of the Christian Bible alone where God reveals God's self. He denied claims to divine revelation in other religions. The Bible shows God as creator, in covenant with Israel, and, most decisively, graciously becoming incarnate in Jesus of Nazareth to atone for human sins. All of this shows that the completely free God is also gracious.

Barth holds that because of the human limitations in knowing anything about God, including even whether God exists, it must be up to God to work in the believer to create the conditions for the acceptance of the truth of the Christian message. In other words, part of God's revelation to humans must be God's creation of the human capacity to accept and recognize that the revelation is true. God's revelation testifies to itself in those who hear the Christian message and come to believe it.

In important ways, Barth reversed the thinking of Enlightenment deists. The deists rejected the God of the Bible who acted in history to embrace the God of the philosophers responsible for the order in the universe. Barth rejected the God of the philosophers known through reason to embrace solely the God of the Bible known through revelation.

Because Barth's theology consists of a positive unfolding of the Christian message exempt from any capacity to question its truth, it is unsurprising that it has had a lukewarm reception in academic contexts. Barth's starting point allows no way to bring critical reflection to bear upon his thought, and academia functions by embracing critical reflection. Barth's thought has had a more positive reception in certain church contexts.

Awareness of God through Ultimate Concern: Tillich

Another significant contemporary path of justifying belief in God is found in the work of Paul Tillich (1886–1965). Tillich regarded himself as working consciously in the stream of thought inaugurated by Friedrich Schleiermacher (1768–1834), a post-Enlightenment theologian whose methods were so original and whose influence was so profound he has commonly been dubbed the father of modern theology.

Following Schleiermacher and over against Barth, Tillich claimed there is a dimension of universal human experience that includes the awareness of God. In their natural state, humans are not completely cut off from God. To Tillich, this dimension of experience can be disclosed through reflection.

Tillich thought the problem with Enlightenment deists, who tried to prove the existence of God on the basis of the order in the world, was that they affirmed humans have a direct experience of the world but no direct experience of God. To Enlightenment deists, God is distant and separate from the world. Barth said that as well, but while Enlightenment deists thought they could prove God's existence rationally on the basis of features of the world, Barth said proofs for God's existence do not work, and one must receive a divine revelation if one is to know God. Tillich rejected them both in claiming that, along with an experience of the world, humans have a direct or immediate experience of God. Instead of focusing on features of the world and getting into the debate about whether God exists, Tillich sought to bring out the dimension of human experience that shows humans have a connection with God already.

Tillich calls the dimension that involves the awareness of God the dimension of "ultimate concern."[15] He claims all people are grasped by such a concern in the course of living their lives. While everyone has a variety of concerns (most basically, concerns for food, shelter, and clothing, but also more complex concerns such as finding a job or a life partner), over and above these limited concerns is a concern that determines one's whole being. Such a concern has the character or quality of ultimacy. It is what provides the ultimate meaning and focus of life. It is that to which an ultimate commitment of life and death is made, and it includes the promise of a surpassing or unconditional fulfillment of one's being.

Tillich points out that anything can potentially become the object of an ultimate concern. It can be a sports team, wealth, power, or the image of an ideal body type. It can also be some concrete idea of God, like the one found in the Bible. In any case, whatever becomes the object of ultimate concern is God for that person because it has the quality of unconditional meaning. Whatever has the quality of unconditional meaning embodies what is meant by God. It is the place where the human is connected with God, or the place where the awareness of God is present.

To put Tillich's claim somewhat differently, his fundamental affirmation is that there is a layer of unconditional meaning in human experience. This layer of meaning is the presence of God to humans. No one can deny the human connection to unconditional meaning because even if one were to despair over meaninglessness, the despair itself implies or is made possible by the fact that one is connected to some unconditional source or ground of meaning. One cannot despair over the lack of concrete meaning without being connected to the source of meaning that makes possible the experience of despair over the lack of meaning.[16] For Tillich, this unconditional meaning expresses itself religiously in the human experience of an ultimate concern where some object is given unconditional meaning. This unconditional meaning is the presence of God and shows that human beings are immediately connected to God in their depths.

Whether or not contemporary theologians accept Tillich's specific analysis of ultimate concern, his general approach, which claims humans have a direct or immediate experience of God along with their experience of the world, has deeply influenced contemporary theology. Implied in Tillich's affirmation of an immediate connection with God is a distinctive and complex understanding of God and God's relationship to the universe. This understanding has also been influential in contemporary theology, and the next section contains an analysis of its similarities to and differences from Enlightenment Deism and theism.

God and God's Relation to the Universe in Panentheism

Prior to the Enlightenment, the universe was thought to be small with the earth at its center. The sun, moon, and stars were seen as moving around the earth in an orderly way, marking the times and the seasons.

With a difference only in details, this was also the biblical view. While extremely profound ideas about God and God's relation to the universe developed in the Middle Ages, it appears that a common unreflective belief remained from biblical times that above the sun, moon, and stars is the realm of heaven, where God resides with the angels. Numerous biblical texts from both the Old and New Testaments portray God as residing on a heavenly throne above the earth, surrounded by angelic beings.

Contemporary people's understanding of the universe has changed. Today, it is recognized that the earth is a small planet circling an ordinary star in a vast, ancient, and expanding cosmos. Despite this change, however, it is still common for Westerners, at least on an unreflective level, to think of God as somehow being above the earth. Heaven is still unreflectively regarded as a distinct place in the sky where God resides. The difference between people today and those from previous ages is that people today know this is not literally true. They know it because of the heritage of this culturally expanded view of the universe. Also, Christians are heirs to a long theological history that affirms God does not have a body, so God cannot literally be located somewhere in a space above.

The knowledge that God is not literally in the space above compels reflection about what is actually meant in considering God's relation to the universe. If God does not literally reside in a heavenly realm in space, how are God's presence and God's relation to the universe to be conceived? These are not only questions about who God is, but also questions of cosmology—the large-scale understanding of reality and what it is really like, in terms of not just its physical properties, but also its meaningful content. The modern period has seen shifts of cosmological understanding and poses compelling alternatives for reflection.

The Enlightenment deists of the seventeenth and eighteenth centuries attempted to sever the connection between God and the universe with the all-important proviso that God was understood to be the originating creator of everything. Enamored with the success of the scientific understanding of the world, they regarded the universe as endowed with a rational, mathematical order. This order and the world's operation were, however, seen as running on their own, independent of God. In this way, the Enlightenment deists differed from many great theologians of the Middle Ages, including Thomas Aquinas, who—influenced by Greek thought—understood God to be the ever-present and ultimate explanation of the order experienced in the universe. For deists, God is not involved in the universe at all after having conceived it in the beginning and setting it in motion. Like a top that continues to spin on its own once the string is pulled, so the universe continues to operate independently of God but according to God's original impetus.

The view of the world as a rational, orderly mechanism that runs on its own was also embraced by many Christian theists of the Enlightenment and beyond. Where Christian theists differed from deists was in their affirmation that from time to time, God intervenes in human history from outside of it. Accepting the idea that God is all-powerful, they affirmed God certainly can intervene in the universe and violate the natural laws God placed there. Accepting the Christian story, they affirmed God needed to intervene most decisively in Jesus of Nazareth in order to overcome the sinfulness and waywardness into which humans had fallen. This understanding of the God-world relation is perhaps best called "interventionist theism." It affirms that God is separate or independent from the universe in God's being, but claims God uses God's power to intervene in the universe periodically.

Deists and interventionist theists hold in common the affirmation that God is separate from or transcendent to the universe. Where they differ is that interventionist theists think God chooses to intervene from time to time, while deists disagree. This important difference is rooted most of all in the question of whether humans need God's intervention. Deists deny the need for such intervention. Interventionist theists believe it is needed because of human sinfulness, and that God graciously performed that intervention in ways revealed by the Christian Bible.

In the contemporary period, some theologians, including Paul Tillich, question whether interventionist theism adequately accounts for the presence of God in and to the universe. In classical theology, the term used to refer to God's presence in and to the universe is *immanence*. Interventionist theism affirms God's otherness or transcendence from the universe but, technically speaking, understands God's immanence as limited to God's active powers engaging human history periodically. While God is certainly presented in the biblical tradition as other and beyond the universe, God is also presented as intimately present to the universe. In the Old Testament, God's glory is said to pervade the universe (e.g., Isa. 6:3). In the New Testament, the writer of Acts has Paul say God is the one in whom "we live and move and have our being" (Acts 17:28). Divine worship, as a regular Christian practice, is about entering into God's presence, presupposing God's immediate availability. How can the immanent presence of God be accounted for theologically?

"Panentheism" is an understanding of God and God's relationship to the universe that seeks to account for God's immanence without sacrificing God's transcendence. This understanding of God was promoted notably in contemporary theology by Paul Tillich, and his ideas help clarify this complicated idea of God and the God-world relation.[17]

Tillich critiques both interventionist theism and Deism for the way they try to separate God from the world and the world from God. While it is difficult to envision, Tillich opposes the idea of God being understood as an independent being separate from or alongside the universe. Instead of a being that exists alongside the universe, God is understood as the unconditional element experienced within the universe. This does not mean, however, that God is understood as somehow limited to this universe—or any possible universe, for that matter. The word *panentheism* is used to describe this perspective because it means everything is in God. It expresses the complicated idea that the world is in God but God infinitely transcends the world at the same time.

Tillich's basic claim about God is that human experience contains an unconditional element, and awareness of this element is awareness of God. This awareness is not a separate or completely independent element from the awareness of other things in the world, but it accompanies the awareness of those things. As shown in the previous section, to Tillich, this awareness is present religiously in an ultimate concern where some object takes on the quality of ultimate meaning. Tillich also points out, however, that an unconditional element is present in ordinary cultural experience. When we hear the voice of conscience demanding we treat other people with respect and not merely as objects for personal gain, that demand contains an unconditional element. When we experience beauty in music or art, an unconditional, infinite, or inexhaustible element is present to us in the finite sounds of the music or form of the painting or dance. When we are driven to seek new knowledge of ourselves and our world, there is an unconditional element drawing us to push forward the limited arena of human understanding. In all these cases, in goodness, beauty, and truth, as well as in relationships of love, an unconditional element accompanies human experience. The unconditional element is, in Tillich's terms, the "depth" or "ground" of that experience. It gives to all cultural experiences their deepest meaning. That element, according to Tillich, is the presence of God in human experience.

The reason Tillich calls this element "unconditional" is that it is an element in human experience that the mind can recognize and acknowledge but is unable to grasp or know in the way the mind ordinarily knows things. Ordinarily, the human mind operates by grasping and applying concepts to the reality experienced through the senses. Humans apply ideas to the world to make sense of it, calling things by their names and organizing human experience meaningfully. However, when the mind confronts the unconditional element of experience—something it confronts only along with the experience of other ordinary things—nothing in the mind can grasp and apply to this element. The mind cannot place its categories or the limited concepts it has from the experience of the world onto this element. It is a surpassing infinity that must simply be acknowledged for what it is. It remains "unconditioned" by the mind, which can condition everything else it experiences but not this ground or depth that is the ultimate source of meaning in those experiences.

The problem, to Tillich, is that while this unconditional element is universally found in human experience, humans often try to make sense of this element by turning it into a discrete object called God, which humans then attempt to condition or upon which they place the limited categories of their minds. To Tillich, this is the mistake interventionist theism makes when it conceives of God as an object alongside the world. In an unsophisticated version, interventionist theism conceives of God as a being in another space above the world, called heaven, where God watches human history and intervenes periodically as a discrete cause. This idea of God is conditioned by the finite categories of human experience, including space, time, and causality. These finite categories of the mind are applied to what is in fact unconditioned and not subject to any finite categories. In a more sophisticated version, God may not literally be conceived as being in a space above the world, but God is still understood as a thing or a being in another realm. Here, God is still conditioned by the human mind that understands individual things as being within some larger whole or some greater realm. When humans think of God as an individual object who is part of a larger whole, they apply finite categories to what is unconditioned and not subject to any finite categories. For God to remain God, thinking of God as an independent being in another world must be avoided. In its place is put an understanding of God as a transcending infinity experienced within the world.

Tillich claims when God is conceived as the unconditional element of experience, God is conceived rightly as both immanent and transcendent. God is immanent because God is present to the mind and determinative of human experience in ultimate concern and the experience of goodness, beauty, and truth. God is transcendent because God remains unconditioned, or ungrasped by the human mind. Another way of putting this is to say that God's transcendence is not something that is just posited or affirmed of God, though humans have no experience of it. Instead, in some sense, God's transcendence is experienced. Paradoxically, it could be said that God's transcendence is an immanent reality for humans. It is present, but it is not something humans can ever grasp or limit. It remains infinite and unbounded beyond the limited experiences that accompany it.

The panentheism Tillich proposes differs from Deism and interventionist theism because Tillich affirms God is a universal presence to humans and not a separate being alongside the universe. As mentioned earlier, interventionist theism disagrees with Deism in embracing the biblical theme that God needs to intervene in history from time to time because of human waywardness. Tillich agrees with this idea in principle, rejecting the confidence and optimism about human behavior displayed by Deism. However, he rejects interventionist theism's interpretation that divine intervention means God as a being of enormous power acts literally as a direct causal agent from outside the universe. He reinterprets divine activity as having another meaning.

For Tillich, God is the transcendent depth present in human experience all the time. God is the unconditioned meaning that gives meaning to all human relationships and all experiences of goodness, beauty, and truth. While the meaning of life occurs only in relation to this depth, human beings still turn from it and turn in on themselves, a condition Tillich calls "estrangement" from the source of meaning.

Given the condition of estrangement, religion is decisively important because it is the place where humans reconnect with the meaningful depth of life. Put differently, it is in religious experiences where the depth of the meaning of life breaks through with a healing power to reorient humans and reconnect them to the source of meaning. Without this reorientation, Tillich thinks human life and human culture would continue in self-destructive estrangement from their depth.

In affirming the need for a continuous reorienting and healing breakthrough of the depth of meaning into human history and human life, Tillich both agrees with and reinterprets the meaning of divine activity in interventionist theism. With this interpretation, he embraces the God of the Bible, understood as an agent of history. At the same time, Tillich embraces the God of the philosophers by affirming that God is the depth of meaning present in all human experiences of meaning.

Human Language about God

According to the Old Testament, the second of the Ten Commandments that Moses received from God on Mount Sinai prohibits the making of any physical image of God. God is not to be identified with anything in the universe, presumably because God transcends and is different from everything in the universe. Despite this prohibition against cast images of God, the Bible is full of rich verbal images of God. Among the host of images, God is called King, Lord, Savior, Father, Husband, Fortress, Light, and Rock. Christian worship is filled with linguistic images of God, with Lord and Father (or heavenly Father) probably leading the way as the most commonly used terms for God in typical Christian liturgies or services.

Theologians have long recognized that while this language is important, it presents a myriad of complications for reflection. If God is transcendent and different from anything in the universe, how can this common language of objects taken from the universe be used to refer to God? This question has been renewed in a particularly potent way in the contemporary period by theologians who have a variety of viewpoints and agendas. One purpose of this section is to examine some of that material. First, however, it addresses the more general theological question of how human language can apply to God at all. This question is approached by engaging in a theological exercise aimed at explaining the issues at stake in the question, and then examining the classical theological answer.

Metaphors of God and the Analogy of Being

To understand how human language might apply to God requires understanding the way metaphors or images work, since calling God "Father" or "Lord" involves taking metaphors or images from common experience and applying them to God. Fathers are biological and social entities in human experience. Because human culture has changed, we do not have lords anymore, but the term comes from cultures that were hierarchically stratified and included lords and servants. In both cases, images from common experience are applied to God.

Part of the richness of human experience lies in the human ability to use metaphors or images to communicate with each other and understand the world. Using a metaphor involves finding and communicating a similarity between dissimilar things. For example, if a teacher refers to a student in her class by saying, "That student is a clown," the teacher is finding some similarity between students and clowns, although they obviously are not literally the same things. Clowns are entertaining and goof around to make other people laugh; most likely, it is this element to which the teacher is referring in comparing the student to a clown.

In some sense, the same idea of finding a similarity between dissimilar things must apply in referring to God with metaphors. If someone says "God is a rock," the speaker is affirming that there is something similar between the dissimilar things of God and a rock. The speaker is not saying God is literally a piece of granite. However, rocks have the quality of being immovable and steadfast; no doubt, that aspect of a rock is being applied to God.

While this seems a simple enough explanation for how human language for God works, it is complicated by the fact that God is supposed to be other than or different from everything in the universe. Ordinarily, in using metaphors, things in the universe are compared by means of ideas or concepts that also apply to the universe. To refer to the earlier example, when a teacher says her student is a clown, the comparison is intelligible because of people's idea or concept of "silly and entertaining behavior." That concept applies to a variety of things in the universe, including, in this case, clowns and a student. However, comparing God to a rock makes the claim that there is a similarity between something within the universe and something that transcends the universe. The claim is that the human concepts "steadfast" and "immovable" apply both to things in the universe and to God. But can the human concepts of things that apply to the universe also apply to God without diminishing God? If God is transcendent and different from everything in the universe, should it not be the case that no human concepts apply literally to God?

To state this dilemma another way, it appears to be the case that in order to preserve God's transcendence, it is important to affirm that none of the ideas in the finite human mind apply to God. God's transcendence means God is different from or other than anything in the universe. However, if none of the ideas in the finite human mind apply to God, how does human language about God make sense or express meaning at all? Conversely, it appears that one way to make sense of human language about God is by claiming that certain human ideas or concepts actually do apply to God. However, if certain human concepts apply to God, does this not reduce God to something finite and fail to regard God as different from or other than everything in the universe?

This dilemma is by no means new to theology. In classical theological terms, this is the problem of simultaneously affirming God's knowability and what is called God's aseity. The term *aseity* literally means "not derived." To apply this term to God means God is not derived from or dependent on anything in the universe. God is the source of everything in the universe, and everything depends on God, but God does not depend on anything. If God did, then God would not be absolute being but a dependent being.

The reason God's aseity is at stake in asking whether human language literally applies to God is that if the human ideas of things in the universe literally apply to God, then God must be in some sense derived from and dependent upon things in the universe. If there are concepts of things that apply both to the universe and to God, those concepts describe things on which God depends in order to have God's being. They are absolutes that define God. God would depend on them, rather than God being absolute and everything depending upon God. Because God has aseity, God must be undefinable. But if God is undefiniable, how can human language apply to God?

In the classical Christian theological tradition, particularly as articulated by Thomas Aquinas, the way the problem is solved is through recourse to what is called "the analogy of being."[18] The analogy of being acknowledges that God is utterly transcendent and different from everything in the universe, and because of this, human concepts, which are derived from things in the universe, cannot apply to God in a direct or literal way. At the same time, the analogy of being says that because God is the source of everything in the universe, there must be some analogy or likeness between God and the things of the universe. God causes the things in the universe to be. As such, God must in some sense be like what God causes. God is not literally like what God causes, because there is a difference between God—who is the source of everything in the universe—and everything in the universe. The analogy of being affirms the fact that human beings cannot know what God is in God's self. However, what can be claimed is that there is some analogy or likeness between the things in the universe and God, since God is their source.

The analogy of being makes possible the meaningfulness of human language for God, while also pointing out the limits of all such language. No human language applies to God literally. At the same time, there must be some connection by analogy between human language and God.

Human Language about God and Contemporary Theology

The increased awareness that human language for God is not literal leads to several implications in contemporary theology. This section covers three important ones.

The first one involves feminist theology. While feminist theology as a movement is covered in greater depth in chapter 7, this issue is important to discuss here, since it is relevant to the discussion of language for God. Feminist theologians have pointed out that while human language for God is not literal, it is important. This is especially the case because the realm from which such language is taken is regarded as valuable, since that language refers to God. If God is called "Father," what is affirmed is that there is a correspondence (by analogy) between fathers and God. This says something valuable about fathers. In some sense, they are Godlike.

As feminist theologians also point out, because human language about God is not literal, flexibility is built into the possible use of such language. Christians today are not just stuck with language from the past if that language comes from another context that is no longer relevant or is potentially harmful. While there are complicated questions regarding the reasons why Christians today may want to change God-language, as well as questions about the new God-language that should be used, the God-language itself comes from finite reality and is not absolute. It is not the case that the only parental metaphor that must be used for God is Father.

Being conscious about the limitations of language for God has led many Christian feminists and other Christian theologians to critique some of the language Christians use for God, especially in worship. Many feminist theologians think at least some contemporary Christian God-language comes from contexts of domineering power, and they suggest such language should be dropped or modified. The common terms *Lord* and *Father* have become especially questionable in these discussions. Many Christian theologians have been moved to explore the biblical and historical tradition anew and to creatively examine the contemporary context, in order to look for and lift up alternative God-language.

One of the most important contributions in examining alternative language for God comes from ecofeminist theologian Sallie McFague. She proposes using the terms *Mother, Lover,* and *Friend* as alternative ways of thinking about God as Creator, Savior, and Sustainer. She claims these terms are more fitting and potentially more healing in the contemporary context than hierarchical terms like *Lord, King*, and *Patriarch*.[19] Whether one accepts these specific suggestions, some Christian denominations are examining the use of alternative language for God, and in an important sense, this examination is based on the awareness of the nonliteral character of all human language for God.

A second contemporary theological development related to awareness that no human language for God is literal is a reemergence of what in the theological tradition is called "negative theology." Negative theology does not refer to a judgment people make about someone's theology; rather, it is a kind of theology that stresses the lack of correspondence between human language and God. It embraces God's utter unknowability. It is called negative theology because it affirms that because of God's otherness, the only thing that can be said about God is what God is not, rather than what God is.

In the contemporary period, negative theology has reemerged in a new way in relation to a philosophical perspective called deconstruction. While deconstruction is complicated and nuanced, one of its emphases is a severe skepticism and critique of human language's ability to grasp reality. This movement is called deconstruction because it deconstructs what it takes as the deepest meanings of the Western intellectual tradition. For deconstruction, all meanings and all affirmations of the Western tradition have hidden within them the seeds of their opposite. When their opposite is brought to light, as occurs in deconstruction, the meaning itself is negated.

The movement's skepticism about language and deconstruction of meaning necessarily involve a critique of the Judeo-Christian idea of God and the traditional language used to refer to God. The meaning of all such language and its referent is deconstructed. As some thinkers see it, what results is simply a kind of nihilism. For others, deconstruction opens up the possibility of an understanding of Deity that is beyond language and representation. The deconstruction of meaning gives way to the possibility of a negative theology.[20]

Finally, the awareness that human language about God is not literal has influenced some contemporary theologians by providing an avenue to understand not only Christian ideas of God, but also the ideas of God found in other religions. The question of the relationship between Christianity and other religions is covered in greater depth in chapter 6, but it is worth mentioning here because of its relevance to the issue of God-language. In the contemporary period, for many Christian theologians, the acknowledgment that all terms for God are analogous and not literal can lead and has led to a certain relativizing of Christian ideas of God vis-à-vis those of other religions. Rather than asserting that Christian ideas of God are absolutely true and non-Christian ones false, there is an awareness that all God-language is nonliteral and must be understood by analogy. Approaching the question of other religions' ideas of God with this understanding has been a bridge in some Christian contexts for greater sensitivity to and appreciation of other religions' ideas of God. The contemporary period has seen significant openness and dialogue between Christians and representatives of other faiths in part because of the insight of the limits of human language for God.

Chapter 4

Christ and History

In the middle of the Gospel of Mark, there is a dramatic moment where Jesus asks his disciples who people say he is (Mark 8:27-30). The disciples answer by claiming people say he is "John the Baptist, . . . Elijah, . . . or one of the prophets" (8:28). Jesus then asks the disciples who they say he is. Peter responds, "You are the Messiah" (8:29). This is the first time in Mark's narrative that a human character recognizes and confesses correctly who Jesus is.

It is clear as Mark's narrative continues, however, that while Peter correctly identifies Jesus as the Messiah, Peter does not understand what that means. In the very next verses, Jesus says he must suffer and die before rising again (8:31-33). Peter takes Jesus aside and begins to rebuke him. Rejecting the rebuke, Jesus calls Peter "Satan" and tells Peter to get behind him.

Peter's identification of Jesus as the Messiah presupposes a long history of Jewish hopes and disappointments, a history out of which an understanding of who the Messiah should be emerges. Jesus' rebuke of Peter inaugurates a new interpretation of what it means to be the Messiah. It is an interpretation that Peter cannot at first understand, but it will become the standard Christian interpretation.

This chapter covers the historical background of Jewish hopes for the Messiah reflected in Peter's confession about Jesus. It also explains the development of the classical Christian interpretation of Jesus. Finally, it covers some developments in the modern period, including contemporary understandings of the historical Jesus and some theological perspectives on Jesus coherent with the insights of contemporary scholarship.

Historical Background: Jewish Hopes for a Messiah

The word *Messiah* is a Hebrew word. While the Christian Old Testament was written in Hebrew, the New Testament was written in Greek, and the same word in Greek is *Christ*. Its translation in English means "Anointed One." When Christians call Jesus the Christ or, interchangeably, the Messiah, they are applying a title to him. They are claiming he is the Anointed One.

The historical meaning of this term comes from an ancient Jewish practice of religious figures anointing their political leaders with oil. To anoint someone literally is to "messiah" them in Hebrew, using the verbal form of the word *Messiah*. The anointing of a political figure by a religious figure signified that the political figure had divine approval upon him to rule.

Most significantly, after Israel gained a king, just over one thousand years before the birth of Jesus, a significant religious figure would anoint the king, signifying God's favor was upon him to rule. Israel's first king, Saul, was anointed by the prophet Samuel (1 Sam. 10:1). Because of Saul's failures, however, Samuel anointed another figure, named David (1 Sam. 16:13). David defeated Israel's enemies and formed a small Jewish kingdom in the ancient Near East around one thousand years before the birth of Jesus.

The history of the Davidic monarchy makes up a significant part of the Old Testament story. According to the book of 2 Samuel, shortly after David became king, an important prophet named Nathan told him in an oracle he received from Israel's God that "your [David's] house and your kingdom shall be made sure forever before me; your throne shall be established forever" (2 Sam. 7:16). As interpreted in Israelite history by the southern kingdom of Judah, this meant God had chosen David's sons to rule the people forever. The Anointed One was a king from David's line who ruled with divine authority and favor over God's people in perpetuity.

For over four hundred years, one of David's descendents was anointed to rule as king in Judah. During that time, considerable hopes for prosperity and peace were placed upon the Davidic king, God's Messiah. About six hundred years before the time of Jesus, however, the nation was defeated, and kingship ended. The plight of the Jewish people, the majority of whom were now scattered throughout other nations, became increasingly troubled. The Jews did not have political independence and could not have their own king. Until the time of Jesus and beyond, the Jews were a pawn in the politics of emerging empires, including the Persian, Greek, and Roman.

Throughout the troubled centuries before the time of Jesus, Jews continued to cling to the promises given them by their God. These promises included promises of blessing and prosperity, a time of justice and peace to be brought about by the Anointed One, the one God chose to rule. The problem, of course, was that the Jews had no king and no chance to govern themselves. They were subject to foreign leaders who often did not have their interests in mind. In these contexts, Jews projected their hopes for good times to come onto the future. They believed God's promises were true and a future Messiah would overcome the troubled context of the present and inaugurate the justice, peace, and blessings promised by God.

Around the time of Jesus, there were a number of different interpretations regarding who the Christ would be and what he would do. Some thought of the Christ as a kingly figure who would defeat Israel's enemies, establish an independent nation for the Jews, and inaugurate a new era of justice and peace. Others thought of the Messiah more as a cosmic figure who would come on the clouds of heaven to defeat supernaturally the enemies of God's people in a worldwide battle. This defeat of God's enemies would culminate in the creation of a new heaven and new earth without suffering and death. It was believed that even the righteous dead would be able to enjoy this new creation, because they would be resurrected from their graves to receive their reward.

Whatever the variation, understood in more modest or cosmic terms, the common element regarding the Jewish hope for the Messiah was that he would bring about a better situation for God's covenant people, the Jews. He would defeat their oppressors with divine power and usher in a new reality. This appears to be Peter's understanding of who the Christ is and what the Christ should do when Peter initially identifies Jesus as the Christ in the Gospel of Mark. That is why Peter is offended and rejects Jesus' claim that as the Christ, Jesus must suffer, die, and rise again.

As far as scholars can tell, there was no Jewish interpretation of the Christ at the time of Jesus that suggested the Christ would suffer, die, and rise again. This was a new interpretation Christians would apply to Jesus, given what happened to him. Equally important, there was no Jewish interpretation of the Christ at the time of Jesus that suggested the Christ was in fact divine or an incarnation of God. This also was a new interpretation born out of the Christian experience of Jesus' suffering, death, and resurrection. The next section unfolds the development of these interpretations.

The Development of Classical Christology

In Christian theology, the term *Christology* refers to what Christians believe and what the church teaches about the claim that Jesus is the Christ. Traditionally, Christology has two parts. One part involves reflection on the meaning of what Jesus did, and the other part involves reflection on the meaning of who Jesus is. While these parts are often separated for the sake of organization, ultimately they belong together. What Jesus did is connected to a claim about who he is, just as who he is makes possible what he did.

In order to understand the classical Christology of the church, it is necessary first to present a historical framework from which the church's affirmations about Jesus as the Christ emerged. This framework forms contemporary scholars' understanding of this period, and it is important for understanding not only the classical Christology of the church but also contemporary reflection about Jesus and contemporary Christology.

Historical Background: New Testament Gospels to the Nicene Creed

It is sometimes assumed, at least by some Christians, that when Jesus was on earth, he taught clearly who he was and the meaning of what would happen to him. While this teaching was hard for the disciples to accept at first, when they saw that what Jesus predicted actually happened, they believed what he had said. Subsequently, they recorded Jesus' teachings in the Bible. The record in the Bible reflects the universally accepted beliefs of the earliest church, which itself is thought to represent a pure strain of unity and faithfulness.

In fact, as contemporary scholars understand it today, the situation was much more complex than this. A detailed reading of the four gospels of the New Testament that attempts to compare them and understand the contexts in which each one was written has yielded a scholarly consensus that they are second-generation Christian interpretations of Jesus. The earliest gospel, Mark, was probably written in the late 60s or so, and the last gospel, John, may have been written in the 90s. This means decades passed between the time of Jesus' ministry, death, and resurrection appearances and the writing of the gospels.

ADDITIONAL INFORMATION

The Four-Source Hypothesis for the Construction
of the Synoptic Gospels

It has long been noticed by careful readers of the gospels of the New
Testament that the first three gospels, Matthew, Mark, and Luke,
share much in common. Broadly speaking, these gospels have the
same structure, in the sense that Jesus goes to the same places and
does the same things at the same times. At points in the gospels, the
wording of the sayings and stories about Jesus is virtually identical.
Because of the commonalities, Matthew, Mark, and Luke are called
Synoptics. This term comes from a Greek word that means "seen
together." In large measure, the Synoptic Gospels can be placed in
parallel columns and read together. Consider the following example
of a brief incident found in all three gospels:

Matthew 8:14-15	Mark 1:29-31	Luke 4:38-39
When Jesus entered Peter's house, he saw his mother-in-law lying in bed with a fever; he touched her hand, and the fever left her, and she got up and began to serve him.	As soon as they left the synagogue, they entered the house of Simon and Andrew, with James and John. Now Simon's mother-in-law was in bed with a fever, and they told him about her at once. He came and took her by the hand and lifted her up. Then the fever left her, and she began to serve them.	After leaving the synagogue he entered Simon's house. Now Simon's mother-in-law was suffering from a high fever, and they asked him about her. Then he stood over her and rebuked the fever, and it left her. Immediately she got up and began to serve them.

The commonalities among the Synoptic Gospels, including the
fact that at times the wording of the sayings or stories is virtually
identical, have led scholars to presume there must be a literary relationship among them. In other words, one of the gospels must have
been written first, and the other writers must have used at least that

gospel, and perhaps others, in crafting their own. The question of who wrote the first gospel, who used whom and how, and what other sources were used in the construction of the gospels is commonly called the "synoptic problem" in New Testament studies.

For centuries in the Christian church, it was assumed that Matthew wrote the first gospel. The church father Augustine (354–430) thought the New Testament order reflected the order of writing, and each successive gospel writer in the New Testament order used the previous gospels in his compositions. However, it was only in the modern period, under the influence of the rigorous, analytical, and critical thinking of the Enlightenment, that a systematic analysis of the Synoptic Gospels was made. Beginning in the eighteenth century, particularly in Germany, scholars compared each passage, looking for a hypothesis that would best explain the literary relationship among the writers and the sources used by each writer. The nineteenth century saw the emergence of a variety of hypotheses as explanations. Over time, one major explanation emerged in the scholarly community as the most compelling alternative. It continues to be the most common explanation embraced by contemporary scholars. It is sometimes called the two-source hypothesis, although a common variant or extension of that hypothesis is called the four-source hypothesis.

According to the four-source hypothesis, Mark was the first gospel writer. Mark was a second-generation Christian who did not come from a Jewish background and who lived outside the land of Palestine, where the stories he described took place. While there is considerable debate about the possible sources available to Mark to write his gospel, much of that debate is of a highly speculative character. Generally, it is thought Mark used oral tradition, or sayings and stories about Jesus that were passed down from eyewitnesses to the Christian community of which he was a part. He may also have had access to some written traditions about Jesus, including perhaps a rudimentary passion narrative. Whatever sources he had, Mark is usually regarded as the first writer who creatively put the variety of sayings and stories with which he was familiar into a comprehensive narrative structure.

Mark is generally considered to have been written sometime between the years 66 and 70. Scholars regard the text as giving evidence of developed ideas about Jesus that must have come from Christian proclamation that took place over several decades. The years 66–70 were ones in which the Jews in Jerusalem revolted against Roman power and the Romans besieged the city. After a long, terrible siege, the Romans took control of the city and destroyed the Jewish temple. Many scholars think Mark's text, especially chapter 13, references this dramatic context, so it must have been written during this time.

According to the four-source hypothesis, Matthew and Luke received their narrative structure and much of their content from Mark. Matthew contains 80 percent of the verses in Mark, while Luke contains 65 percent of Mark's verses.[1] The main argument for Mark being the source for Matthew and Luke is that Matthew and Luke almost never agree with each other when they diverge from Mark. It is far more common to have Matthew diverge from Mark while Luke agrees with Mark or, conversely, to have Luke diverge from Mark while Matthew agrees with Mark. This means Mark is probably the common basis of the other two gospels. Along with this, Matthew and Luke smooth out some of the linguistic difficulties in Mark and fix some of Mark's presentation of information that appears difficult to assimilate or understand.

Matthew and Luke are each considerably longer than Mark. While following Mark's basic narrative structure, Matthew and Luke have a significant number of passages in common that are not in Mark. In fact, more than 220 verses are in both Matthew and Luke but not in Mark.[2] Most of these verses are sayings of Jesus, rather than stories about him and what he did. Some of the most famous verses are included in what is called the Sermon on the Mount in Matthew 5–8. They include the beatitudes, teaching about the law, and the Lord's Prayer.

While Matthew and Luke share many sayings of Jesus in common, they do not put them into their gospels in the same way. Matthew tends to organize the teachings of Jesus into longer speeches, while Luke tends to disperse them throughout his narrative. This has led to the hypothesis that Matthew and Luke must have independently used another document besides Mark as a source when constructing their gospels. This hypothesized document is commonly called Q, from the German word *quelle*, which means source.

Most of the content of Matthew and Luke comes from Mark and Q. However, Matthew and Luke also have material not found in any other gospel. It is hypothesized this material comes from sources each one had independently. These sources are labeled M and L.

In summary, the most commonly accepted scholarly hypothesis for the construction of the Synoptic Gospels argues that four sources were used: Mark, Q, M, and L. Mark wrote the first gospel and did not have access to Q. Matthew and Luke wrote their gospels independently of one other. They used Mark's narrative structure and much content from Mark. They also incorporated material in their own way from another document they had, called Q. Finally, they used material from sources to which each one had independent access, called M and L.

As this brief summary suggests, the arguments for the four-source hypothesis are the result of tremendous scholarly effort. One value of this scholarly activity is that it has reinforced the importance of reading each gospel in and for itself. Ultimately, of course, Christians embrace and value all four gospels. However, sometimes the valuing of all four has led to fusing them in such a way that the distinct portrayal of Jesus in each one, and the distinct message of each one, is lost. The approach behind the four-source hypothesis insists that each gospel must on some level be seen in and for itself as a creative telling (and retelling) of the message about Jesus. This approach claims it is truer to the gospel texts and the authors' intentions to understand the gospels in their creative individuality, rather than simply fusing all the gospels into a conglomeration without distinctions.

The decades between the ministry, death, and resurrection appearances of Jesus and the writing of the gospels were times of creative and ongoing interpretation of what the events of Jesus' life meant and who he was. Recall that Jews during the time of Jesus had no expectation that the Messiah would die and rise again. This had to be understood from scratch. It is also the case that all four of the gospels in some fashion present the resurrection of Jesus from the dead as a surprise to his followers. In the Gospel of Mark, for example, the disciples had abandoned Jesus during his suffering and death, and some female followers were going to anoint his dead body with spices when, to their shock, they discovered an empty tomb. This surprising event needed to be understood. Who Jesus was, given this event, needed to be explained.

What appears to have happened is that as faithful followers of Jesus began to interpret and proclaim who Jesus was, they fused two decisive elements. On the one hand, there was the memory of what Jesus said and did, and what happened to him, that was passed on by followers who experienced him as a historical figure. On the other hand, there was the interpretation of who Jesus was and what he meant insofar as he was experienced in a new way as resurrected from the dead. In other words, the early believers not only transmitted a historical memory of Jesus but engaged in a creative interpretation of who he was as their living Lord that was based on a postresurrection experience of him. The gospels of the New Testament are streams of this ongoing and creative interpretation of the resurrected Lord fused with the transmitted historical memory of the person Jesus.

This can be stated another way by comparison with contemporary types of writing. It is sometimes the case, at least for some Christians, that the gospels of the New Testament are read as if they were newspaper accounts. What a newspaper does, at least ideally, is tell you what happened just after it happened, and it does so with standards or expectations of accuracy regarding its recounting of events and quotes. Contemporary scholars of the New Testament reject this understanding of the gospels, given the decades of distance between the events and the writing down of those events. At the same time, however, contemporary scholars also reject the idea that the New Testament gospels are to be read as if they were contemporary history books. History books inform the reader of what happened either in the distant or recent past with a broader understanding and hopefully a deeper interpretation than the analysis of a daily newspaper, but still with standards or expectations of accuracy regarding the recounting of events, stories, and quotes. The gospels are not history books in that sense either, although they do contain historical memories.

Rather than newspaper accounts or history books, the gospels are creative theological interpretations of the meaning of Jesus that are placed in narrative form. They contain some real historical memory of the person Jesus who grew up in Nazareth in Galilee and had a relatively brief teaching and healing ministry before meeting his fate on a cross in Jerusalem. However, they also contain creative interpretations of who Jesus was, given the fact that his followers experienced him as resurrected and, with this, claimed their allegiance to him as Lord. Both of these elements—historical memory and creative postresurrection interpretation—are fused together in the text as one. The communities and writers responsible for the text maintained some historical memory in putting together the text. At the same time, they were to some extent free to shape the ordering of events in the stories and even create new stories and new sayings reflecting their postresurrection understanding of Jesus.

If it is the case that the gospels contain creative interpretations of the meaning of Jesus by the believing community after his resurrection, one might expect to find some differences among them. After all, the community of early Christian believers was diverse. Fairly quickly, it consisted of both Jews and non-Jews, and it was spread through different regions of the eastern part of the Roman Empire. In fact, when we look at the gospels in the New Testament, we can see variety in their understanding of who Jesus was. How extensive and how significant the variety are matters of ongoing debate by contemporary scholars.

While there is recognized variety in the canonical gospels, in the contemporary period we have been fortunate to discover a whole series of gospels, as well as other early Christian writings, that did not make it into the New Testament. Dating these works is a matter of considerable debate among contemporary scholars. Most scholars think most of these works come from the early part of the second century, although a number of these works appear to contain older material. To be sure, these gospels present an even greater array of perspectives about Jesus. At minimum, they show that in less than a hundred years from the time of Jesus, there was a wide array of diverse and often conflicting interpretations of who Jesus was in the early Christian communities.[3]

ADDITIONAL INFORMATION

The Nag Hammadi Library and the *Gospel of Thomas*

While there have been a number of important contemporary discoveries of early Christian writings that did not make it into the New Testament, no single discovery has been more important than the discovery of what is commonly called the Nag Hammadi Library. The discovery was made in 1945 by a farmer who was looking for fertilizer in a cave near the Egyptian town of Nag Hammadi. In the cave, he discovered an ancient sealed jar. As it turned out, the jar contained fifty-two separate writings, the majority of which were gospels and other Christian writings that did not make it into the New Testament canon.[4]

The texts themselves were written in the ancient Egyptian language of Coptic and date from the third and fourth centuries. They are thought to be translations of Greek texts, the vast majority of which are lost, but most of which are believed to date to the second century. It is hypothesized these texts were buried sometime in the fourth or fifth century by monks from a nearby monastery called Saint Pachomius. Most likely, the monks buried the texts because they had been banned. They represented a view of Christianity that was considered heretical. This heretical view, called Christian Gnosticism, is explained in the next section. The discovery of these texts has proved invaluable to the contemporary understanding of Christian Gnosticism.

Of all the texts discovered in the Nag Hammadi Library, the one that has provoked the most attention is the *Gospel of Thomas*. It is purported to have been written by Jesus' disciple Thomas. It is intriguing in both form and content. Unlike the gospels of the New Testament, which are organized around a narrative structure, this gospel contains no narrative but a series of 114 discrete sayings of Jesus. It begins in the following way:

> These are the secret sayings which the living Jesus spoke and which Didymos Judas Thomas wrote down. And he said, "Whoever finds the interpretation of these sayings will not experience death."[5]

This quote, along with the fact that the gospel is a collection of sayings of Jesus, suggests that what is important to the gospel writer is not the story of Jesus' suffering, death, and resurrection, but an interpretation of Jesus' sayings. It is the interpretation of Jesus' sayings that leads to life.

An examination of the content of these sayings is striking, because many of them have similarities to what Jesus says in the Synoptic Gospels. At times, the sayings are identical to the Synoptics, or virtually so. For example, in saying 34, Jesus says, "If a blind man leads a blind man they will both fall into a pit."[6] This is virtually identical to Matt. 15:14. Many other sayings have parts that are similar to the Synoptics yet diverge. For example, in saying 31, Jesus says, "No prophet is accepted in his own village; no physician heals those who know him."[7] Jesus says something close to the first phrase in Mark and Luke, and also in John. The second phrase is not found in the canonical gospels.

While a number of sayings in the *Gospel of Thomas* are similar to those of the Synoptics, many are not comparable to the Synoptics at all. At times in the *Gospel of Thomas*, Jesus speaks in esoteric terms that most scholars identify as early or proto-gnostic teaching. For example, at times Jesus emphasizes escaping the evil world of the flesh for the sake of the world of the spirit. An example of this emphasis is in saying 37:

> His disciples said, "When will you become revealed to us and when shall we see you?" Jesus said, "When you disrobe without being ashamed and take up your garments and place them under your feet like little children and tread on them, then [will you see] the son of the living one, and you will not be afraid."[8]

The similarities between the *Gospel of Thomas* and the sayings in the Synoptic Gospels raise important questions about how to date the *Gospel of Thomas*. Did the writer of this gospel simply lift some sayings from the Synoptics at a time after they had already been written and adapt them in certain ways to create his gospel? If so, why include the particular divergences from the Synoptics, many of which are unique and striking, and many of which do not necessarily support gnostic ideas? If this gospel was not simply created from the Synoptics, then does it contain at least some independent material that either predates the Synoptics or is contemporaneous with them? Does at least some of that material go back to Jesus himself? These are questions with which scholars continue to wrestle.

By the middle and end of the second century, there is ample evidence of earnest efforts by some important Christian leaders to weed out what were regarded as false interpretations of Jesus and separate them from true ones. It appears these leaders represented an emerging mainstream group in Christianity, and their efforts decisively shaped the direction of Christian history. Among other things, they affirmed that a certain set of books, believed to have come from Jesus' apostles, represented true Christianity. Other books and other gospels were rejected as falsely claiming to have been written by the apostles. This process would eventually lead to the formation of the New Testament canon. While the entire New Testament canon was not decided until the middle to end of the fourth century, by the end of the second century, it appears this emerging mainstream group had accepted what could be regarded as a canonical core. This core consisted of the four gospels of Matthew, Mark, Luke, and John, the book of Acts, the letters of Paul (including Hebrews), 1 Peter, and 1 John.[9] Other books remained debated in different churches and different locales.

Leaders in the emerging mainstream church also stressed the importance of the formation of creeds and the affirmation of church order.[10] Creeds are succinct statements of belief, and one of the ways the emerging mainstream group of Christians defined who they were vis-à-vis other Christian groups with other beliefs was by articulating their beliefs in creeds. Finally, members of the emerging mainstream group separated themselves from other Christian groups by the affirmation that their churches were founded by Jesus' original apostles, to whom Jesus had given the authority to lead. Those apostles in turn had started the churches of the mainstream group and passed on to the current leaders their authority to lead. They were the ones to whom one was to listen in theological debates.

With this threefold process of canon, creed, and church authority, the emerging mainstream church eventually excluded other Christian interpretations in favor of theirs. This did not mean all debates ceased in the church. It did mean, however, that the range of options in the debates was narrowed. The debates occurred within what became an agreed-upon framework of interpretation accepted by the mainstream church.

This framework of interpretation set forth by the emerging mainstream church was finally given its most decisive formation in the writing of the Nicene Creed in 325. The formation of this creed occurred just over a decade after the watershed change in the church brought about by Emperor Constantine in 313. Constantine legalized and favored Christianity, placing it on a path whereby it would become the religion of the empire. As emperor, Constantine wanted the church to be united in its affirmations, especially its claims about Jesus. He called a council, or a meeting of important church leaders, whose purpose was to write a succinct statement of belief. Out of this council came the Nicene Creed.

While there was considerable controversy about the acceptance of the Nicene Creed in the decades after it was written, eventually it was affirmed by the church everywhere in the East and West. This affirmation continued through the Middle Ages, when stating the creed at worship services was common practice. The main Protestant Reformers of the sixteenth century, including Martin Luther, Ulrich Zwingli, and John Calvin, all accepted the Nicene Creed. Their debates with the church of their day lay elsewhere. To this day, the Nicene Creed remains the most important creed in Christianity for articulating what it means to claim that Jesus is the Christ. The next section explains the meaning of that affirmation in the creed by examining the historical and theological context out of which the creed emerged.

Jesus the Christ in Classical Christology

There can be little doubt that Jesus impressed himself mightily upon his followers as a person of God. While Jesus' mission was limited primarily to the rural villages of Galilee, it appears that fairly significant numbers of Jewish residents of this small area heard about him, and some witnessed firsthand what he said and did. As a result, a few were moved enough to devote their lives to him and his message. They believed he represented the Jewish God and this God's will. What a shock it must have been for Jesus' followers to see him at the end of his life get ground up by Roman power as if he were nothing but a common criminal. He was tortured and executed on a cross in typical Roman fashion as an enemy of the state.

This was not the end of the story for his followers, however; they experienced him resurrected from the dead, an experience that is difficult to interpret by any account. The earliest New Testament writer, the apostle Paul, who did not know the historical Jesus but was converted to Christianity several years after Jesus' death, never explicitly mentions an empty tomb. He does say Jesus was raised on the third day and appeared to his followers, including Paul himself. By Paul's account, he was the last person to witness an appearance of the resurrected Christ (1 Cor. 15:3-8). Paul gives few details about what the experience involved, sidestepping the question of what Jesus' resurrected body is like, other than to say it is a spiritual body that is imperishable and from heaven (1 Cor. 15:42-49). The New Testament gospels all claim the tomb in which Jesus' dead body was laid was empty. In their description of the resurrected Jesus, they do not merely affirm he was the same physical person with the same body resuscitated. He was changed—so much so that some of his followers had a hard time recognizing who he was when they first saw him (Luke 24:13-32; John 20:11-17). He appeared to his followers in a different form and with different powers that, among other things, allowed him to be present and vanish in mysterious ways that ordinary physical bodies cannot do (Luke 24:31, 36; John 20:26).

The meaning of the suffering, death, and resurrection appearances of Jesus needed to be interpreted. As we have said, not all of Jesus' early followers interpreted this event in the same way. Still, an important framework of interpretation was present early. We see this framework in the New Testament in the letters of Paul and the gospels. This framework became the predominant one because it was accepted by the emerging mainstream church in the second century.

The hope for a Messiah was a powerful theme in the Judaism of Jesus' time; however, in Jewish interpretations, the Christ was supposed to make a difference for the condition of the Jewish people in the world and not die and rise again. The main difficulty of interpretation was making sense of the fact that the promised Messiah died and rose again.

One way this was done was to connect the idea of a dying and rising Messiah with the idea affirmed in the cosmic understanding of the Messiah in Judaism, mentioned earlier, which claimed the Messiah would overcome evil and death. In the cosmic understanding of the Messiah, the Christ was the one who would bring in a new world where evil and death were defeated and justice and peace reigned for the righteous. While Jesus' resurrection had not brought in a new world, for those who experienced him as resurrected, he had overcome evil and death. He submitted to them at the height of their powers in the agony of the cross, and he overcame them in the resurrection.

For the followers of Jesus, this overcoming of evil and death meant something more than the fact that, as an individual, Jesus was now granted immortality. With Jesus identified as the cosmic Messiah, the one who was to bring in the new world without evil and death, his overcoming of evil and death showed God's decisive power and God's victory over these enemies in human life and human history as a whole. These enemies were not yet defeated in fact everywhere in history, but in Jesus' resurrection, they were disarmed and displayed as powerless.

As cosmic Messiah, Jesus was affirmed by Christians as the one who would also eventually bring in the new world devoid of evil and suffering. The resurrection appearances that Jesus' followers experienced lasted only for a brief time, after which it was affirmed that Jesus ascended to God's right hand, the arena of God's power (Acts 2:33). From this position, already triumphant over evil and death, Jesus would soon return to defeat those enemies in history itself. Many early Christians, including Paul, believed this would occur in their lifetimes (1 Thess. 4:15-17; 1 Cor. 15:51-52). In the meantime, believers could be assured of this coming victory and could share in some limited triumph over these powers in their lives as they awaited his return.

As seen in the New Testament, especially in the writings of Paul, this framework of interpretation was part of an understanding of universal history rooted in distinctive Jewish ideas about God as creator of the universe and actor in the arena of human history. In Jewish fashion, it was affirmed that God had made a good creation. A new stress was placed on the fact that humans had tainted this creation by an act of original disobedience. As a result of this original act of disobedience, evil and death infected all human history and all creation. God's merciful plan to overcome them included a covenant with the Jews and, finally, the sending of Jesus as the Messiah who defeated them in the cross and resurrection. Rising from the dead, Jesus ascended to God, from where he would soon return in God's power to defeat evil and death in history. This would result in the creation of a new heaven and a new earth in which believers would enjoy an endless age of justice and peace.

Within this important framework for understanding what Jesus as the Christ had done, there remained ambiguity about who Jesus as the Christ was. This framework claimed Jesus was the cosmic Messiah who fulfilled God's plan by defeating evil and death and who ascended to God and would return to bring history to a close with a new heaven and new earth. However, was this cosmic Messiah necessarily God or an incarnation of God? Was this cosmic Messiah human? These questions about Jesus' identity would engage the church for centuries.

It appears that at least some early believers in Jesus and some of the New Testament writers would have thought it odd to claim Jesus was an incarnation of God. They believed Jesus was a faithful human who was selected to be the Messiah and in whom God's Spirit came to dwell mightily. As God's agent and with God's power, Jesus overcame sin and death in the resurrection, after which he was exalted and ascended to be with God. At the close of history, he would return to usher in God's kingdom.

In this view, called adoptionism, Jesus was certainly understood as special. He was uniquely God's agent, specially chosen by God, who acted at God's behest. He performed a role no one else did or could. However, he was not an incarnation of the preexistent Word of God. He was a human agent of God, exalted to special status by God.

ADDITIONAL INFORMATION

Adoptionism in the Early Christian Movement

Adoptionism is the idea that Jesus was not the incarnation of the preexistent Word of God, but a human being who was adopted by God. Jesus became the son of God because of his faithfulness. He was adopted by God and gained an exalted status.

Many scholars see evidence of adoptionism in the New Testament. They point to two main types of adoptionism evidenced there. In one type, Jesus is adopted as the son of God at his baptism by John in the Jordan. The primary example given of this type is the Gospel of Mark. Mark's gospel begins with Jesus as an adult, making no mention of the virgin birth. Throughout the gospel, no claims are made by Jesus or the narrator that Jesus is the incarnation of the preexistent Word of God. Early in the gospel, in 1:9, the reader is told simply, "Jesus came from Nazareth of Galilee and was baptized by John in the Jordan." After his baptism, Jesus alone, and not those around him, sees "the heavens torn apart and the Spirit descending like a dove on him" (1:10). This is the moment of adoption, in which God declares, "You are my son, the Beloved; with you I am well pleased" (1:10).

In the second type of adoptionism, Jesus is adopted to be Son of God and exalted by God at his resurrection. One notable passage many scholars claim represents this view is Rom. 1:3-4. In this passage, the apostle Paul is writing, though many scholars think he is not necessarily expressing his ideas but quoting an early Christian confession about Jesus. The confession says Jesus was "descended from David according to the flesh and was declared to be Son of God with power according to the spirit of holiness by resurrection from the dead." Jesus' human descent is from the line of David. The resurrection is the point of his adoption as Son of God.

Whether adoptionism is traceable to the New Testament, it was certainly promoted in certain Christian contexts in the second century. It was the position of a popular Christian writing from the early or mid-second century called the *Shepherd of Hermas*. While valued in many Christian circles in the second century, the book was eventually excluded from the New Testament canon, perhaps in part because of its adoptionist views.

Standing in some tension with this view was the idea Jesus was in fact an incarnation of God. The development of this view is complex, especially given the fact that in Judaism at Jesus' time there was no expectation the Messiah would be an incarnation of God. What had developed in Judaism, however, was the idea of what could be called an "outgoing aspect" of God, referred to as either the Word of God or the Wisdom of God. While God in God's self remained transcendent, this aspect was the source of the order of the universe. It was that through which God created the universe.

Alongside this Jewish development stood the pagan religion of Rome, which had never shied from the idea of incarnation. Roman polytheism did not draw such a sharp line between God and the world as had the Jews and Judaism. The idea that humans could be incarnations of God, or that at death they would become Gods, was common.

In one important stream of Christian interpretation, it was affirmed that the Word of God, or the outgoing aspect of the one true God, had become incarnate one time in the person Jesus. The preexistent Word of God, which is responsible for the order of the universe and is that by which creation was made, took on flesh in Jesus.

While there are some passages in Paul's writings and other parts of the New Testament that either support this view explicitly or can be interpreted as consistent with this view (see Phil. 2:5-11) , it is especially in the Gospel of John where this view is preeminent. The prologue of John states that the preexistent Word of God became flesh in Jesus (1:1-18). In John, Jesus has an awareness of his preexistence, saying that he has "come down from heaven" (6:38) and that he is "from above" (8:23), and claiming, "Before Abraham was, I am" (8:58). At different points he says, "The Father and I are one" (10:30), and "Whoever has seen me has seen the Father" (14:9). Throughout the gospel, in various forms, Jesus refers to himself as "I am," the mysterious title for God in the Old Testament (see 8:12, 24, 28, 58).

While the adoptionist position would question whether Jesus was really God, a reading of the Gospel of John could lead one to question whether Jesus was really human. In fact, it appears that in the community that produced the Gospel of John, some claimed Jesus was not really human, causing a crisis and a split within the community. This split is evidenced in the letters of John in the New Testament (see 1 John 2:18-27; 4:1-3), which come either from the same person who wrote the Gospel of John or from someone within the same community responsible for that gospel.

The letters of John come at the end of the biblical period, approximately 100 c.e. At this time and during the following century, there arose to prominence an interpretation of Jesus that denied or seriously minimized Jesus' humanity. This movement, called Christian Gnosticism, affirmed an anti-Jewish interpretation of what it meant for Jesus to be the Messiah. Christian Gnosticism denied that the material world is good, while also denying that the Jewish God who made this world is either wholly good or all-powerful. Rather, an inferior God made this world, and the true God is purely spiritual and not connected with the material world. In some forms, Christian Gnosticism affirmed that Jesus was not really material but only appeared to be so. Jesus was understood as the Savior or Messiah because he came from the true, immaterial God to provide the secret knowledge necessary to escape the material world and all of history, which is the goal of human striving.

ADDITIONAL INFORMATION

The Gnostic Gospels of Mary and Judas

While the Nag Hammadi Library is the most complete source of Christian Gnosticism available today, other Gnostic gospels have been discovered that were not included in that library. Two of the most important ones are the *Gospel of Mary* and the *Gospel of Judas*.

The *Gospel of Mary* is purported to have been written by Jesus' follower Mary Magdalene. It was first discovered in Cairo, Egypt, in 1896. This version was written in the ancient Egyptian language of Coptic and dates from the fifth century. Unfortunately, the text is incomplete. Out of a total of eighteen pages of text, less than eight pages survive. Since the time of the original find, two other fragments from the gospel have been found that were written in Greek. This provides evidence of scholars' suspicion that the fifth-century Coptic version is a later translation of an earlier Greek text. Most scholars date the gospel to the second century.[11]

The gospel consists of three scenes. In the first scene, the resurrected Jesus is speaking to the disciples, answering their questions about the nature of matter and sin. Jesus stresses that sin is the result of people not knowing their true spiritual nature but giving way to bodily passions. Jesus encourages the disciples to teach his message, and he leaves. In the second scene, at Peter's request, Mary teaches the disciples what Jesus told her in a vision. While the teaching is complex, it appears to be advice about how the soul can find salvation by ascending beyond the powers of the material realm. The final scene consists of disputes among the disciples about whether Mary's teaching was actually from Jesus. Andrew and Peter claim it was not, while Levi defends Mary's legitimacy.

The teaching of the text shows the antimaterialism that is characteristic of Christian Gnosticism. One of the fascinating elements of the text is the way it elevates a woman as teacher of the disciples, and the conflict this elevation causes.

For those familiar with the canonical gospels, it is surprising to learn of the discovery of a gospel purported to have been written by the disciple Judas. In all four gospels in the New Testament, Judas betrays Jesus to the authorities, leading to Jesus' crucifixion. In Matthew, Judas repents for what he has done and hangs himself (27:3-10).

The *Gospel of Judas* was found with other documents in a cave near Maghagha, Egypt, in 1978. Because of political and economic intrigue, it was not published until 2006, making it one of the most recent pieces of literature to come to light about early Christian Gnosticism. The manuscript of the *Gospel of Judas* is nearly complete. The version discovered was written in Coptic. This version is probably a translation of a Greek original from the second century.[12]

The content of the *Gospel of Judas* is a series of conversations between Jesus and his disciples in the days before Jesus' arrest and subsequent crucifixion. While the discussions are often lengthy and difficult, it is clear that except for Judas, the disciples do not understand Jesus or his message. In the climax of the text, Jesus takes Judas aside and teaches him secret truths about the nature of reality. Among other things, Jesus teaches Judas that this world was created by inferior deities. One must realize this and transcend the limits of this world to find salvation from the true God. In a surprising twist on the gospel story, Jesus affirms that Judas is a faithful disciple who will gain prominence among the saved. By turning Jesus over to the authorities, which leads to Jesus' eventual death, Judas is not harming Jesus so much as he is helping Jesus get rid of his mortal body and attain salvation.[13]

In both the *Gospel of Mary* and the *Gospel of Judas*, the protago-
nists understand Jesus in a way the rest of the disciples do not. They
get knowledge from Jesus that the other disciples either do not have
or do not accept. This reflects an important tendency in Christian
Gnosticism, which presented Jesus as giving secret knowledge of
salvation. It also reflects the tension between gnostic groups and the
emerging orthodox church of the second century. In these texts, the
gnostics are claiming that the followers of Jesus' other disciples, who
represent the emerging orthodox church, are ignorant and miss out
on Jesus' true meaning and message.

Christian Gnosticism was critiqued by the emerging mainstream
church of the middle and end of the second century. The emerging mainstream church affirmed the Jewish background of Christianity, including
the idea that the one God made creation and it was good. They affirmed
that God acted in history with a plan. Making a covenant with the Jews
and becoming incarnate in Jesus were decisive parts of this plan. With
their affirmation that the material creation was good, they affirmed also
Jesus' humanity and the idea Jesus would come again to bring a new
heaven and new earth. The goal of life is not simply to escape the material world for a spiritual one, as in Gnosticism, but to look forward to a
perfected remaking of this world.

This critique effectively pushed Gnosticism out of the church, or at
least silenced its public voice, by the end of the third century. The concrete means used for defeating Gnosticism have already been mentioned,
including the creation of a canon of authoritative books, the formation of
creeds, and the affirmation of church authority.

At the dawning of the fourth century, while Gnosticism was silenced
and the New Testament was virtually formed, there remained no universally acknowledged creed that clearly articulated Jesus' identity. This
situation led to the rise of yet another prominent interpretation of Jesus
in a movement called Arianism. It was the debates over Arianism in the
church that led Emperor Constantine to call a church council in 325 out
of which came the Nicene Creed.

Arianism is named after a Christian priest and popular teacher
named Arius (256–336). While he was notable in his time and context,
little is known about his life or the true range of what he taught, since his
thought and that of his followers was rejected in the debates at Nicaea.

Having been rejected, his writings were ordered to be destroyed. What is known of his teaching comes almost exclusively from the writings of his opponents who were criticizing him.

In Arius's understanding, Jesus was more than human but less than God. Arius accepted the idea that Jesus was uniquely an incarnation of the Word of God. This meant Jesus was more than human. Arius claimed, however, that the Word of God incarnate in Jesus was not fully God. The Word of God was itself a creature made by God before the creation of the universe. In Arius's theology, what existed from all time was God alone. At one point, God created the Word. After this, through the Word, God created the universe. At the right time, God sent the Word to be incarnate in Jesus. Since Arius regarded Jesus as the incarnation of the Word of God, we can assume Arius affirmed that Jesus' death and resurrection accomplished salvation and that he would return to bring about a new heaven and new earth. In Arianism, Jesus was the unique incarnation of the Word of God who came for human salvation, but the Word of God was not fully God.

It appears Arius thought it necessary to claim that the Word incarnate in Jesus was less than God in order to preserve monotheism for Christianity. To him, if Jesus were God, then there would be more than one God, and Christianity would lose its monotheistic affirmation.[14]

The opposition that challenged the Arian position at Nicaea staked the claim that the Word of God incarnate in Jesus was fully God, while holding to the affirmation that Jesus was human as well. This position, which became enshrined in the Nicene Creed, says Jesus was of the "same substance" as God. Jesus was an incarnation of God who "became human."

In the generations after the creed's acceptance, the church affirmed with even greater clarity that Jesus was fully God and fully human by talking about the divine and human natures of Jesus. The relationship of these two natures was clarified in yet another important creed decided upon at a council of the church in Chalcedon in 451. This creed claims that the two natures in Jesus are neither confused nor separated. In other words, the divine and human natures in Jesus are not blended together into something that is neither fully God nor fully human. Jesus is not some freaky third thing that is a fusion of divinity and humanity but not fully either one. At the same time, the two natures are not in Jesus as two separate things. There is no identifiable "divine part" separated from the "human part," because this would mean Jesus was not a unity.

ADDITIONAL INFORMATION

The Creeds of Nicaea and Chalcedon

The Nicene Creed is the most important creed in the history of the Christian church. After its formulation and eventual acceptance, it became commonplace to repeat the creed in worship services, a practice that continues in most liturgical traditions today.

The Nicene Creed is called an ecumenical creed. The term *ecumenical* comes from a Greek word meaning "whole" or "all." In this context, it refers to a creed of the whole church. It was written in 325 and became accepted in Christianity before Christianity split into the Orthodox branch and Roman Catholic branch.

The following version is the original version from 325. The version that is commonly said in churches today is a slightly modified version, with most of the modifications coming from another church council in 381.

> We believe in one God the Father Almighty, Maker of all things visible and invisible; and in one Lord Jesus Christ, the only begotten of the Father, that is, of the same substance of the Father, God of God, light of light, true God of true God, begotten not made, of the same substance with the Father, through whom all things were made both in heaven and on earth; who for us men and our salvation descended, was incarnate, and was made man, suffered and rose again the third day, ascended into heaven and cometh to judge the living and the dead. And in the Holy Ghost. Those who say: There was a time when He was not, and He was not before He was begotten; and that He was made out of nothing; or who maintain that He is of another hypostasis or another substance [than the Father], or that the Son of God is created, or mutable, or subject to change, [them] the Catholic Church anathematizes.[15]

When the creed was written, the main issue of contention was whether Jesus was fully an incarnation of God, or whether the Son of God who became incarnate in Jesus was a creature who was less than God. The latter view was held by the Arians. The creed goes to great lengths to stress that what became incarnate in Jesus was fully

God. The end of the 325 version contains anathemas or condemnations of the Arian position.

The Creed of Chalcedon from 451 is an important ecumenical creed because it addresses the relation between the divine and
human natures in Jesus. Famously, it claims these natures are neither separated nor confused:

> Following, then, the holy fathers, we unite in teaching all men to
> confess the one and only Son, our Lord Jesus Christ. This self-
> same one is perfect both in deity and in humanness; this self-
> same one is also actually God and actually man, with a rational
> soul and a body. He is of the same reality as God as far as his
> deity is concerned and of the same reality as we ourselves as far
> as his humanness is concerned; thus like us in all respects, sin
> only excepted. Before time began he was begotten of the Father,
> in respect of his deity, and now in these "last days," for us and on
> behalf of our salvation, this selfsame one was born of Mary the
> virgin, who is God-bearer in respect of his humanness.
>
> We also teach that we apprehend this one and only Christ—
> Son, Lord, only-begotten—in two natures; and we do this
> without confusing the two natures, without transmuting one
> nature into the other, without dividing them into two separate
> categories, without contrasting them according to area or func-
> tion. The distinctiveness of each nature is not nullified by the
> union. Instead, the "properties" of each nature are conserved
> and both natures concur in one "person" and in one reality.
> They are not divided or cut into two persons, but are together
> the one and only and only-begotten Word of God, the Lord
> Jesus Christ. Thus have the prophets of old testified; thus the
> Lord Jesus Christ himself taught us; thus the Creed of the
> Fathers has handed down to us.[16]

The Nicene Creed with its clarification in the Creed of Chalcedon
expresses the classical Christology of the church with regard to Jesus'
identity. Jesus is fully God and fully human. The two natures are neither
confused nor separated in him. Implied in this articulation of Jesus' identity is the affirmation that God is a Trinity. God is not only the transcendent Father, but became incarnate in Jesus and is present in the church
in an ongoing way through the Spirit.

It is important to note that while the classical Christology of Nicaea affirms that Jesus is fully God and fully human, it does not say how it is possible for one person to be both, nor does it say why it is necessary that Jesus must be both. Each of these questions would be taken up by subsequent theologians and prove fertile theological ground in Christian history.

The latter question, regarding why Jesus had to be both fully divine and fully human, while not explicitly stated in the creed, was an important issue in determining the affirmations at Nicaea. We can see the reasoning for this in the writings of the main defender of the Nicene Creed, a bishop from Alexandria named Athanasius (296–373).[17]

Athanasius said Jesus had to be both divine and human to accomplish human salvation securely. He understood salvation as an exchange of properties between God and humans. Humans received the goodness and immortality of God, while God took on and overcame the sinfulness and mortality of humans. For this salvation to occur, God had to become fully human in Jesus so that the qualities of goodness and immortality would genuinely be imparted to humanity. If God did not become fully human, then human nature would not be transformed. At the same time, Jesus had to be fully God in order to bring the qualities of goodness and immortality to humans in a way that securely overcomes humans' sinfulness and mortality. Anything less than God would not be able to bring these qualities to humans in a definitive and secure way, so salvation would not be guaranteed.

The Historical Jesus and Christology in the Contemporary Period

In the modern period, a series of transformative ideas about Jesus have emerged. The best way to understand these developments is to recall the contemporary approach to the construction of the New Testament gospels, given earlier in this chapter. For contemporary academic scholars, the gospels are neither newspaper accounts nor history books. They are a combination of real historical memories of Jesus, memories that passed through the Christian community in various locales, and the creative postresurrection interpretation of who Jesus is that was put forward by early believers.

One of the implications of this understanding of the gospels is that Jesus had a limited consciousness regarding who he was and what would happen to him. This view can appear shocking, at least initially, to Christian belief. It is deeply ingrained in Christian understanding that Jesus was God, and with this affirmation is very often connected the assumption that Jesus had God's mind, or divine knowledge. The gospels themselves reinforce this view in significant ways. This is especially true of the Gospel of John, where Jesus is presented as not only knowing what is going to happen to him in detail in advance, but knowing what it all means and even knowing about his own preexistence in heaven with God. At the same time, however, the classical Christology of the church affirms that Jesus was fully human. To be fully human means not only to have a human body but to have a human mind. This emphasis on the human mind of Jesus characterizes typical academic scholarship on Jesus in the contemporary period.[18]

According to the contemporary scholarly view of the construction of the gospels, when Jesus is presented as having supernatural knowledge, this is not the Jesus of historical memory. Instead, it is the postresurrection Jesus creatively projected back onto the Jesus of history by the early Christian community and gospel writers. In other words, after the resurrection, when the church came to understand Jesus as its exalted Lord and therefore in some sense more than human, the church created stories of Jesus as knowing in advance what would happen to him and the meaning of those events. In fact, as a historical figure, Jesus had a human consciousness. This means he did not know any more about the future and what would happen to him than any other observant person would or could.

This understanding of the gospels invariably raises the question about who in fact the historical Jesus was. If Jesus had a limited consciousness and did not know either precisely what would happen to him or how the church would end up interpreting him after the resurrection, then who was he as a living figure of history? How did he understand himself, and what was the message he delivered to others as he moved through the Galilean villages among the poor Jewish peasantry under Roman occupation at the end of the third decade of the first century?

This has been a potent question in scholarship on the Bible in the modern period. In contemporary biblical studies, it is commonly referred to as the "quest for the historical Jesus." This quest itself has an intriguing history, and while the details of this history are too numerous to recount, there is a main outline that is informative for showing some of the discoveries and debates of the distinctively modern approach to the New Testament.

The Quest for the Historical Jesus

The quest for the historical Jesus involves the attempt to separate the real historical memory of Jesus in the biblical text from the church's post-resurrection interpretation with which that historical memory is fused. If one can clearly distinguish the historical memories from the church's constructions, one would presumably have material by which one could reconstruct the historical figure of Jesus himself.

Answers to who Jesus was that have come out of this quest have a history that reaches all the way back to the Enlightenment Deism of the seventeenth and eighteenth centuries. In the American context, for example, the deist Thomas Jefferson (1743–1826) engaged in an early version of the quest for the historical Jesus. Jefferson denied the supernatural elements in the biblical accounts of Jesus. To Jefferson, Jesus was not a healer, an exorcist, the incarnation of God, or someone who rose from the dead. When you take out these elements, Jefferson thought, what you have left is a moral teacher, and Jefferson was convinced that Jesus' moral teaching was of the highest caliber. It was Jesus' refined moral teaching that was most to be admired about him.[19]

The nineteenth century saw the quest for the historical Jesus take a more systematic turn, and it involved considerable creativity in thinking about the New Testament text. Still, the view of Jesus that predominated during this time was that of a moral teacher.

The beginning of the twentieth century brought a revolution of this view. Credit for this revolution primarily belongs to the German scholar and humanitarian Albert Schweitzer (1875–1965). He published a widely read and widely discussed text called *The Quest of the Historical Jesus* in 1906.[20]

In Schweitzer's interpretation, understanding Jesus in his context means seeing Jesus as a radical prophet-like figure who anticipated the end of the world in his own time. Like other Jews of his day, Jesus thought God would soon intervene in history to defeat the evil powers represented by the Roman Empire and bring about a new era of justice and peace for God's righteous people. Jesus regarded it as his special mission to proclaim this event, and he understood himself as an important figure in bringing about this event. For Schweitzer, Jesus' sayings and deeds should be interpreted in light of his anticipation of an imminent cosmic apocalypse, not as principles of a refined universal morality.

This view has been refined and transformed in a variety of ways through the twentieth century and into the present, but broadly speaking, it has remained the predominant scholarly view on the historical Jesus. Jesus is regarded as anticipating the end of the world in his lifetime—an event that is to be brought about by the dramatic intervention in history by God to defeat evil. Jesus' authentic sayings and deeds promote this understanding and are to be interpreted in light of it. Precisely how Jesus understood himself and his role in the anticipated intervention and triumph by God are matters of considerable debate. Still, it is claimed that, as the result of the postresurrection experience, the early church proclaimed that Jesus was the one who would soon return and bring about the new world Jesus himself proclaimed and anticipated during his life and teaching.[21]

While the view of the historical Jesus as expecting the end of the world in his lifetime has been the predominant one in the contemporary period, it is not without its challengers. In particular, a great number of scholars claim that the entire project of seeking the historical Jesus is bankrupt. They say it is impossible to determine what in the New Testament comes from the historical Jesus himself and what comes from the creative interpretation of the church. The attempt to make this distinction invariably involves irresponsible historical analysis, so the attempt should not be made.[22]

At times, this view has predominated in the academic community, and the quest for the historical Jesus has lain dormant. It is, however, difficult to think the quest will ever be abandoned. Previous failings aside, once it is understood that the New Testament contains both historical memory and creative interpretation of the church, it seems inevitable that some scholars will try to separate out the historical memory and coherently reconstruct the actual history behind the text, including an interpretation of the sayings and deeds of the historical Jesus.

Another challenge to the view of the historical Jesus as someone who expected the end of the world in his lifetime has arisen in the scholarly community from the latter third of the twentieth century to the present. A number of scholars claim the passages in which Jesus speaks about the imminent end of the world never came from Jesus himself, but were part of the church's creative interpretation of him.

If the historical Jesus was not a radical prophet-like figure who expected the apocalypse in his time, who was he? Differing interpretations have been put forward to answer this question, but generally he is regarded in his words and deeds as a teacher of a kind of subversive wisdom. His wisdom was one in which he sought to overturn the power structures and the hierarchical divisions between people that were prominent in his day. He called people to shared fellowship beyond the abuses of power and the divisiveness of human culture that set groups above one another and against each other. His message was radical as a new vision for society, but it was not something he anticipated God would enact by dramatically intervening in history and bringing about the end of the world in his time. He simply encouraged people to start living in this new way now. To do so was to make the kingdom of God a reality in the present.[23]

This alternative version has enjoyed some scholarly popularity, but it remains a serious question whether it can adequately account for the fact that, in Jesus' context, the anticipation of an apocalyptic end of the world was a powerful theme. This theme was an important part of early Christian teaching about Jesus. Many scholars remain convinced that if the early church taught an apocalyptic end of the world was soon to occur in Jesus' second coming, the church must have gotten an apocalyptic message from Jesus, albeit in a different form. In other words, the alternative interpretation of the historical Jesus appears to have a harder time connecting its understanding of the historical Jesus with the early church's message about Jesus than does the position affirming that Jesus himself thought the world would end in his lifetime.

Directions in Contemporary Christology

Many creative Christologies have appeared in the contemporary period. Rather than attempting a comprehensive summary, this section covers three major directions in Christology, showing how these directions relate both to the question of the historical Jesus and to the classical Christology of the church.

LIBERATION THEOLOGY

The importance of the words and deeds of the historical Jesus has reemerged in a number of contemporary Christologies. This is true especially in feminist theology and liberation theology. Since feminist theology is covered in chapter 7, this section focuses on liberation theology and its understanding of the historical Jesus.

Liberation theology is indigenous to Latin America, where it first emerged in the 1960s. Its concrete context and focus are the condition of the lower classes in the developing world of Central and South America, particularly those whose daily lives are stuck in grinding poverty. This is a kind of poverty with which those living in the developed world are often unfamiliar and may have a hard time understanding. It is poverty in which the basic necessities of food, shelter, clothing, and medical care are often lacking, and even if one has them, life is lived on the razor's edge of losing them. It is the kind of poverty that is devoid of opportunity. There is little or no chance for a decent education and safe, well-paying jobs. For the tens of millions stuck in this kind of poverty, there seems to be no way of escape, because there is no opportunity to garner the resources to change their condition.

In this context, certain Roman Catholic theologians began to embrace a Marxist analysis to understand the condition of the lower classes. They claimed the lower classes were not poor because they were lazy or unintelligent, and they were not poor because God had poured special blessings or favor upon the handful of wealthy elites in Latin American society or among the great masses of well-off people in the developed world of the United States and Western Europe. They were poor because the well-off wanted to maintain their wealth. To do so, the wealthy set up economic systems backed by political power that required cheap labor from the poor of the developing world and the cheap extraction of raw materials from their countries.

In this context, liberation theologians describe the main problem of the lower classes in Latin America as oppression. This oppression is seen as structural, involving economic and political systems beyond any individual's control. The main problem of the poor is not that as individuals they behave badly. It is that they are trapped by economic and political systems that are oppressive, and it is those systems that need to be changed. The answer to oppression has to be liberation, and liberation has to mean concrete changes in the structural conditions causing oppression.

Embracing a Marxist analysis of the problem, liberation theologians claimed Christianity needs to provide a solution to this situation. They developed a powerful new understanding of Christianity in which they affirmed that God favors the poor versus the powerful and desires the relief of their oppression.[24] They looked for support in biblical themes such as the exodus in the Old Testament, where God freed the Hebrew slaves from the powers that dominated them in Egypt, or the Old Testament prophets, who sounded the call for the concrete enacting of justice in God's name. They also looked anew at the life and ministry of Jesus.

From their vantage point, liberation theologians saw that Jesus' social and political context mirrored their own. There was a deep identification with Jesus as a historical figure, including his message and his fate. Jesus was a member of an oppressed class in the powerful Roman Empire. Liberation theologians including Leonardo Boff understood Jesus as a radical, prophet-like figure who called for the kingdom of God to be realized in history and symbolically enacted the presence of the kingdom in his deeds. The call for the realization of the kingdom of God meant the overthrow of the powerful oppressors and the inauguration of God's justice in a context of oppression.[25]

Jesus' call for the kingdom was courageous, because he inevitably faced opposition from the social, political, and religious forces who had an interest in keeping the oppressive systems intact. Jesus called his followers to show that same kind of courage, even if it meant facing death.

Jesus was eventually killed by the oppressive powers of the world, but his resurrection meant God vindicated him. His life and his message were ones that God favored. Moreover, the resurrection means God's power is still present in an ongoing way in the community committed to his vision and built on his message.

On the whole, liberation theologians have been concerned to show that their ideas about Jesus fit with the classical two-nature Christology of the church. However, their emphasis is not so much on right belief about Jesus (orthodoxy), but on following Jesus (orthopraxy). For Latin American liberation theologians, right action primarily means identifying with Jesus and taking a courageous stand as he did in affirming the need for enacting God's justice in history.

While liberation theologians accepted a Marxist analysis of the problem of the poor, they did not necessarily accept Marx's utopian solution to this problem. Marx thought a utopian society would emerge from the tension between owners and workers when workers revolted and controlled the means of production. Most liberation theologians have been more circumspect, affirming that a utopian society will always remain a future goal even while affirming the need for changes now.

While liberation theology has been undergoing rethinking since the fall of the Soviet communist system, its importance remains undiminished in the context in which liberation theologians live and work, and in the contemporary Christian theological world. They have raised important challenges to developed-world theologians regarding what it means to enact God's justice today in a global context, and they have provided keen insights into the biblical literature. These insights include raising awareness of the fact that the context of the interpreter influences what is seen and what is emphasized in interpretation of the Bible.

EXISTENTIALIST THEOLOGY

Liberation theology embraced the historical Jesus and his message about the kingdom of God, calling for right action in following Jesus in the work for social change that would overcome the structures of oppression. Existentialist theology lacks these emphases. It denies the significance of the historical Jesus for faith, and its transformative concern is directed toward the individual and the individual's realization of authentic existence, rather than the transformation of oppressive social structures.

The father of existentialist theology is Rudolf Bultmann (1884–1976), a German theologian who in his early career was known primarily as a New Testament scholar. After writing several groundbreaking works on the New Testament, he spent the last few decades of his life developing a theology based on his understanding of the Bible and the existentialist philosophy of Martin Heidegger (1889–1976).[26]

Bultmann was well aware of the scholarly quest for the historical Jesus. In certain ways, he contributed to it in his New Testament scholarship by helping delineate criteria by which one can determine whether a saying attributed to Jesus actually came from the historical Jesus or from the early church. As a New Testament scholar and historian, however, Bultmann thought there was not enough information to create a reliable construction of the historical figure of Jesus. As a Christian theologian, he was convinced that whatever one might discover about the historical Jesus is ultimately insignificant. To Bultmann, the historical Jesus can never be more than a model for people to emulate, and he thought Christianity consists fundamentally or primarily in the fact that the resurrected Christ is savior or redeemer, not that the historical Jesus was a model.

Bultmann was convinced the worldview of the writers of the New Testament and the early church that formed the classical Christology of Christianity differed significantly from the worldview of contemporary people. The New Testament writers and the early church accepted a mythological worldview in which supernatural powers located both above and below the earth directly intervene in our time-and-space world. Bultmann thought the classical Christology of the church expresses this worldview, wherein a preexistent divine being became incarnate as a human to overcome satanic powers and return to the divine realm. To him, contemporary people cannot accept such direct divine intervention, and the classical Christology in which it is expressed is not to be understood literally. At the same time, Bultmann wanted to proclaim that the meaning of Christianity is salvation, not that the historical Jesus is a model for human action.

While Bultmann himself never puts it quite this way, for him, Christianity is about salvation because the resurrection experience is a saving and transformative religious experience. The resurrection is not something that happened to Jesus' body, but something that happened to Jesus' disciples. They experienced new life or a transformed existence despite the defeat of the cross. In this awakening of new life, a power was available that overcame any obstacles to living authentically. The early church interpreted this new life in the mythological worldview of their day as the supernatural appearances of a glorified Christ. Over time, the mythological worldview completely took hold, and the idea of the incarnation of a divine being who died, rose, and ascended to be with God became normative Christian belief. However, according to Bultmann, contemporary people do not need to accept the mythological worldview in order to access the realization of new life that is contained in the message about the Christ. Contemporary people can still have the experience of new life and transformed existence, which is ongoing in the Christian life and message, without accepting literally the mythology of the New Testament.

For Bultmann, the experience of new life or salvation is understood as the change from inauthentic to authentic existence. While the category of authentic existence is complex, most basically it means for Bultmann that one does not seek to secure one's existence out of finite or available things, but lives one's life on the basis of the transcendent power of God that is beyond the finite. Bultmann thought human beings cannot live this way on their own. They will always fall back into trying to secure their lives through finite things unless freed through the message of Christianity. That message is most fundamentally a message about the cross and resurrection, which means dying to those things that would keep one from an authentic existence and being reborn to a new life reconciled with God.

Bultmann never seriously dealt with the question of other religions. He thought Christianity has life's answer, in the sense that authentic existence is made possible through it. He sought no analysis beyond that affirmation. However, since his time, it has become clear that his understanding of how Christianity operates to bring about authentic existence needs to be analyzed from a universal religious framework. In other words, there is no necessary reason to presuppose that the transformation about which Bultmann speaks, or something like it, is possible only in Christianity. It is possible there, but it certainly may be available elsewhere, and to understand fully how it is possible in Christianity requires an analysis using categories that can potentially be applied elsewhere.

Bultmann has been soundly criticized on many levels. To some, he is wrong to ignore the historical Jesus and his power as a model for Christian living. For others, Bultmann seems to ignore a needy world and reduce the meaning of Christianity merely to an individual transformative experience. For many, Bultmann's denial of direct divine intervention in history means he has rejected something essential to Christianity, since Christian belief invariably includes belief that God acted directly in history. While criticized by some, Bultmann is seen as a heroic pathfinder by others. He sought to make sense of Christianity in a modern context with its new intellectual challenges. For such reinterpreters, whether or not one fully agrees with Bultmann's analysis, the only way Christianity itself will be saved and continue to exist is if it meets fully the challenges of the modern world.

THEOLOGY OF HOPE

While the "theology of hope" is a full-fledged movement with influences in many directions, it is most often associated with the early work of the German Reformed theologian Jurgen Moltmann (1926–), who wrote a book by that title.[27] Like Bultmann, Moltmann minimizes the importance of the historical Jesus for faith, at least in his early work, and focuses much more on the meaning of the saving events of Jesus' cross and resurrection. He criticizes Bultmann, however, for limiting the meaning of salvation to the existential transformation of individuals. Moltmann affirms a historical and cosmic meaning of the cross and resurrection of Jesus. For him, the cross and resurrection of Jesus are the concrete hope of all of human history and the universe as a whole.

Moltmann claims humans are hopeful creatures who live in relation to future possibilities. The biblical revelation in the Old Testament, which Moltmann takes as foundational to God's decisive historical interaction with humanity, needs to be understood in that context. The Old Testament revelation is most centrally a series of promises by which God draws the Jewish people to new possibilities that would not otherwise have been seen or realized in history. God's promises open a new future that draws the present to it. For Moltmann, this is the way distinctively theological hope, or hope in which God is active, operates. In it, something new emerges that is more than what was contained in the given context of the old. This "more" is found always in the direction of healing and wholeness and the overcoming of suffering and evil.

The promises of the Old Testament move from promises of the flourishing of the Hebrew community in history under God's blessings to the promise of the resurrection of the dead and the remaking of the universe without evil and suffering. It is in the context of the latter promise that Moltmann thinks the death and resurrection of Jesus need to be understood. For Moltmann, the resurrection of Jesus in particular is a fulfillment in the middle of history of the hopeful promise of what will happen to all humans and to the entire cosmos at the end of history. Unlike Bultmann, Moltmann claims that the resurrection of Jesus was actually the reanimation and transformation of the historical figure of Jesus. Jesus was changed into what all humans will become when God's promise for the universe is realized.

On the basis of the resurrection, Moltmann affirms Christianity has a worldwide mission. It is uniquely in the Christian proclamation and no other religion that the realization of the future direction of the cosmos is contained. Moltmann also affirms that the realization of the resurrection has a resounding ethical influence on believers. The resurrection is the overcoming of evil, suffering, and death. While humanity and the cosmos must wait for its final realization in the future, knowing that history is moving in that direction motivates believers to work actively for the overcoming of evil and suffering in history. Finally, the resurrection has ecological implications because, in the resurrection, Jesus is transformed as a whole person, thus signifying what the entire creation will become. Living in light of the hopeful possibility of this transformation means to care for the natural world, which itself will be transformed at the end of time.

While Moltmann does not focus on the historical Jesus, one can certainly see connections with liberation theology in his thought. As in liberation theology, Moltmann emphasizes the importance of healing transformations in history, especially in his emphasis on the ethical implications of Christian hope in the resurrection, and he promotes social activism toward justice in a manner similar to liberation theology.

Moltmann embraces the classical Christology of the church explicitly and develops what he takes to be the implications of this theology in an important early work titled *The Crucified God*.[28] In this text, he emphasizes that since Jesus is an incarnation of God, the suffering, crucifixion, and death of Jesus must be understood as an event in the life and experience of God. With Jesus' suffering and death, God experiences and identifies with the suffering of all humans and all the cosmos. At the same time, the resurrection guarantees victory over suffering and death.

The understanding of God that Moltmann develops in his explication of Jesus' suffering and death can be contrasted to the idea of God in classical Greek thinking. In classical Greek thinking, God is said to be impassible, or incapable of suffering or pain. If God were capable of suffering and pain, it would make God limited in some way and not absolute. For God to undergo suffering would mean God must undergo change in the movement through suffering. In Moltmann's understanding of God becoming incarnate in Jesus, he stresses that God does undergo change understood in a specific way. While God's character is unchanging, God's experience is deepened through the incarnation, suffering, death, and resurrection of Jesus.

Moltmann is criticized in differing directions. Those sympathetic to existentialist theology criticize his historicizing of Christianity. By literalizing the resurrection and affirming that it tells us of the future of the cosmos, they claim he has absolutized Christianity vis-à-vis other religions. Others think his rejection of divine impassibility endangers God's transcendence or absoluteness, making God subject to a historical experience for God's own development. In any case, his analysis of the importance of hope for human life, his understanding of the resurrection as the realization in history of the ultimate hope of the cosmos, and his understanding of God as identifying experientially with suffering and death in the cross have contributed significantly to the contemporary theological discussion and remain lasting resources for theological reflection.

Chapter 5

Heaven, Hell, and Anthropology

As self-conscious beings, humans live their lives aware of finitude, aware of the fact that all individual lives are inexorably moving toward death. Reports of near-death experiences aside, it remains that what lies beyond death cannot be determined on the basis of experience. Instead, humans project ideas of what happens beyond the grave based on their understanding of the nature of reality. Beliefs about what happens beyond death are rooted in humans' understanding of what they are, how they are related to the rest of the world, who God is, and how God regards humans.

Historically, a variety of options in the Old and New Testaments and in Greek thought about what happens after death helped shape the development of classical Christian theology on this issue. This chapter covers these historical developments. It also looks at the way some contemporary theologians are rethinking the afterlife as they reexamine how humans are related to the world, who God is, and how God regards humans.

Biblical and Greek Views of Humanity and Human Destiny

Mainstream Old Testament Belief in Sheol

Given the importance of belief in the afterlife for many Christians today, it can be surprising to realize that throughout the majority of the Old Testament, from the time of Abraham (approximately 1750 b.c.e.) until about two hundred years before Jesus, mainstream Jewish belief did not include belief in a vital afterlife. Instead, Jews believed in an abode of the dead called Sheol, where all people went when they died.

While Sheol is never explicitly described, belief in Sheol is assumed throughout the Old Testament narrative, and at various times, the writers comment on aspects of that belief. Sheol was thought to be underground, because people were said to go down to it (Gen. 37:35; Num. 16:30-33). It was a place of neither punishment nor a reward. It was simply the place where all people went when they died, regardless of how they had lived. It was a place of quietness and rest where people were in a sleep-like state, though not completely obliterated. In a famous passage in the Hebrew Bible, a medium calls the prophet Samuel up from Sheol. When Samuel comes up, he appears annoyed for having been awakened (1 Sam. 28:15). Samuel was not annihilated, yet in Sheol, he was not conscious, active, and vital. Sheol was a place of silence but also a place of darkness (Ps. 115:17; Job 10:20-22). The people there were unaware of what was happening on earth, and they were not able to praise or remember God (Ps. 6:4-5).

Rather than individual immortality, what was most important to the ancient Hebrews when they considered the future beyond the life of any individual or any generation was the survival of the covenant community on earth. They had what is called a collectivist culture. What was valued primarily was not the individual as such, but the clan, tribe, and nation. Regarding the future, the individual identified with the continuation of the group over time, rather than hoping for his or her own personal immortality. The individual regarded him- or herself as a finite creature whose days would end while the community continued.

In the mainstream theology of the Old Testament, the community was assured to exist over time if it remained faithful to the covenant with its God. This covenant called for exclusive worship of the God Yahweh, and it contained a series of concrete religious, moral, and purity laws by which the people were to organize and lead their lives. Faithfulness to the covenant would mean blessings and continuation of the community. Unfaithfulness to the covenant would mean punishment and risk of the community's annihilation.[1]

Most of the great prophets of the Hebrew Bible, including Isaiah of Jerusalem, Jeremiah, and Ezekiel, interpreted the fate of the nation in light of this theology. They regarded the defeat of both the northern kingdom, Israel (721 B.C.E.), and the southern kingdom, Judah (587 B.C.E.), to be the result of Yahweh destroying Yahweh's own people for their unfaithfulness to the covenant.

These same prophets, however, saw Yahweh as the kind of God who would not give up on the people. Almost without exception, the prophets affirmed that through punishment would come blessing, and through unfaithfulness would come faithfulness. The writings of the prophets resound with visions of a bright future to be realized in history in which the nation is exalted and secure, and where justice and peace are established.

Development of Apocalypticism and Belief in Resurrection

The Jewish view of the afterlife began to change as the people's social and political situation changed following their defeat as a nation and their exile. After the defeat of Judah in 587 B.C.E., the Jews were not allowed political autonomy and for centuries were used as pawns in the political game played by the empire-building powers of the day. In this context, the old interpretation of national defeat and suffering—that God was punishing the people because of their unfaithfulness—was not an adequate answer. Approximately two hundred years before the time of Jesus, a new interpretation called apocalypticism took shape.

Apocalypticism is a worldview that also spawned a special kind of literature. This literature is represented in the Bible particularly in the books of Daniel and Revelation, but other apocalyptic books that did not make it into the Bible were written in the centuries before and the century after the time of Jesus. The reason Jews were oppressed, according to the apocalyptic worldview, was that the world was under the sway of evil powers aligned against God. These evil powers oppressed God's righteous people. While these powers would have their way for some time, finally, when it looked as if they would win, God would decisively intervene in history on the side of God's righteous people, and they would triumph.

ADDITIONAL INFORMATION

Apocalyptic Genre in the Bible

The word *apocalypse* comes from a Greek word that means "to reveal." In the biblical context, it refers most commonly to a revelation of the end of time. Both the Old and New Testaments contain apocalypses in the form of statements about what will happen at the end of time. Each also contains a book written in an apocalyptic genre. In the Old Testament, this is the book of Daniel (especially chapters 7–12), and in the New Testament, it is the book of Revelation. Apocalyptic genre

---

is a special kind of literature that developed and flourished several hundred years on either side of Jesus' birth.

Apocalyptic literature has several distinct features. It involves a human subject being transported to a heavenly realm, where the subject is shown visions of the end of time. The visions are invariably exotic and highly symbolic. They involve fantastical creatures with multiple heads, limbs, and horns. The creatures and their features all represent earthly realities of some sort. The visions also invariably involve a violent clash between forces of darkness and light. Exotic and terrifying beasts represent the forces of darkness. They engage in wicked acts, lead others astray, and are in control of history, oppressing God's chosen people. God allows this to occur for a time, before God intervenes through the agency of some figure or figures who represent the forces of light. God's decisive intervention culminates in a violent clash with the forces of darkness that brings about the end of ordinary history. The defeat of evil ushers in a new age of peace for the righteous.

In the book of Daniel, the one who receives the visions is the character Daniel. In Revelation, it is an individual named John. In both books, the ones receiving the visions are initially confused about them. Daniel and John rely on heavenly interpreters to explain the visions. The explanations make some connections between the fantastical creatures of the visions and known earthly kings and kingdoms. However, there is always some level of mystery about precisely who or what the visionary creatures represent.

The fact that this literature purports to speak about the end of time but does so in symbolic or coded language makes the literature both intriguing and difficult to interpret. Christian history is filled with suggestions regarding who or what the fantastical creatures represent, and this includes suggestions from the contemporary period.

The rise of historical criticism has led to another approach to this literature by academically oriented biblical scholars. Among other things, historical criticism stresses that the biblical writers were in some sense limited by their time and place. The writers worked from a certain understanding of who God is, and in their contexts, they tried to interpret faithfully what God was doing. Still, they had no absolute transcendent standpoint from which they could see the future and write about it even in coded language.

The mainstream interpretation of apocalyptic literature from a historical-critical perspective claims that the authors of this literature were writing about their own contexts in the coded language they used. In both Daniel and Revelation, the context was one of persecution. In Daniel, it was persecution of the Jews under a second-century foreign king who had political control over the region of Palestine. The king, Antiochus IV Epiphanes, forcibly tried to destroy the Jewish religion. He desecrated the Jewish temple in Jerusalem in 167 B.C.E. by sacrificing swine on the altar and setting up a statue of the God Zeus. He forbade Jews from following the distinctive elements of the Jewish law, including circumcision and worship on the Sabbath. In the book of Daniel, Antiochus is presented as the ultimate force of evil in history. The book is written to assure Jews who are resisting Antiochus that God is on their side and will not allow him to be victorious.

The book of Revelation is widely believed to have been written at a time of Christian persecution. Part of it may come from Christian persecution under the Roman emperor Nero, who ruled from 54 to 68 C.E. Part may also come from persecution under Domitian, emperor from 81 to 96 C.E. In any case, the book is written with a vivid expectation that God will soon intervene in history. Jesus Christ will return and defeat the oppressive evil powers that rule history, ushering in a new era of righteousness and peace.

Christians who embrace the historical-critical approach to these texts do not regard them as containing detailed information in secret code about what will happen in the future. The literal referent of the mysterious creatures in the texts is the ruling powers at the time of the author. For such Christians, however, the books can still be regarded as valuable. Among other things, they were written from the theological conviction that God is ultimately in control of history and God's justice will triumph in history. Christians can affirm this theological conviction while believing that details about the future remain unknown.

As it developed in apocalypticism, the defeat of evil powers and the inauguration of a new age for the righteous were understood in cosmic terms. The apocalyptic vision went far beyond the vision of the Old Testament prophets, whose hope was for an endless historical age of peace, justice, and blessings for the community. The apocalyptic vision, to use a phrase from the book of Daniel, was about "the end of days," or the end of ordinary history (Dan. 10:14).

In apocalyptic thought, history as we know it will end with the destruction of the present order and the re-creation of the world for the righteous without evil, suffering, and death. The righteous who live to see the coming of this new world will be transformed and not die, and those who died before this event will be resurrected from their graves to experience it. In the clearest affirmation of resurrection in the Old Testament, the book of Daniel makes the astonishing claim that "many of those who sleep in the dust of the earth shall awake, some to everlasting life and some to shame and everlasting contempt" (Dan. 12:4).

The idea of resurrection means the righteous who live in times of oppression will be able to share in the glorious victory of God at the end of time. Although they are not rewarded for their righteousness during their lives but instead face suffering, they will receive their reward beyond the grave. Conversely, the wicked who get away with their evil deeds while alive will have to face their just punishment after death. This assures that God's justice will triumph even in those times where it seems impossible, with the righteous suffering and the wicked flourishing.

While apocalypticism brought a new view of history and the afterlife, it is important to recognize that this new view stood in continuity with the mainstream view of the Hebrew Bible in significant ways. Like the old view, apocalypticism affirmed the importance of the prosperity of the covenant community in history. It expressed this in grander terms than the old view, as the inauguration of God's everlasting kingdom in a new world at the end of history. Like the old view, apocalypticism regarded human beings as finite creatures whose days will end and who will inevitably die. What was added was the possibility of resurrection in which God will bring the individual creature back to life in a transformed existence. Like the old view, apocalypticism affirmed that God is faithful to God's covenant people and God's justice will triumph in history. This triumph does not just involve the people finally becoming faithful and being rewarded, however, but also God actively defeating evil and re-creating the world for the righteous without suffering and death while punishing the wicked who at least seemed to get away with their wickedness.

Ideas about the resurrection of the dead and the new age to come were not universally agreed upon by Jews at the time of Jesus and the writing of the New Testament. At the time of Jesus, there were still some

Jews, including the Sadducees, who denied the resurrection and clung to the Sheol idea of the afterlife. Many other Jews, such as the Pharisees, accepted the idea of resurrection but did not necessarily agree about what it involved. They debated issues such as whether everyone would be raised or only some, what the resurrection body would be like, how it would be connected with the old one, and what resurrection implies for the creation as a whole.

Greek Thought and Belief in an Immortal Soul

While apocalypticism was developing in Judaism, Greek thought was spreading throughout the Mediterranean region as a result of the conquests of Alexander the Great in the latter part of the fourth century. Alexander sought to bring Greek culture to the territories he conquered, and this included the lasting influence of Greek philosophical thought. Of particular interest is the Platonic idea of the afterlife, which exerted a deep influence on both Judaism and Christianity.

In Plato's view, the human being is more than merely a finite creature whose days will end in death. Humans have a preexistent immortal soul that is trapped in a finite, changing body. Plato thought the soul is like the forms or essences of the things it knows; it is eternal and unchanging. The body is like everything else in the universe that is made of matter; it is finite and changing, and will fade away.[2]

In this understanding, the human being is a conflicted combination of an immortal soul and a mortal body, which are two utterly different kinds of things. The goal of life, as Plato understood it, is to discipline and/or deny the things of the body so that, at death, the soul can separate from the body and ascend to a purely spiritual, eternal, and unchanging realm, the realm of the forms. Those who do not manage to separate their souls from their bodies in this life still have immortal souls, but because their souls are fused with the material realm in the form of their bodies, they will again become stuck in a body and be reincarnated. From there, they will have to begin again and try to release themselves from the material world.

Notice how this Greek view of salvation and the afterlife differs significantly from the Hebrew view. In the Greek view, human beings naturally have an immortal soul, although it has become trapped in a mortal body. Salvation is separation of the soul from the body. The soul alone is immortal. In the Hebrew view, human beings are not naturally immortal. They die, and according to apocalypticism, some (or perhaps all) are resurrected by an act of God. Resurrection involves the reconstitution of the whole person, mind and body, to a new kind of immortal existence that is envisioned in earthly terms as a remade heaven and earth without suffering and death. Also of importance is the fact that the Greek view lacks a stress on the community's destiny in history under God's guidance. In the Greek view, history is ultimately unimportant. It is part of the finite, changing realm from which one seeks to escape. In the Hebrew view, history is of vital importance. Salvation comes through God's acts in history at the end of history.

Classical Christian Eschatology

Eschatology is the doctrine of the end times. The classical Christian conception regarding eschatology fused the apocalyptic Hebrew view with the Greek anthropology inherited from Plato. The combination of these elements took shape within the distinctive Christian understanding of salvation history that developed in the early church and became inscribed in its theology and creeds.

Fusion of Greek Anthropology and Hebrew Teleology

Many New Testament writers, including the apostle Paul, were deeply influenced by the apocalyptic worldview. Apocalypticism can be connected with messianism, or the hope for a Messiah, and this was the case for Paul. Apocalypticism affirms that God will defeat evil and bring about a new world without suffering and death. Messianism says this will occur through the Messiah, God's Anointed One. As a messianic apocalypticist, Paul affirmed that Jesus was the Messiah and interpreted Jesus' death, resurrection, and second coming in apocalyptic categories.

Paul thought Jesus' resurrection in the midst of history showed a triumph over the evil powers that ran history. Faith in Jesus and his conquest of the powers guaranteed that when Jesus returned at the second coming, the faithful would be resurrected if they had died, or transformed and given a new spiritual body that would not die if they were still alive. Paul thought Jesus' return was imminent, expecting it in his own lifetime (1 Thess. 4:15-17; 1 Cor. 15:51-52). He thought it had cosmic implications, in the sense that all creation would be made anew at Jesus' return and creation groaned for that day (Rom. 8:18-22). Those who died with faith in Christ slept until the day of their resurrection at Jesus' second coming (1 Thess. 4:14; 1 Cor. 15:22-23). It is unclear whether Paul believed in a general resurrection and punishment for the wicked, or simply believed in the resurrection of believers. Other New Testament authors, including the writer of the book of Revelation, did believe in a general resurrection that would include punishment of the wicked and rewards for the righteous (Rev. 20:11-13).

The delay of Jesus' return and the influence of Greek thought on developing Christian theology led to the acceptance of certain Greek ideas. Although it was never formally incorporated into an ecumenical creed, the Greek anthropology that affirmed that people have immortal souls gained widespread acceptance within Christianity. Since people have immortal souls, it makes sense that when people die, they do not just sleep, but go either to heaven- or hell-like states immediately. This view eventually became normative.

While accepting the idea that humans have immortal souls, Christians also continued to affirm the Hebrew/apocalyptic view that history is moving in a direction toward some final consummation. In Christian categories, this culmination was understood as the second coming of Christ, which would bring about the end of the world. When Christ returns, evil and death will be defeated, the dead will be raised, a final judgment will be given, and a new heaven and earth without suffering and death will be created.

Many early Christians bore an expectation that the second coming of Christ would occur soon. During its first three centuries, Christianity was a minority faith, and its believers were subject to periodic persecution by the Roman Empire. It must have been relatively easy for Christians, especially during times of persecution, to hang on to the apocalyptic interpretation of reality, hoping for the imminent end of the world, which would include the defeat of the evil Roman Empire and its replacement by God's kingdom of righteousness.

The context shifted dramatically, however, when Emperor Constantine legalized and favored Christianity in 313, setting it on a path to become the religion of the empire. With this transformation came a new emphasis on the belief that the kingdom of God is not just a future reality that is supposed to come through God's dramatic acts in history against the evil powers that ruled history. The kingdom of God is also something to be realized here and now in the world.[3]

The expectation that Jesus would return soon and bring the evil powers of the world to an end died down for all but schismatic groups as Christian civilization was built. Still, the idea continued in Christianity that history is moving toward a final consummation in the second coming of Christ. Classical Christian eschatology affirms that at the second coming, when history comes to an end, the souls of those who have died, which are already in heaven- or hell-like states, will be reunited with their resurrected bodies, which are renewed immortal bodies. Everyone will then receive judgment and go to his or her final destiny: believers to paradise and unbelievers to eternal damnation.

That this reconciliation of Greek and Hebrew ideas was extraordinarily successful is attested by the fact that the Greek anthropology, in some modified form or other, united with the Hebrew view of the directionality of history predominated in Western thinking until the contemporary period. Even after the Protestant Reformation of the sixteenth century and the splitting of the church in Europe between Roman Catholicism and Protestant factions, all sides continued to affirm an eschatology whose main features combined Greek and Hebrew thought.

ADDITIONAL INFORMATION

Purgatory

One of the main differences between Roman Catholic and Protestant views of the afterlife is the Roman Catholic belief in purgatory. In traditional Roman Catholic teaching, purgatory is a place of temporal punishment after death for those who have received the grace of salvation in life. Since those in purgatory have already received saving grace, their sins are forgiven and the issue of the ultimate salvation of their souls is not in question. In traditional Catholic teaching, however, while having one's sins forgiven by God's saving grace is decisive, it is not the end of the process regarding what must happen to a person because of his or her sins. One must not only have one's sins forgiven but also undergo the appropriate punishment for those sins. Purgatory is the place where believers suffer punishment after death for sins not confessed in life or sins for which one did not receive punishment in life. Traditionally, this punishment is understood as a purging fire. Understood literally or metaphorically, it is an undesirable condition keeping one from the full joy of unity with God after death.

The belief in a place of purgation for sins after death is ancient. The main biblical passage on which Roman Catholics base this doctrine is 2 Macc. 12:39-45. There it is said that Judas Maccabaeus "made the propitiation for them that had died, that they might be released from their sin." New Testament passages used as evidence for the doctrine are Matt. 12:31 and 1 Cor. 3:11-15, although there is serious debate among biblical scholars whether these passages in fact validate the doctrine.[4]

A number of important second-century Christian theologians mention a place of purging fire after death. It appears that a major influence in the development of the doctrine was the early practice of praying for the dead that was part of Christian liturgy.[5] Why should the living pray for the dead unless those prayers are able to influence the dead person's soul in some way?

In the Western church, the doctrine of purgatory was notably developed and promoted by Pope Gregory, who was pope from 590 to 604. He formalized many of the beliefs and practices surrounding purgatory that became normative in the Middle Ages.

During the Middle Ages, the doctrine of purgatory was a deeply ingrained belief in the Western church, which continued to develop explicit ways of expressing regulatory control over it. Purgatory was connected with the liturgical practices of praying for the dead and supporting masses for the dead. Since the church understood itself as mediator of grace, the church also developed what were called "indulgences," which were said to help release the souls of the dead in purgatory. As mediator of grace, the church drew on the merits of Christ's sacrifice along with the merits of the saints and the faithful to give indulgences to help release souls from purgatory. These indulgences in effect paid for the consequences of sins that the dead person still had remaining on his or her account, keeping him or her from the blessedness of the heavenly state.

Even before the sixteenth century, the church had already taken the extraordinary step of selling indulgences. It was in the sixteenth century, however, that the selling of indulgences was promoted widely in a major fund-raising campaign of the church. This provoked the ire of a young Augustinian monk named Martin Luther. To him, the selling of indulgences meant the church had put at least one aspect of God's grace on sale to the highest bidder. This practice, more than any other, initiated Martin Luther's public critique of the church. His critique continued to deepen and expand, eventually leading to the Protestant Reformation of the sixteenth century.

Over the course of the sixteenth century, as Protestant groups broke from Rome and Protestant ideas developed, all of the Protestant branches rejected the doctrine of purgatory. Protestants argued that the doctrine was not supported by scripture. Protestants and Roman Catholics accept somewhat different books as sacred scripture. Protestants do not regard the set of books that contains 2 Maccabees as canonical scripture. Protestants call this set of books the Apocrypha, meaning false writings, while Roman Catholics call it the Deuterocanon, or second canon. As already noted, 2 Maccabees contains the most explicit reference of support for purgatory.

Most significantly, in the classical articulation of Protestant theology, Protestants affirm that an individual's status before God is determined by faith alone. Faith is accepting grace, or accepting the grace of forgiveness of sins offered to one on account of what God has done for one in the atoning act of Jesus Christ's death and resurrection. For Protestants, the internal act of acceptance is sufficient to guarantee right standing before God. No further act of penance is required for one's sins, and there is no further act of punishment for sins, at least regarding one's standing before God. Before God, one is accepted, even though in the world one may still have to face the consequences for sins, especially sins that hurt other people or violate social laws. Given Protestant belief in one's right standing before God coming through faith alone, understood most basically as internal acceptance, there is no need for purgatory. At death, the right standing before God that one has in life is made real. This right standing is actualized by God's acceptance of the soul into a heavenly state. Like Roman Catholics, Protestant groups also classically accept the idea that the soul will be reunited with a remade body at the end of historical time, after which the person's ultimate destiny is realized.

Original Sin, Grace, and Human Destiny

The ancient Hebrews understood God's action in history in relationship to God's covenant with the Jewish people. Interpreted through the covenant relationship, God was conceived as both just and loving. In the mainstream interpretation of the Hebrew Bible, God forgave the people's faults time and again, but when the people's violation of the covenant became so great as to be irreparable, God destroyed God's own people in an act of justice. God did not give up on God's people, however, but in love continued to work with them and promised to bring them to a bright future.

Hebrew apocalypticism interpreted the operation of God's love and justice somewhat differently. In its view, God's justice and love meant the righteous who were oppressed at the hands of the unrighteous who controlled history should be rewarded. They would be resurrected to enjoy an eternal existence without evil and death. At the same time, God's justice demanded that those who did evil should receive judgment for it, even if they seemed to get away with it in this life. They would be resurrected for judgment.

Yet another angle on the operation of God's justice and love developed in Christianity. Decisive for this development in Western Christianity is the towering theological figure of Augustine of Hippo (354–430).[6] Augustine's thought on universal human history and human destiny shaped the Western theological tradition more than the work of any other single Christian theologian.

To Augustine, humans were initially created perfect and placed in a paradise without sin and death. The primal human ancestors, Adam and Eve, willfully disobeyed God and, as a result, were punished with suffering and finitude owing to God's justice. This primal sin also brought about a perversion of human nature. All humans are born with twisted desires such that they cannot avoid sinning or escape the power of sin over their lives. Because of God's justice, humans inherit guilt not only for the sins they are bound to commit in their lives but on account of the original sin of their primal ancestors. For all humanity, coming into being with a twisted nature means they incur God's wrath on them whereby they justifiably deserve eternal damnation.

From this context, the saving work of Christ is understood. A blanket of condemnation covers everyone under God's justice, but as a result of Christ's atoning death, some have received salvation as a free gift of God's love. They will inherit paradise rather than the damnation they deserve. They will also receive the power to overcome the twisting and entrapping character of sin in their lives.

Augustine's idea of original sin warping human nature and making all people deserving of damnation became normative in Western Christianity, as did his idea of salvation coming as a free gift of grace. Augustine himself thought access to this grace comes through the sacraments of the church, including infant baptism, which washes away original sin, and the Eucharist. This paved the way for the development of the sacramental system of the medieval church, which formally recognized seven sacraments in 1215. The Protestant Reformers of the sixteenth century agreed with Augustine's ideas of original sin and grace. Against the sacramental system of their time, however, they tended to stress that grace comes through an individual encounter with God. While there are many nuances in interpretation and individual theology, classically, both Protestants and Catholics accept the idea of original sin blanketing all humanity with guilt and condemnation, and salvation coming through God's free gift of grace.

Contemporary Alternatives Regarding the Afterlife

The Interdependent and Evolutionary Understanding of Human Beings

There is no comprehensive unity of thought in the contemporary period in the West regarding human anthropology and the afterlife. There are, however, important tendencies in progressive thought regarding the contemporary understanding of human beings. One of those tendencies is a rejection of the Greek anthropology, or the idea that humans have an immortal soul trapped in a finite body. One reason for this rejection involves questions about this position's intelligibility. It was never clear in the Greek anthropology how the mind and body could come together and interact if they were such thoroughly different kinds of things. Another reason is a new understanding of the universe and the human relation to other living things brought about by discoveries in contemporary science.

Contemporary people no longer think of the universe as young and small with the earth at its center and God in a realm above it. The universe is billions of years old and immeasurably vast. Quite possibly, it contains other life-forms. Perhaps they also have self-consciousness. Whatever life-forms exist in the universe, including human beings, evolved over vast reaches of time through natural selection. The fact that humans evolved from lower life-forms does not necessarily deny the fact that humans may be unique and special in some way. It also does not necessarily mean evolution was merely a chance or random process. It does, however, imply a renewed sense of connection or interrelationship of humans with everything else that exists.[7]

This sense of interrelatedness with everything distinguishes contemporary thinking from much Enlightenment thinking that understood humans in the dualistic categories of Greek anthropology. The Enlightenment philosopher René Descartes famously claimed there are only two kinds of substances, "thinking" substance and "extended" substance.[8] He claimed thinking substance is found only in human beings and is immortal. He sought to differentiate humans absolutely from the lower animals that he regarded merely as instances of extended substance. He denied that animals have feelings or any sense of an internal reality that approaches human consciousness.

On the whole, progressive thinkers today no longer think this way but understand human beings as unique and yet standing on a continuum of relationality with everything else. Like everything else, humans have a material basis. Like all other carbon-based life, human bodies come from ancient stardust. Humans share the mysterious quality of "life" with single-celled organisms and plants, while sharing with higher animals an internal sense, even while they take that sense to a different qualitative level that makes human culture possible. Moreover, as a species, humans are dependent on the larger network of life that sustains them. Human beings cannot cut themselves off from the ecological system of the planet or destroy this system without destroying themselves.

This relationality and connectedness with everything that exists, which is characteristic of much contemporary thought, means that human beings are conceived as mind-body unities rather than a conflicted combination of two different kinds of substances. In theological terms, one could say there is a renewed emphasis in the contemporary period on the human being as a finite creature, a view that in many ways is closer to the understanding of the human being in the Hebrew Bible than in Greek thought.

Understanding humans in light of the evolutionary process has implications for thinking about original sin and human guilt, which, as previously mentioned, are important ideas in the classical Christian conception of salvation history and the determination of people's status in the afterlife. Augustine thought all human beings are descendents of an original pair who were given eternal life, something they forsook through disobedience. The evolutionary understanding of humans denies there was a single pair of human descendents or that eternal life ever was an option for our human ancestors. To Augustine, suffering and death are punishments resulting from human sin. The evolutionary understanding sees suffering and death as built into the nature of things. Evolution through natural selection operates on the principle that more individuals with slight variations are produced in every generation than can survive, so that over time, those best adapted to given conditions are selected. It requires the ongoing death of individuals and generations to operate. Augustine thought twisted human nature and the divine condemnation that comes with it and blankets all humans are owing to an original human choice for which all subsequent humans are held responsible. From an evolutionary perspective, there was no original choice or willful disobedience of our primal parents that twisted human nature and made everyone deserving of condemnation.

Understanding humans as creatures that emerged from a long evolutionary process requires reading the Genesis story regarding the fall of humans into sin in a nonliteral way. It is a story that describes the discovery all humans experience in emerging to full consciousness of finitude, aware of the harshness of reality. It is still possible to hold that there is something twisted about human nature, but this twistedness has to be understood as the heritage of the evolutionary process or some developmental problem humans face, rather than the result of a willful act of disobedience by our first parents.

Resurrection or Determined Agnosticism

Many contemporary theologians affirm that the resurrection of Christ in the middle of history is the firstfruits of a general resurrection to come at the end of history. This general resurrection will involve more than the resurrection of people. It will mean a transformation of the cosmos as a whole as the cosmos is freed from suffering and death.

This position is represented in the previous chapter under the theology of hope. This theology does not require the Greek anthropology or a literal reading of the Genesis story. Its understanding of God is of a power drawing all things to a perfect fulfillment overcoming evil, suffering, and death. Its understanding of Christ, and particularly of the resurrection, is of a glimpse into that fulfillment in the middle of history.

Many who embrace this position argue it has important implications for social justice and environmental activism. Their claim is that precisely because people have an eternal destiny of harmony, we are called to work for justice and peace now and enact it in our time. Also, precisely because the creation has an eternal destiny freed from suffering and death, we are called to work for ecological healing now. In other words, for this position, the fact that all people and the creation as a whole will be transformed means that everything finite has an eternal meaning. This eternal meaning reflects back on the present and calls for transformative action now in terms of social justice and ecological healing.

In contrast to this position is the emergence in the contemporary period of what could be called a determined or committed agnosticism regarding the afterlife among some Christian theologians. A level of openness or skepticism regarding the veracity of one's affirmations about the afterlife is common for all theologians, but the position described here makes a more determined case for agnosticism or simply avoids all discussion about the afterlife, diminishing the significance of the issue altogether.

This position is evident especially in some feminist and ecological theologies, and there are both theoretical and practical reasons for it.[9] The theoretical side involves a renewed emphasis on understanding humans as part of a greater whole that includes all living things. This understanding includes a critique of the dualism characteristic of the Greek anthropology that would separate humans as utterly distinct and special from the whole, on account of their immortal souls. Humans are understood as creatures with limited lives. On the practical side, there is an emphasis on the interpretation of salvation as having a this-worldly meaning and as involving the ecological healing of the planet as well as the enacting of social justice for humans in this world. This position sees a danger in the affirmation of an afterlife: such an affirmation invariably leads to a lack of concern with social justice and ecological healing of the planet in the present. For this position, if everything is going to be remade by God in the end, why should we necessarily care about improving it now? Only if things are finite and limited are we aroused to make sure justice is enacted for everyone now, and moved to work now to make sure the planet is preserved for all living things for the indefinite future.

There is, then, a paradox in contemporary theology: Some theologians, including those influenced by the theology of hope, regard the affirmation of an afterlife as an argument in favor of social activism and ecological healing. At the same time, other theologians regard the affirmation of an afterlife as a threat to social activism and ecological healing. Those who believe in the resurrection and transformation of all things ultimately trace their belief to the apocalyptic worldview, although they minimize the typical cataclysmic aspects of that worldview in which the new comes only through a catastrophic destruction of the old. In general, the determined agnostics about the afterlife view the future in the same way as the mainstream position of the Hebrew Bible. What is important is not individual immortality but the thriving of the community over time in history. It is affirmed that this thriving will occur when justice is enacted. For this position, the envisioned future often involves the thriving of all life-forms, not just human beings.

Progress in the Afterlife: John Hick

John Hick (1922–), a British theologian and philosopher of religion who is notable for his clear and creative thinking, has made significant contributions to contemporary religious reflection in several areas. One unique contribution in his early work is his understanding of the afterlife.[10]

As claimed earlier, one's understanding of the afterlife is shaped by how one understands human beings and their relation to everything that exists, as well as God and the way God relates to people. This is certainly true for Hick. In his early thought, one of the major issues with which he grapples is whether there can be a good and all-powerful God and whether life can have a purpose given the reality of evil, suffering, and death. Traditionally, in Christian reflection, this issue is called theodicy. The term literally means "justification of God" and refers to how one can justify a good and all-powerful God making a world with evil, suffering, and death in it.

Hick critiques the Augustinian explanation of evil, suffering, and death in a way similar to the critique just given. Augustine thought suffering and death are punishments that resulted from Adam and Eve's disobedience in the garden of Eden, and he thought humans have a warped nature bound to do evil because of this disobedience. For Augustine, this means all evil, suffering, and death are ultimately the result of a misuse of human free will, and humans for all time are responsible for this misuse. In contrast, Hick thinks humans must be understood as having evolved from lower life-forms. Humans never existed in a perfect state with the opportunity for an everlasting life without suffering that was sacrificed by their free will. Suffering and death are built into the nature of the universe. They are not punishments, but insofar as one believes in a good and all-powerful Creator, they must have been put into the universe by God for a purpose. Similarly, whatever problem there is with human nature must in some sense be the consequence of the evolutionary process from which human beings came, rather than a result of Adam and Eve's sin.

While Hick's critique of Augustine on the origin of evil, suffering, and death moves him outside the mainstream of Western Christian thought, Hick claims that an alternative explanation for evil to Augustine's is found in the history of Christian reflection. He roots this alternative position in the thought of the second-century church father Irenaeas, although he admits he develops suggestions from Irenaeas that go well beyond Irenaeas's own ideas.

The main idea Hick takes from Irenaeas is that human beings were not created in a perfect and immortal state from which they fell and which they need to recover. Instead, humans were created in a child-like or immature condition. This condition involves the potentiality for growth into religiously and ethically mature individuals and into just and peaceful societies, but that potentiality is not realized at creation. It must be realized in history.

Hick thinks this insight is compatible with an evolutionary view of humans wherein humans emerge from the long evolutionary process as immature but with the capacity for moral and religious life. To Hick, God must not simply give perfected moral and religious life to humans. It must be earned or developed in a historical process, because only insofar as it is won through human development is it genuinely valuable for the creature who earns it. In Hick's terms, the purpose of human life is "soul-making," whereby human beings overcome their selfish nature in the development of moral and religious character. It is the development of this moral and religious character that is the purpose of human life. Insofar as this position is Christian, it views Jesus as the embodiment of the goal of human life in the middle of history.

Hick claims that if moral and religious development is the goal of human life, then suffering and death must be built into the universe. If the universe always immediately responded to our desires and there were no dangers and no death, there would be no moral and religious growth. We would always get what we wanted, but we would not develop virtues that can come only through struggle or obstacles. One can develop patience, determination, courage, temperance, and other virtues only if one faces real hurdles against which these virtues are honed. One develops an understanding of one's own limits, as well as compassion and understanding for others, in relation to the real challenges of suffering faced in the world. Moreover, if there were no death, we would never develop anything, for no matter what happened, good or bad, our lives would always go on endlessly.

Hick understands the root of moral evil as selfishness and sees it as the heritage of the evolutionary process. The harsh environment out of which we evolved required selfishness, or the limitation of our selfless-ness to some immediate group or clan in order to survive. These are the limitations we need to overcome in the historical process of soul-making.

While evil, suffering, and death are necessary, Hick recognizes the tragic consequences of their reality. Diseases and accidents strike down people early in life before they have an opportunity for complete moral and religious development. The inhumane actions of people toward each other destroy moral and religious potentiality instead of developing it. Moreover, with the possible exception of the saints of the various reli-gious traditions, few people, actually develop their moral and religious character toward something close to perfection. This acknowledgment leads to Hick's unique understanding of the afterlife.

The purpose of human life insofar as it is made by a good and all-powerful God is for all humans to come in relation to this God with a developed moral character. For the vast majority of people, this devel-opment cannot be accomplished in one life. Under these assumptions, Hick argues, it is reasonable to posit an afterlife or a series of afterlives in which the soul-making process can continue.

A unique feature of Hick's afterlife perspective vis-à-vis the main-stream view of Christian history is his idea of postmortem moral and reli-gious development. This view is not entirely novel in Christian history, as it was affirmed also by the third-century church father Origen, although many of his ideas were later declared heretical by the church. The idea of postmortem development is certainly not novel in world intellectual history. Wrapped up in the idea of reincarnation, a fundamental belief in Hinduism and Buddhism, is the notion that one must make moral progress from one life to the next to achieve the highest human moral and religious goal. The Enlightenment philosopher Immanuel Kant also posited postmortem moral development as essential to humans' ability to achieve the fundamental purpose of life, which he regarded as perfected moral development.

Ecological theologians would find troubling Hick's too-exclusive focus on the meaning of creation as human moral and religious develop-ment. Other theologians critique Hick for not having biblical evidence for his view or for not understanding that the heavenly reward deemed essential to Christianity is a reward, not a further process. Still, Hick's position raises important questions for Christian reflection on the after-life. In all of its major forms, Christianity affirms that sanctifying grace, or grace that makes one holy, is a vital part of the Christian life. Christian theology affirms that sanctification is a process that is begun in this life. Different theologians disagree, however, about how much one can be perfected in this life, and the majority position is that one never becomes perfectly holy in this life but continues to struggle with sin on some level. If this is the case, while one's sins may be forgiven, the character that created those sins is not perfected at death. This does raise the question of how that character can be made perfect while still respecting the integrity of the individual. Hick's positing of development after death is one way of answering that question.

Process Theology's Limited God and the Afterlife

Process theology developed in the middle of the twentieth century and continues to exert a significant influence on Christian thought, especially in the area involving dialogue between science and religion. Process theology developed from the ideas of Alfred North Whitehead (1861–1947), a British mathematician and philosopher who is most notable for his important text *Process and Reality*, published in 1929.[11] In this text, he provides a metaphysic, or a vision of the fundamental character of reality, including God.

Process theologians think Whitehead is important because his vision of reality is both relevant to the times and compatible with the biblical tradition. They claim Whitehead fulfills the contemporary demand for an understanding of reality that involves the interdependence of all things, and that grasps dynamism and change as inherent features of reality, a contemporary requirement, given our understanding of evolutionary history. They also claim Whitehead's view of God is compatible with the biblical view and corrects the errant view of God in Christianity that is a heritage of Greek thought.

Whitehead understands change or process as fundamental to reality. In an interdependent way, all entities draw from the past and emerge toward the future. This emergence involves freedom, and it is a basic part of Whitehead's thought that in an interdependent way, individual entities and the universe as a whole must be understood as having an independent integrity or freedom to go the way of their own choosing. At the same time, the emergence of things is not simply random or chaotic. It is toward greater intensity and complexity, and also toward greater harmony and order. There is a greater intensity and complexity in the full self-consciousness of humans than there is in the limited awareness of an animal, plant, amoeba, or atom. In human experience, the capacity for joy, love, beauty, and truth is embodied in a way and at a depth that cannot be experienced at other levels. Human experience involves an emergence beyond the other levels, and Whitehead regards this emergence as not simply chance or random, but intended and fundamental to the character of reality.

For Whitehead, the emergence of the new in the process of reality takes place by the directing creativity of God, but he has a distinctive understanding of how God's directing creativity works. At every state of change or process, God provides opportunities to reality and lures or draws it toward a direction that involves both greater intensity and greater order. In their freedom and independence, given entities can always resist God's draw or lure. Whitehead's claim is that God is limited in the sense that God cannot stop that resistance. God does not use coercive power to get God's way with creation, not just because God does not choose to use coercive power, but also because God does not have that kind of power. God's power is persuasive, providing opportunities and luring creation toward greater good. This luring has created evolutionary history and the history of human culture, but there is always the capacity for resistance by the creation.

With human beings and their realization of complete self-consciousness and freedom, we have the full development of the capacity for great good and great joy, as well as the capacity to resist God's luring influence. From this position, we can see process thought's understanding of evil. On the one hand, evil comes from human resistance to God's influence, a resistance enacted by human freedom refusing to listen to God's call of harmony. On the other hand, evil is the consequence of there being a limited God and an undeveloped universe. In process thought, God is not absolute and all-powerful, nor is God understood as having created the universe out of nothing. God formed the order of the universe out of chaos, and God is drawing the universe to greater states of intensity and harmony in the ongoing process of the universe, but that process is not complete.[12]

It is informative to compare the understanding of evil in process thought with Augustine and Hick. Like Hick, process theologians would critique the Augustinian idea that there was a time in which humans and the creation were created perfect and without evil. Like Hick, they would disagree with Augustine that evil, suffering, and death are punishments for human disobedience. Hick, however, assumes that an all-powerful God created a world with suffering and death in it as necessary for human soul-making. For Hick, while God is all-powerful, God must back off and allow the historical process to proceed without intervention, even if it involves the eruption of great evil, because the development of moral character is valuable finally only if it is achieved by humans and not imposed by God. Process theologians deny that God intentionally created a world with suffering and death for a positive purpose. Suffering, death, and evil due to human choices are the consequence of a limited God having formed the universe out of chaos. While God is drawing the universe to greater harmony, that process is not complete, so suffering, death, and evil remain.

Whitehead did not develop any distinctively Christian implications of his thought, but Christian process theologians have done so. Notable among them is John Cobb (1925–), who developed a distinctive process Christology, or understanding of the meaning of Jesus as the Christ from a process perspective.[13] Cobb points out that according to process thought, God never forces things but always draws the universe to greater goodness. The aspect of God by which God is ever present and ever drawing the universe to greater goodness is considered by Cobb to be the "Word of God," which is referred to in the Bible. The Christian claim is that the Word of God became incarnate in Jesus, and Cobb develops this idea to affirm that Jesus embodies the meaning and goodness to which God seeks to draw all creation. In Cobb's Christology, God's Word is effective everywhere and at all times, with Christians having a peculiar insight into that Word in Jesus.

One of the distinctive elements of process thought is that it denies God is all-powerful or absolute. This distinguishes process thought from the majority position in Christian history. For process thought, while God has a consistent character that is always good, because God is not absolute, God is subject to the ultimate metaphysical principles of creation and the ongoing process of creation. God and the creation are interdependent in such a way that God is subject to time and lives through the world and the experience of the world. This means that whatever happens to the world also happens in and to God. Put differently, not only is God the lure of the world, drawing it to greater goodness, but God also co-experiences everything that happens in the world or in the historical process from the inside.

The idea that God experiences everything in the world from the inside means God is affected by the world, and because of this, in some sense, God changes with the process of the world. What happens in the world changes God, not in terms of changing God's character, but in terms of deepening God's experiences and providing material to and for God's being. When a new species of animal emerges, for example, this adds to the richness of God's experience. Similarly, it adds to God's suffering when species are extinguished. When humans create a new work of art, this adds not only to human culture but also to the depth of God's experience. Likewise, when humans destroy one another, not only human suffering and pain are registered, but also God's suffering and pain.

According to process theologians, this understanding of God is closer to the biblical idea of God than the absolute God of Greek thought. Conceived as absolute, God is regarded as unchanging and impassible. Technically, God's impassibility means God is incapable of suffering. To suffer means to undergo changes, and whatever undergoes change has some sort of limitation or lack of fullness of being. As absolute, God is considered complete fullness or complete realization to which nothing can be added. If God is this complete fullness, God may be able to draw the world toward God, but God can never undergo the ups and downs or the joys and sorrows of the world with the world. God remains detached from the ongoing process of the world. Process theologians claim this is not the God of the Bible. The God of the Bible is intimately engaged with the joys and sorrows of the world. This God broods over the world, seeking to draw it to new levels of fulfillment while respecting its integrity.

While there is no single view of the afterlife in process theology, there is a common or notable view developed by the process thinker Charles Hartshorne (1897–2000). As process theology envisions it, God co-experiences everything that happens in creation. Because God is everlasting, this makes God the ultimate and final repository of all experiences. Everything that happens in the world, from every creature that lives and dies to every human experience of joy or sorrow, is eternally recorded in God's memory and becomes part of God's everlasting being. To Hartshorne, it is in this sense that human beings live on after individual death. The afterlife does not involve personal immortality in the sense that one's body or one's consciousness continues so that one has new experiences, but it does involve the taking up and eternal recording of everything that one was into God.[14]

There are process theologians who think other alternatives for the afterlife are possible under process assumptions. They think some sort of personal immortality can be realized as God develops the processes of the universe.[15] In an important sense, settling this issue would seem to rest on what one thinks of God's power vis-à-vis creation. If one grants that God is not all-powerful, can one still think of God as having enough power to overcome individual death for created entities or the creation as a whole in the future? Some process theologians are confident enough in God's power to answer yes to this question.

The issue of the degree of God's power and how it affects not just personal immortality, but the future consummation of creation, remains an important one for process thinkers. If God is not all-powerful, is God nevertheless powerful enough to guarantee that God's purposes will ultimately be realized in the history of creation? Or could it be, alternatively, that chaos will ultimately overwhelm the order God has made? This chaos could come in the form of overwhelming natural disasters that destroy all life and halt the evolutionary process at least on this planet, or it could come in the form of human freedom resisting God's call to harmony and goodness and annihilating all life in a nuclear holocaust. Perhaps a mediating position could also be envisioned in which there are eras of progress over chaos, followed by eras of regress with regard to chaos, in a virtually endless oscillating cycle.

The question of assurance regarding a positive future given a limited God is a serious question for process theology, and it is often brought to bear on this theology by its critics. The response of process theologians is to claim that while their God is not all-powerful, their God is risk-taking in forming and trying to perfect creation. God is willing to be vulnerable to failure in this process. The alternative, they say, is an uninvolved God or a God of coercive power, neither of which would be humanly desirable.

Part Three

Christianity and Cultural Transformations

Chapter 6

Christianity and Other Religions

The emperor Constantine transformed Christianity when he legalized and favored it in the year 313. At the time, legalizing and favoring Christianity were radical moves. What was not radical, however, was the idea that the emperor should support religion. It was taken for granted that a political leader would use his or her political power and tax money to promote, regulate, and enforce religion. By the end of the fourth century, Christianity was technically the only religion of the empire. Christianity, an exclusive monotheism, had taken over Roman religion, which was a diverse polytheism.

While the historical details are different, the same pattern occurred in the seventh century with the emergence of Islam. Islam was also an exclusive monotheism tied to political power. In a relatively short period of time, it effectively took over the diverse polytheism of the Arab peoples and then expanded to other ethnic groups and areas.

This pattern reveals a logic in monotheism that, when it is tied strongly to political power, excludes other religions, or at least tries to do so. Monotheism says there is only one God. This God is transcendent, different from anything in the universe, and not to be worshipped in carved images. Moreover, monotheism affirms that God has revealed God's self in history to some specific individual or group. The different forms of monotheism, whether Jewish, Christian, or Muslim, have traditionally claimed they are the bearers of the true revelation over against the claims of the other groups. If there is only one God, who is known and to be worshipped according to how God has revealed God's self, then insofar as a political leader understands him- or herself as charged with promoting and enforcing true religion in his or her realm, it is understandable that this leader would exclude other religions with their Gods and forms of worship.

The logic of monotheism can be contrasted with the logic of polytheism. If you believe there are many Gods who manifest themselves in different ways to different people, you would expect there to be different religions with a diversity of practices in the world. You could worship one or perhaps more of these Gods without denying the legitimacy of others. If you were a political figure with this belief, you could support many religions in your realm, as long as they were not hostile to your rule.

Broadly speaking, this kind of polytheistic tolerance was the official position of the Roman Empire at the time of Jesus. Also, in many Far Eastern cultures that historically have a polytheistic basis to their religious life, a variety of religious traditions have often coexisted in ways that are mind-boggling to Westerners reared in monotheism. In Japan, for example, the vast majority of people do not choose between being Buddhist and Shinto. They claim both. They worship freely at both types of shrines and claim the Gods and traditions of each for various aspects of their lives.

While monotheism has a logic that tends to make it exclusive, historically Christianity upped the ante of this exclusivism with its doctrines of original sin, incarnation, and salvation. The doctrine of original sin says because of the sin of the first human parents, all human beings are not only warped in their desires but deserving of damnation. They need to receive the grace offered by Jesus Christ's atoning act to avoid perdition. This atonement was made possible by the one God becoming incarnate as a human being for one and only one time. Human history before the incarnation and atonement points to the incarnation and atonement and is preparatory to it. The incarnation and atonement make grace and forgiveness real, and human history since the incarnation and atonement is lived in light of that central reality and in anticipation of the second coming of Christ, where ordinary history will end, the dead will be raised, a final judgment will be given, and the kingdom of God will begin.

It is not surprising that in the centuries after Constantine, with the logic of monotheism, the exclusivity of salvation through Christ, and the idea that the political ruler should support and enforce true religion, Christianity developed a civilization that excluded other religions. Historically, the only religious diversity allowed in medieval Christian contexts was Judaism, and Jews often did not fare well in those contexts. Jews were not allowed to be full participants in civic life, and whether it was officially sanctioned or carried out at unofficial levels, Jews were subject to periodic persecution at the hands of Christians.

The modern period in the West brought dramatic changes to this pattern with the emergence of freedom of religion as a norm resulting at least in part from the influence of Enlightenment thought. Breaking through to freedom of religion was a long and difficult process in Western

Europe and the American colonies, a process fraught with conflict. As Christianity in Western Europe split apart in the sixteenth century into Protestant factions and Roman Catholicism, these groups had to learn to tolerate each other in the seventeenth and eighteenth centuries. The freedom of religion that eventually emerged as a political position was the outward expression of that hard-won tolerance.

While Protestant factions and Roman Catholics were learning to tolerate each other in Western Europe, the civilizations they created made advances in science and technology that allowed them eventually to dominate the world. In this domination, Western Christians often related to indigenous cultures in ways that were not favorable to the indigenous people or their religion. At various times and places, political conquest and forced religious conversions were the norm.

In the nineteenth century, an imperialistic fervor was maintained in the West that often continued the pattern of running roughshod over the religious and cultural practices of non-Christian peoples. The twentieth century, however, brought new kinds of considerations. There was a renewed emphasis on the right of people to determine their own destiny, ending strictly political forms of colonialism, even while economic dependence and oversight based on political interest remained (and remains) a problem. In some contexts, there was a growing understanding that our knowledge is to some degree historically or culturally relative. This made possible a new kind of appreciation of those who were different. It was not automatically assumed that representatives of other religions should convert and be like Western Christians.

The period from the late twentieth century to the present has brought a host of concrete changes in the relationship among religions. Most especially, there is a frequency and intensity of interaction between previously isolated cultures and religions that was unthinkable in the past. The Internet and other communications media provide instant global access, including access to representatives of the world's religions. Businesses are multinational and, with this, often contain representatives of a variety of religions. Travel of Westerners to sites in which other world religions are predominant is more and more commonplace. Scholarship, often of the highest caliber, makes the ideas of the world religions accessible. In the United States, with changes in immigration policy since 1965, there has been a dramatic increase in the numbers and visibility of representatives from the world religions, an increase that continues into the present.[1] Today, not just urban centers but also many rural areas of the country are home to significant religious diversity.

For many in the United States, these factors, along with intellectual transformations that promote the appreciation of diversity, have led to a new and significant valorization of the world religions. What does this new appreciation mean for Christianity, given its historical stance as a monotheistic religion that promotes salvation exclusively through Jesus Christ? Do classical Christian doctrines need to be reconsidered and reshaped in light of the value perceived in the various world religions? Should Christians try to persuade representatives of the world religions to convert to Christianity in order to find salvation, or should they encourage members of other religions to remain faithful practitioners of their own traditions? These are potent questions for contemporary Christian thought, and it appears they will only become more significant with the increasing interaction between Christians and devotees of other world religions around the globe.

This chapter addresses these questions by proposing a commonly used typology or framework for thinking through the relationship between Christianity and other religions. It analyzes the arguments of contemporary thinkers and groups who represent positions within this framework, seeking to uncover the reasons for the positions taken on the relationship between Christianity and other religions, and asking what the position implies not only for the understanding of other religions, but also for the understanding of Christianity.

A Framework for Understanding Christianity's Relationship to Other Religions

Since its introduction in the early 1980s, a framework containing a threefold typology has become commonplace in religious studies for understanding the relationship between Christianity and other religions.[2] Despite significant criticism of this framework over the decades, it remains widely known and widely used because of its ability to illumine important issues. In this chapter, this framework is used in a modified form.

This framework proposes that Christians regard other religions in one of three main ways. The first way is called exclusivism. It claims there is no salvation except the salvation known and experienced in Jesus Christ. In Jesus Christ alone, and therefore in Christianity alone, humans may receive the grace of God by which they can attain salvation. The second way, called inclusivism, affirms that grace, even grace of a saving type, is present in religions other than Christianity. That grace, however, is ultimately the grace Christians know and experience in Jesus Christ. In other words, the grace brought to humanity fully in Jesus Christ is understood as including or being effective in other religions so that devotees of those religions may experience it and be saved by it, even though they do not explicitly know or accept Jesus Christ. The final way is called pluralism, and it claims salvation is equally available in all religions. The experience of salvation Christians have in Jesus Christ is only one form of salvation among other forms that are equally present and equally effective in the various world religions.

The strength of this framework is that it focuses on the decisive question of whether devotees of non-Christian religions can be saved. The focus on this central question, and the way the framework provides a range of logical options in regard to it, is at least part of the reason it continues to be used. With that being said, the framework has two weaknesses that require clarification and expansion.

The first weakness is that the framework does not explicitly engage options for salvation for devotees of non-Christian religions besides the one that saving grace is or is not present in their religion in this life. Numerous Christian theologians, historically and at present, hypothesize that God provides an opportunity at death for devotees of non-Christian religions to hear the gospel and attain salvation, but this position does not fit neatly into the framework. Such people could be considered exclusivists, since they claim grace and salvation are known exclusively through Jesus Christ, or they could be considered inclusivists, since they claim this grace includes members of non-Christian religions with the proviso they receive it only at death. In this chapter, this position is analyzed under the category of exclusivism, limiting the definition of inclusivism to those who affirm saving grace is present in non-Christian religions in this life.

The second weakness is that in focusing exclusively on salvation, this framework does not account adequately for what Christians may think regarding the truth of other religions. The question of whether Christians think there is some truth in other religions, even if it may not be saving truth, is in many ways a broader and more complex question than the question of whether there is salvation in other religions. If one asks whether there is salvation in other religions, for the most part, one seeks a direct yes-or-no answer. Asking whether there is truth in other religions, however, calls for a more complicated analysis involving a continuum. One could claim, as some Christian theologians do, that there is only the smallest fragment of truth in non-Christian religions. Or one could claim, as other Christian theologians do, that non-Christian religions contain a fairly high degree of truth and Christians may even be able to learn things from them, while stopping short of claiming that salvation occurs in them. One could also claim that the levels of truth vary in the different non-Christian religions. Finally, asking about truth in non-Christian religions reflects back on one's theology and theological presuppositions in important ways and helps uncover the reasons for the position taken. While the focus on salvation provided by the framework is valuable, in this chapter it is supplemented and deepened by a discussion of what Christian theologians think regarding the truth of other religions.

Historical Exclusivism and Articulation of the Issues

As mentioned in the opening section, the mainstream position of Christianity through most of its history has been exclusivism. Exclusivist passages are certainly found in the New Testament. Two of the most famous are John 14:6, which has Jesus say, "I am the way, and the truth, and the life. No one comes to the Father except through me," and Acts 4:12, which has Peter say, referring to Jesus, "There is salvation in no one else, for there is no other name under heaven given among mortals by which we must be saved." Christians of the Patristic period in Christian history (100–450) certainly understood themselves as having a worldwide mission of converting members of other religions to Christianity in accordance with the charge of the resurrected Christ in Matt. 28:19 to "make disciples of all nations." The development of the doctrines of original sin, incarnation, and atonement made the exclusivist position the norm in Western Christianity.

A difficulty faced by the exclusivist theology of the early church was the question of the status of righteous pagans, including the Greek philosophers admired by many church fathers, who lived before the time of Jesus in a culture isolated from Judaism. Different suggestions were made to include them in salvation; these involved either some form of inclusivism or a postmortem opportunity to hear and respond to the gospel of Jesus Christ.

In the Middle Ages, despite the exclusivist thrust of Christian teaching, sophisticated ways were developed to affirm there is at least some truth in other religions. The preeminent and historically most significant example of this approach is in the thought of Thomas Aquinas.[3] Thomas draws a clear distinction between theological truths that can be known by reason and those that can be known only by revelation.[4] To Thomas, the truths of reason are universal and rationally demonstrable. Anyone with a sound mind reflecting on the world outside of them can know them. They include the ideas that God exists, God is one, God has certain attributes, humans have immortal souls, and humans are called to proper moral behavior. Standing above these truths but not in conflict with them are truths that can be known only by accepting the self-revelation of God recorded in the Bible and interpreted by the church. They include the ideas that God is a Trinity and that Jesus was an incarnation of God whose death and resurrection brought salvation.

In the theological tradition that developed after Thomas, the first set of truths knowable by reason came to be called "natural theology" or "general revelation," since it refers to what is revealed or known about God by the natural mind reflecting on reality. The second set of truths known only through God's self-revelation in history came to be called "revealed theology" or "special revelation," since it refers to what is revealed and known about God by God's special acts in history on humans' behalf.

While Thomas was isolated from the religions of the Far East, he was in contact with the Muslim civilization that bordered the Christian. By means of natural theology, he was able to affirm a connection with certain teachings of Islamic monotheism, as well as Judaism. Jews, Muslims, and Christians, however, all also affirm specific revealed truths that stand in some level of conflict with one other. Regarding the revealed truths of Christianity, Thomas said they cannot be demonstrably proven by reason. All he could do was give probable arguments for them that provide "training and consolation" to those who have already accepted the Christian revelation.[5] The arguments for the truth of the Christian revelation are not strong enough to convince someone who has accepted a different revelation.

Thomas's theological approach has outstanding historical significance because it became the standard approach to theology in Roman Catholic contexts, as well as Protestant ones when Protestants formalized their theology after the Reformation of the sixteenth century. Upon analysis, this approach involves certain tensions or problems regarding what it implies about non-Christian religions. These problems were not potent enough in Thomas's context or the post-Reformation context to transform the theological thinking of the time, but their importance has impressed itself on contemporary reflection.

The first tension is that the truths of revealed theology, which are the saving truths of Christianity, are particular historical truths and are not knowable universally. One does not have access to these truths simply by using one's mind and reflecting on reality, but one must be in a certain historical position to know about them. In Thomas's time, there were human civilizations not only of the Far East but also of the New World that had no opportunity to know about the Christian message. Throughout history, this has included millions upon millions of people.

For some Christians, the idea that certain people in the world are not in a position to hear the saving message of the gospel has served as a motivator to bring the gospel to those people. However, it also raises a serious question regarding the fairness of what happens to those people. Strictly speaking, according to the Christian doctrine of original sin, without access to the saving grace of Christ, those people are damned. But is it fair they are damned, given the fact that on the most basic level, their damnation is rooted in the fact that they were not in a historical position to hear the gospel message? In this text, this issue is called the "historical contingency" problem. It refers to the fact that one must be in a certain historical stream to hear the gospel, and whether or not one is in that stream rests on the contingent conditions of the time and place of one's birth.

The second tension is that the truths of revealed theology, which are the saving truths of Christianity, are not strictly provable by reason. To Thomas, at least, the most important truths—those that have to do with one's ultimate standing before God and one's eternal destiny—must on some level be accepted and cannot be convincingly proven as true to people who accept other revelations. However, if revealed truths must first be accepted and cannot be convincingly proven as true outside this acceptance, how can one expect people who accept other revelations to give up their revelations and accept the Christian one? Unless the truths of the Christian revelation can be universally proven as true in a convincing way, it would seem there are no grounds for expecting non-Christians to convert to Christianity. If there is no basis for them to convert, how can they be held accountable for not believing the Christian revelation? If no revelations are rationally provable, how can one revelation claim authority over the others?

In this text, this issue is called the "revelation acceptance" problem. It was not a problem for Thomas, who was nestled securely in a Christian civilization and had what appears to be an unquestioned certainty regarding the truth of the Christian revelation vis-à-vis other revelations. It becomes an issue in the Enlightenment of the seventeenth and eighteenth centuries, and it remains one today.

When we put these two issues together, another problem emerges that is actually a development of the historical contingency problem. On the one hand, simply hearing the message of Christianity depends on historically contingent circumstances. On the other hand, the Christian revelation must in some sense be accepted and cannot be universally proven as true. Given these factors, if we ask why most people who accept Christianity are Christians, we have to say it is because of the accident of where they were born. Most people who are Christians embrace Christianity because they were born in a Christian context, whether the narrow context of their immediate family or the broader context of their social group or nation. This is not to deny conversions in and out of Christianity, and it is certainly not to deny the fact that historically there have been major changes by groups of people from one religion to another. It is to say, however, that statistically speaking, the most significant factor in determining whether one will be a Christian is whether one was born in a Christian context. And what is true for Christianity is true for all of the world religions. Statistically speaking, chances are that if you were born in Pakistan to Muslim parents, you would be a Muslim; if you were born in India to Hindu parents, you would be a Hindu. It does not follow necessarily or logically from this that Christianity is untrue. It does, however, deepen the question of how one can fairly hold members of non-Christian religions accountable for not accepting Christianity.

This point has implications for interpreting the meaning of the Christian proclamation to non-Christians. Sometimes it is claimed in Christian contexts that if the gospel message is brought to devotees of the world religions and they reject it, then those people can rightly be held accountable for their damnation. They had a chance to hear the message of salvation and rejected it, so their damnation is upon their own heads, and God is not being unfair in condemning them. However, if one's belonging to a religion is based primarily on the accidental factor of one's birth, then it seems that members of other religions cannot be held so easily accountable for not converting when they hear the Christian message. They are only doing what most people, including Christians, do when they learn about another religion: they are remaining in the religion to which they were born. Since this is the case, it means the historical contingency problem involves not only the fact that one must be in a certain historical context to hear the message of Christianity, but also the idea that simply hearing the message of Christianity cannot be judged a sufficient reason for people to leave their religion and convert to Christianity.

As stated already, these problems were not serious issues in the Middle Ages or in the Reformation era. In certain ways, they become important in the Enlightenment of the seventeenth and eighteenth centuries. They gain new significance in the contemporary period with the increased interaction of world cultures and a new appreciation, at least by many people, of the world religions. The remainder of this chapter analyzes the positions of exclusivism, inclusivism, and pluralism, asking in each case how proponents of these positions would respond to these two problems.

Types of Contemporary Exclusivism

Contemporary exclusivism takes a variety of forms. Without making a claim to be exhaustive, this section examines several of these forms. The examination includes representative groups and individual thinkers.

Christianity Is Exclusively True and the Exclusive Place of Salvation: Sectarian Protestantism

The strongest form of exclusivism unites the idea that Christianity is the exclusive place of salvation with the idea that Christianity is exclusively true. While this position is not popular in academic circles and is not generally found in Christian groups that are significantly integrated into American culture, it is represented by some sectarian Protestant groups.

Sectarianism is a sociological term that refers to the capacity of a group to insulate itself from the larger world, drawing a sharp line of demarcation between members of the in-group and the culture in which they live. In certain Protestant groups, the drawing of this line occurs through the promotion of a worldview that regards the outside world as under satanic forces that are at present ruling history. In this view, only the limited members of the sectarian group can truly escape these forces and hold to the truth and a chance at salvation.

In its extreme forms, this view of the world regards big business, big government, other Christian denominations, and the world religions as all being under satanic influences. These groups often maintain an apocalyptic orientation, expecting and promoting the imminent physical return of Jesus, which will be followed by the destruction of the world and most of its inhabitants while the members of the group are spared and vindicated as God's faithful remnant.

Viewing the world as under the sway of evil powers from which only their group is free does not allow for the influence of the kinds of

considerations discussed with regard to the historical contingency problem and the revelation acceptance problem. Asking about these problems
seriously would itself be regarded as threatening or dangerous, since the
group's focus is on holding on to the truth in what is perceived as a hostile world. Consequently, these groups exempt themselves from the kind
of discussion that is germane to this chapter. At the same time, however,
they also isolate themselves from a sympathetic understanding of others
who are different, including members of the world religions. Perhaps the
most troubling manifestation of this isolation is in the fact that they are
willing to affirm that the vast majority of the world's inhabitants will be
destroyed in the imminent end of history they await.

Christianity Is Exclusively True, but Salvation Is for Everyone: Karl Barth

One of the most renowned Protestant theologians of the early and middle
twentieth century, Karl Barth, is notable for denying there is any connection between God and humans except the one God creates through
revelation. For Barth, humans have no natural awareness of God, and
God cannot be known by the mind reflecting on reality as proposed by
natural theology. God must be known by revelation alone, and the only
revelation he deems viable is the one testified to in the Old and New
Testaments, in which God reveals God's self in covenant with the Jews
and becomes incarnate in Jesus Christ to redeem sinful human beings.
Since human beings are utterly cut off from the knowledge of God and
the only viable revelation is the Judeo-Christian one, the world religions
must of necessity be completely false.

In his writings on the truth of Christianity vis-à-vis other religions,
Barth is concerned to show that the exclusive truth of Christianity is
not something that extends in a full-fledged way to Christianity as an
institution in the world.[6] As an institution in the world, Christianity
involves ministers and priests, seminaries, denominations, and individual
churches with their different modes of worship and variety of teachings
and influence on culture and politics. Christianity is not exclusively true
in the sense that every aspect of its institutional life is true. It is exclusively true only in the sense that the true revelation from God comes to it
and nowhere else. As an institution in the world, it can always be wrong,
and it continually needs to be judged by the revelation it bears.

Because humans have no natural knowledge of God, Barth affirms
God must create the belief in the revelation affirmed by Christianity.

This leads to a peculiar idea regarding how Christianity is true. For Barth, Christianity is not true in the sense that once it is revealed, its doctrines can be scrutinized by any rational mind and found to correspond to reality. Instead, Christianity becomes true in the sense that the Holy Spirit, effective in the preaching of the message of Christianity, creates the condition for the believer to acknowledge its truth. Christianity cannot be determined to be true outside the self-validating work of the Holy Spirit in the believer.

This understanding of Christianity's truth gives us Barth's answer to the revelation acceptance problem. This problem asks why one should accept the Christian revelation as true versus any other revelation if the Christian revelation cannot be rationally verified. Barth says the Christian revelation testifies to its own truth in those who hear and accept it, and he is satisfied to leave it at that.

While Barth was satisfied with this answer, many in his own time were not, and many in the generation that followed him have not been satisfied either. The fact he was even able to give this kind of an answer tells us something important about his context. Even in the early and middle part of the twentieth century, Barth was satisfied to think and work within an insular and, one could even say, isolated Christian context. While he wrote volume after volume of theology for the Christian church, he almost never comments on a religion other than Christianity, with the one exception to this rule being Judaism. He displays no serious knowledge about, insight into, or even concern with the Far Eastern religions and Islam. The fact that he could do this and still be a renowned theologian says something important about how different his context was from our own, and how dramatically and rapidly our context has changed.

Although Barth denied other religions were true, his theology pointed to the idea that all humanity will eventually be saved. In Christian theology, the position that all humanity will eventually be saved is called "universalism." It is a minority view in Christian history, but it is based on the idea that God loves all humans equally and that God will realize God's purpose for the entire creation, which is to bring everyone and everything into a fulfilled relationship with God's self. For God not to do so would mean that God's purpose in making creation would ultimately remain frustrated or unfulfilled. Universalists claim that an all-powerful God will certainly fulfill God's purpose for creation.

While Barth admitted his theology points toward universalism, on theological grounds he denied directly holding this view. What troubled him was the idea that if he affirmed that everyone eventually will be saved, he would be telling God what God must do. If everyone will be saved, then God must save everyone. To Barth, such a position offends God's freedom, and he wanted to maintain that God is free to do what God will do.

Although he did not directly hold universalism, it was nevertheless Barth's conviction that the revelation in the New Testament teaches that God chose all humanity to receive grace in Jesus Christ. Jesus Christ reveals God's "yes" to the whole world, not just to a certain number of people whom God has chosen to elect for salvation, and not even just to those who are in the historical position to hear and receive the Christian message.

Since Barth did not think God's saving grace is operating in the world religions outside the explicit acceptance of salvation in Jesus Christ, his affirmation that God embraces everyone in salvation means salvation somehow has to be offered to members of the world religions other than Christianity at death. This idea shows how Barth responds to the historical contingency problem articulated earlier. Those who are not in a position to hear about Christianity, or who hear about it and remain committed to their own religion in this life, have a chance to hear and respond to the gospel at death. Presumably, in the postmortem proclamation of the gospel, it will be clear that Christianity is the one and only true revelation.

The position that non-Christians have an opportunity to hear and respond to the gospel at death is one way to reconcile the tension between the affirmation that salvation comes only through Christianity and the apparent unfairness of God damning or excluding people who did not have a chance to hear the Christian gospel, or who may have heard it but were embedded deeply and faithfully in their own religious traditions so they did not convert in their lifetimes. One does not have to go as far as Barth in affirming the exclusive truth of Christianity or in pointing to universal salvation to maintain this position.

One of the main questions about the affirmation of a postmortem opportunity at Christian salvation for members of non-Christian religions is whether this position solves the problem of Christianity and other religions, or whether it ignores the problem essentially by failing to engage other religions seriously. Does the Christian who takes this position have an unshakable prejudgment that Christianity is exclusively true and the only place of salvation, so affirming the possibility of postmortem salvation to members of other religions solves a fairness problem but keeps the Christian from engaging these other religions in an open-minded way that could potentially be transformative? Other significant questions arise with this one. Is it good or problematic for a Christian to have unshakable confidence and work from the immovable presupposition that salvation and final truth are in Christianity alone? Does such unshakable confidence display positively the strength of one's commitment to Christianity, or does it show a kind of closed-mindedness that keeps one from a serious examination of the world religions that may end up calling for a transformation in the nature of one's Christian commitment?

These are enormous and difficult questions that many professional theologians and lay Christians alike are taking seriously today. As for Barth, he lived at a time and in a context that enabled him to avoid the seriousness of these questions and, with them, a serious exploration of the world religions. He did not try to understand the world religions for what they are, and he appears not to have thought they had anything of significance to say to him. He kept them at arm's distance while interpreting them through his own Christian lens.

The World Religions Have Some Truth, but Christianity Is the Exclusive Place of Salvation: Evangelical Protestantism

Evangelical Protestantism is a significant movement on the American religious landscape. It constitutes just over one-fourth of the American population and consists of several major denominations and independent churches.[7] While Evangelicals are theologically conservative, they are significantly integrated into American culture, which distinguishes them from the more sectarian Protestant groups mentioned previously. On theological matters, they affirm that God's revelation is found uniquely in the Old and New Testaments of the Bible, and they tend to read the Bible literally. They also affirm the importance of a born-again or conversion experience as a key element of Christian salvation. For Evangelicals, it is through this experience that one becomes justified or right with God.

While Evangelicals do not have a single view of other religions, an analysis of the dynamics of the conversion experience reveals one position taken by many Evangelicals regarding members of non-Christian religions. The conversion experience has a typical pattern in which a person becomes convicted of his or her own sinfulness before God. This is an inner, heartfelt conviction that involves the sense of God's disfavor or judgment, even wrath, upon one as a sinner. At the same time, coming in and through this sense of sinfulness and unworthiness are God's grace and acceptance made possible by the substitutionary death of God's son, Jesus Christ, for one's sins. Testimonies about conversion typically involve an overwhelming sense of thankfulness for this act of pure mercy on God's part that saves one from the condemnation one deserves.

As interpreted by Evangelicals, the awareness in a conversion experience that one is a sinner deserving God's wrath expresses the state, known or unknown, of unconverted people. This includes the irreligious within a culture influenced by Christianity, as well as devotees of other religions. In typical Evangelical terminology, there is a gulf or chasm separating unconverted people from God and from salvation, whether those people are fully aware of this chasm or not. Insofar as one may have a dim awareness of one's guilt and its seriousness, instead of seeking grace, one may engage in acts of good works to attempt to make oneself right before God. It is typical for Evangelicals to regard other religions and also other forms of Christianity as examples in which people are seeking to make themselves right before God by their own efforts. However, for Evangelicals, such good works are never enough to bridge the unbridgeable chasm between the individual and God. Only the conversion experience, in which there are both acknowledgment of sin and reception of grace given through Christ, can do this.

Because of the importance of a conversion experience to bridge the unbridgeable gap between the person and God, many Evangelicals deny that salvation can occur in non-Christian religions.[8] That does not mean Evangelicals necessarily think the world religions are completely false. Many also affirm the possibility of natural theology, so that outside of the conscious awareness of the Christian message, one could come to some true theological positions.

An example of Evangelical theologians who affirm natural theology is found in the work of Douglas Geivett and Gary Phillips.[9] They argue on the basis of universal reason that humans can know there is a personal loving God, so any religion that affirms this, even if in a confused way, contains some truth. Geivett and Phillips go on to claim that because all human beings have a natural sense of the moral law and human failings with regard to it, humans can also expect that a loving God would meet humanity's "darkest aspects" in some concrete way with a divine revelation.[10] In other words, their understanding of natural theology goes so far as to pave the way for the expectation of a saving revelation, which, they claim, is found exclusively in Christianity. This shows how they would respond to the revelation acceptance problem identified earlier. Even though one cannot strictly prove the truth of the Christian revelation through natural reason, the truths of natural reason anticipate it.

Geivett and Phillips respond to the historical contingency problem by referring to the doctrine of "middle knowledge."[11] This doctrine says that part of God's omniscience is that God knows what all individuals would do if in fact they were presented with different situations than the ones with which they are presented in their lifetimes. If this is the case, God knows what people who never had the chance to hear the Christian gospel would have done if in fact they had had a chance to hear the gospel. If one adds to this a belief in God's sovereignty, or control of the events in the universe, one can make the argument that Geivett and Phillips apparently support: that God has arranged things so that all those who in fact would have responded positively to the Christian gospel were put in a position to hear the Christian gospel, and all those who did not hear the Christian gospel would have rejected it anyway.

While the doctrine of middle knowledge appears theoretically to be a possible resolution to the historical contingency problem, one has to ask whether it strains credulity in the attempt to solve this problem. In the course of human history, over thousands of years, many human cultures arise in relative isolation from each other, and major world religions develop in these relatively independent cultures. Christianity develops in the middle of one of these cultures and makes exclusive claims. Is it most reasonable to think people who are outside Christianity are in fact people God knows would have rejected Christianity if they had heard it, so God placed them in a position outside the Christian message? Or is it most reasonable to think they are simply people doing what most Christians also do, which is quite naturally accepting the religion into which they were born?

This question can be made concrete by considering a Native American woman living on the plains of the American Midwest in the fifteenth century, completely isolated from Christianity. Is she aptly conceived as someone God knows would have rejected the Christian message if she had had a chance to hear it, so God had her be born in a time and place outside Christianity? Or is thinking of her this way, while logically possible, forcing her into a mold constructed from one's own presuppositions, and is it one's presuppositions that need to be changed?

In our earlier analysis of Barth's position on the non-Christian religions, it was asked whether Barth adequately accounts for the world religions and takes them seriously, or whether he presupposes the truth of Christianity in an unshakable way and fails to take the world religions seriously. This question can be expanded here. Without attempting to diminish the importance of the conversion experience for Evangelicals, does this experience in its particularity provide an adequate norm by which all other religions can and should be judged? If other religions promote human transformation in a way that is different from the specific dynamic involved in the Evangelical conversion experience, is it really the case that all those alternatives can and should be interpreted merely as attempts at works righteousness—people vainly trying to make themselves right before God by their own efforts? Might they not be genuine and transforming responses to some transcendent reality? Moreover, many of the world religions speak of the importance of receiving divine grace or mercy. Is that grace or mercy not real because it is not in the Christian form? Again, these are large and difficult questions, and while they do not yield easy answers, they are also not easily avoided in our increasingly diverse religious context.

Inclusivism

Inclusivism affirms that members of non-Christian religions can find salvation in their own religions outside the explicit knowledge and acceptance of Jesus Christ. With this claim, it differs from exclusivism and agrees with pluralism, since pluralism also says there is salvation in religions other than Christianity. However, inclusivism also affirms that Christianity is special in relation to all other religions because the salvation in Jesus Christ is the goal or ideal of salvation, a goal that other religions have in an inferior way. This makes it like exclusivism and unlike pluralism, since exclusivism also affirms Christianity's superiority over against other religions, and pluralism puts all religions on an even par.

The idea that there is salvation outside of the church and outside of the explicit acceptance of Jesus Christ as savior is not completely new in Christian history. Its contemporary form, however, emerges in a novel context as part of a unique framework of theological reflection. The next section traces the outline of the emergence of this framework in order to explain both contemporary inclusivism and contemporary pluralism, the latter of which follows the same framework but takes it to different conclusions.

Emergence of Inclusivism

The contemporary social context that has led to new questions and considerations about Christianity's relationship to the world religions has already been examined. While these transformations of social context were occurring, at least in some wings of Christian theology, theoretical transformations also were occurring and led to new ways of thinking about the world religions. These theoretical transformations go to the core of what it means to do theology.

As noted in the discussion of exclusivism, one of the common ways of doing theology, which ultimately goes back to Thomas Aquinas and was adopted and adapted by both Protestants and Catholics after the Protestant Reformation, was to distinguish natural theology or general revelation from revealed theology or special revelation. Natural theology contains truths about God, the soul, and the moral law that can be known simply by the mind reflecting on reality. Revealed theology contains truths known only by God's self-revelation in history recorded in the Bible and taught by the church. While the truths of general revelation are said to be universal, they are not the saving truths of Christianity. Essentially they have to do with a more distant God, or a God who is not involved in history. The truths of special revelation are the saving truths of Christianity, where God is involved in history, in the giving of grace, and in personal transformation.

Traditionally, in this framework, claims to special revelation by religions other than Christianity are simply deemed invalid. In Christianity alone, it is affirmed, is the special channel of grace that can only be known and realized in special revelation. Because of the affirmation of the uniqueness of revelation in Christianity, there was never a serious analysis of what it means to experience and accept this revelation that would or could have universal applicability. Grace comes only in Christianity, so no serious analysis of the reality and experience of grace was made that refers to any religious experience outside Christianity.

This changed with a shift in theological focus adopted by some Christian theologians in the early contemporary period. They began to analyze religious experience, including the Christian experience of grace, in a way that shows this experience has some universal element. Put differently and more broadly, what these theologians did was analyze human experience in such a way that they were able to show that a religious directedness, and with it a connection to God, is a structural part of human experience. Their claim was that everyone in his or her immediate consciousness is connected to God, and they sought to show how this connection to God impinges upon all human beings.

If everyone has an immediate connection to God as a structural part of what it means to be human, this breaks down the old view that says religions other than Christianity have only a distant relation to God through general revelation, while only in Christianity is there an immediate and transforming relation to God of special revelation. Instead, everyone must be understood as having an immediate and at least potentially transforming relationship to God, and the salvation and grace spoken about in Christianity must be understood as one specific way in which that relationship is expressed and realized. In other words, for this contemporary approach, natural theology or general revelation is replaced by an analysis of human experience in general, and religious experience in particular, which shows that everyone has a living connection to God. What it means to be human is to be connected to God in a potentially transforming way. Special revelation is replaced by an examination of the concrete ways in which this living relationship is manifest in human history in the religions of the world. Each religion is a different concrete manifestation of the universal connection to God that is part of what it means to be human.

Clearly, this approach to theology implies a different attitude toward non-Christian religions than the previous approach. For this approach, the question is not whether non-Christian religions have a transformative relation to God, but whether their relationship is equal to that of Christianity or in some sense inferior to Christianity. This question is precisely where inclusivists and pluralists differ. In an important sense, both inclusivists and pluralists come out of this transformation of thinking in theology. They differ because pluralists think all religions express an equally transformative relationship to God, while inclusivists think Christianity is the highest realization of the relationship to God and other religions remain inferior in some way.

Salvation Occurs in All Religions, but Christianity Is Completely True: Karl Rahner

This shift in theological approach occurred among some Protestant and Roman Catholic theologians. As a result, inclusivist theologians can be found in both traditions in the contemporary period. Probably the most notable inclusivist, however, is the German Jesuit Karl Rahner (1904–1984); this section analyzes his position.

While Rahner was a brilliant theologian who wrote prodigiously on an immense range of topics, his writings themselves do not contain in-depth analyses of the world religions, with the exception of Judaism. Certainly he showed familiarity with world religions other than Christianity, but he displayed no serious expertise about them, nor did he engage in any

concrete comparative work in relation to them. Instead, he talked about
the world religions from the point of view of his own Christian theological perspective. The presuppositions of his perspective, more than actual
analysis of what the world religions say, informed his position. This does
not necessarily mean he was wrong. It means what he was doing was providing a framework of thinking that needed to be carried out or applied
to the world religions to see whether it was viable.

In an important and widely read lecture on Christianity and other
religions, the foremost reason Rahner gives for his affirmation that there
is salvation in non-Christian religions is that his Christian perspective
informs him that God wants to save everyone.[12] If God really wants to
save everyone, but millions upon millions of people throughout history
have no access to the Christian message, then, Rahner says, God must
be bringing salvation to those people in some other way. The best way to
understand God's bringing of salvation to them is to affirm that God uses
the same means as God uses to bring salvation to Christians: God uses
some concrete, social religion. The religions must be the place where
God's grace is universally available. This means, in Rahner's words, non-
Christian religions are "positively included in God's plan of salvation."[13]
This is Rahner's solution to the historical contingency problem.

To understand how Rahner thinks it is possible for God to enact
salvation in other religions requires a deeper analysis of his theology.
One of his main theological bases is that the human subject is invariably
and immediately connected to the presence of God. Rahner thinks his
analysis of the human subject and his or her connection to God on this
level is universal. In his language, all human beings are "elevated" to a
relationship with God as part of the structure of their being.

For Rahner, this connection to God is realized through the fact that
humans experience their lives as pervaded by a sense of mystery. One of
the ways he points to the presence of this mystery is in ordinary human
cognition of the world. Immediately, before one even thinks about it, the
mind grasps the objects experienced through the senses with concepts.
This allows one to identify conceptually those things perceived through
the senses, like a table, desk, pen, and paper. Through this immediate
grasping of objects, one makes sense of the world. As Rahner analyzes
it, in every act of grasping the world with the concepts and categories of
the mind, the mind always extends beyond the concepts and categories
to something more that transcends them. The mind is open to this more,
which is the mystery of being that surrounds human life and understanding. This mystery is the universal presence of God to the human subject,

immediately present in a way that is ungraspable and that transcends all categories of thought and knowledge.

For Rahner, the presence of God is always the presence of grace, which means all human lives are surrounded by the mysterious grace of God. However, this grace must be specifically articulated in order for it to be more than some ungraspable and vague otherness. Human beings are concrete social creatures and, as such, need concrete and social articulation of this mysterious presence of grace. The world religions, with their concrete ideas of God or the Gods and their communal rituals and worship, provide the context for the mysterious presence of grace.

While Rahner thinks grace and, therefore, salvation are available in all religions, he is unflinching in holding to the idea that Christianity is the fulfillment of salvation. Rahner calls Jesus the "absolute Savior." In the incarnation, death, and resurrection of Jesus the Christ, God gives God's self to humanity in a complete and total way. This means it is here that grace is manifest in its full, final, and complete form. All other religions have salvation, but they express it in a lesser and to some extent confused way. They have salvation, but they do not really know what the final meaning of salvation is all about.[14]

Because non-Christian religions have salvation, even though they do not have it in its finality, they point to the fullness of salvation in Christianity and are oriented toward it. This means, according to Rahner, that eventually in the encounter of Christianity with other religions, those other religions will realize they are lesser instances of salvation and will give way to Christianity. Since the salvation of other religions is real but inferior, when other religions encounter the fullness of salvation in Christianity, that inferiority should become clear. This is the way Rahner solves the revelation acceptance problem identified earlier. He thinks in the ongoing and increasing encounter of Christianity with other religions, the fullness and finality of Christianity will become evident.

This complex of ideas is what Rahner means when, in an intriguing use of language, he calls members of non-Christian religions "anonymous Christians." They are Christians in the sense that they are saved by the same grace of the same God by which Christians are saved, although they do not have this grace in its fullness. They are also Christians in anticipation, in the sense that it is anticipated that all religions in the encounter with Christianity will see the superiority of its salvation.

Because Rahner's position is between exclusivism and pluralism, he can be and has been critiqued from both perspectives. Exclusivists critique Rahner's idea that God's grace is effective in the world religions. Rahner thought God's graceful presence enfolds all lives, is embodied inadequately in the world religions, and is disclosed fully in Christian salvation. This can be contrasted with the Evangelical perspective, where those outside the Christian experience of grace face an unbridgeable chasm between themselves and God. For Evangelicals, Christian salvation is not the completion or fullness of the inadequate forms of salvation in the world religions. In an important sense, Christian salvation is the contradiction of the attempts at self-salvation, or the attempts to bridge the unbridgeable chasm between themselves and God, that occur in the world religions.

Because pluralists regard all religions as equal avenues of salvation, they agree with Rahner in affirming there is salvation in all religions, but they maintain he is mistaken in claiming Christianity as the ideal of salvation. For pluralists, Rahner sees salvation too narrowly through the Christian lens. The pluralist critique of Rahner claims that his perspective was formed by a presumption that Christianity is the highest truth, a presumption Rahner never seriously questioned and was not willing or able to transcend. In the end, Rahner wants to turn everyone into a Christian, rather than seeing salvation as bigger than Christianity, as the pluralists do.

Pluralism

Pluralism affirms that salvation occurs in all religions in a relatively equal manner. It denies the claim of any religion to be the exclusive locus of salvation or the pinnacle of salvation.

For Christianity, this implies a considerable rethinking of many of its doctrines, including the ideas of incarnation and atonement. The need to reshape doctrines to embrace pluralism extends to non-Christian religions as well, insofar as they affirm their superiority to other religions. This chapter is limited to the impact of a pluralist stance on Christianity, but it is notable that acceptance of the theory of pluralism would lead to important transformations in virtually all of the world religions. Paradoxically, while acknowledging the legitimacy of all religions by affirming salvation is equally available in them all, pluralism also calls for significant change in the self-understanding of the religions.

Salvation Occurs in All Religions, and No Religion Is Exclusively True: John Hick

The most notable contemporary Christian theologian to propose a conscious and sophisticated version of pluralism is John Hick, whose ideas regarding theodicy and the afterlife were summarized in chapter 5. In the latter decades of his career, Hick has promoted what he calls a "pluralist hypothesis" on the religions. Coming from a Christian perspective and writing for what is mostly a Christian audience, Hick argues for a "Copernican revolution" regarding Christianity's relationship to other religions. As Copernicus put the sun in the center when he showed that the earth revolves around the sun and not vice versa, so Hick wants to put God, rather than Christianity, in the center of the religious universe and have all the religions including Christianity revolve around God.

Hick refers to two empirical insights in multiple writings that provide evidence for Hick's pluralist hypothesis. One of these insights is what was described as the historical contingency problem. Hick points out that, on the whole, the biggest factor determining whether one is a member of a certain religion has to do with whether one was born into that religion.[15] Individual conversions aside, most people belong to a certain religion because of the contingent factor of their birth. A tension exists, then, between acknowledging this contingent factor and the tendency of representatives of various religions to elevate their religion as the exclusive or highest truth. Hick understands that, from a strictly logical standpoint, it could be the case that all religions are adopted contingently but one of the religions is nevertheless completely or exclusively true. In other words, this insight is not a platform on which to logically deduce his pluralist hypothesis. Instead, it raises suspicion about the potential arbitrariness of the exclusivist position and, insofar as people have become culturally conscious of it, partly explains why so many Christians have become open to the possibility of genuine truth in other religions.

Hick's second insight is that all religious traditions, or at least all of the great historical world religions, are contexts of human transformation in about the same degree of effectiveness.[16] Hick understands the function or purpose of religion as being the transformation of people from a self-centered state to a state in which their lives are grounded in what he calls the Real. In general, for his pluralist hypothesis, Hick avoids using the term *God* and prefers instead to speak of the Real, since the term *God* can be limited to a Christian or monotheistic interpretation. The transcendence of egoism and grounding in the Real realizes itself in basic religious and moral fruits, or transformed lives. Hick understands this as the essence of salvation, and his claim is that insofar as it can be judged, all religions do this with about the same degree of effectiveness. This is true whether what is examined is a religion's ability to produce saints, who are superlative examples of this transformation, or the ability of a religion to affect the lives of ordinary devotees, or the moral character of the world historical civilizations shaped by a major religion. In all cases, the religions are operating to bring about transformation and moral fruits in a relatively equal way.

Hick recognizes that, once again, from a strictly logical standpoint, it could be the case that while human transformation or salvation is occurring equally in all of the religions, one of the religions has the hidden source of that salvation for all. If one religion held the meaning or completion of salvation for all religions, it would be the truest religion theoretically. However, as Hick points out, when human transformation occurs equally in all religions, the claim that this transformation is explained by the truth in one religion invokes suspicion and appears arbitrary.

Because of the apparent arbitrariness in other positions, Hick proposes his pluralist hypothesis as an explanation of the religions that best accounts for the two insights just described. The task of his hypothesis is to explain how all of the religions can be equally true, though none of them exclusively true, given the enormous diversity within their belief systems. Each major religion has its own particular conception of God, the Gods, or ultimate reality. In Judaism, Christianity, and Islam, there is one God conceived in personal terms. In some versions of some Eastern traditions, ultimate reality is conceived in impersonal terms. If transformation is occurring equally in all of them, how can they also all be true, though none exclusively true, when they have such different ideas about the highest reality?

Hick's hypothesis is that there is a universal presence of the Real that affects all human lives, and this universal presence is understood in a variety of ways in different historical and cultural streams. All religions are equally true because all are mediations of the same universal reality in the same degree of effectiveness. None of the religions is exclusively true, because each is a particular historical, cultural, and categorically formed way of expressing and relating to this reality.[17]

Hick explains the variety of understandings of the Real in the world religions by affirming the philosophical and religious insight that the human mind is limited in relation to the Real, which transcends all of the categories of the mind, but the mind is also always active in shaping the reality it encounters. This shaping includes the mind's relation to the Real. The mind never just passively accepts and simply re-presents any reality given to it. Instead, the mind is always actively engaged in the formation of a meaningful reality. For Hick, this includes the formation of the different concrete understandings of the Real or God or ultimate reality expressed in all of the world religions.

This hypothesis enables Hick to distinguish between what he calls the "Real in itself" and the "Real as variously experienced and thought by different human communities."[18] The Real in itself is the universal divine presence that remains unknown and transcends all mental categories and historical formations. The Real as experienced by different human communities is the idea of ultimate reality grasped in and through human mental categories and in and through a cultural and historical tradition, or one of the world religions. This distinction means that no conception of ultimate reality in the world religions is true in a literal sense. God is neither personal nor impersonal in God's self. However, all conceptions of ultimate reality are true as mediators of the universal Real in itself insofar as they bring about genuine human transformation.

In a variety of places in his writings, Hick points out that the distinction he makes between the Real in itself and the Real as experienced by human conceptual and historical formations is in fact affirmed in some way by all the great religious traditions. They all recognize that ultimate reality transcends the human mind and the human attempt to represent it. At the same time, they offer particular forms for understanding and relating to ultimate reality. This serves as evidence for Hick's position, in the sense that while his pluralist hypothesis may require the reformulation of some exclusivist elements in the religious traditions, it does not simply impose itself on those traditions as an entirely foreign element. Its structure is already contained in the idea of ultimate reality in the traditions themselves.

Hick's pluralist hypothesis resolves the two issues identified earlier as the historical contingency problem and the revelation acceptance problem. If Christianity is only one way of salvation among others that are equal, as Hick postulates, then people without access to Christianity have as much of an opportunity to experience salvation in its fullness as do Christians. And if the revealed truths of each religion are equally true, as genuine mediations of the universal Real that bring about transformation, and equally false, since none literally describes the Real, then no one in any religion needs to give up his or her idea of ultimate reality or way of relating to ultimate reality for any other.

Writing primarily for a Christian audience, Hick is concerned to show the way in which Christianity can and must be reinterpreted to meet the demands of a pluralist position. In particular, Hick has focused on reformulating the Christian ideas of incarnation and atonement.

Regarding the incarnation, he understands that the formulation of classical Christology that claims God literally became incarnate in Jesus so that Jesus has both a divine and human nature is unacceptable from a pluralist perspective. It means that Christianity alone was founded by God and is superior to other religions. In its place, Hick proposes what he calls an "inspirational" or "degree" Christology.[19] Such a Christology affirms that Jesus was a human in whom the Spirit of God was present in an extraordinary degree. Jesus was completely open to God's presence in his life, words, and deeds. He reflected God's love in a particularly powerful way. However, this does not mean he literally had a divine nature. Jesus was not literally God in terms of his nature, but was full of God in terms of his religious character. This understanding of Jesus enables Hick to affirm that Jesus was a potent religious figure, but it also allows him to claim there can be other such figures in other world religions.

Hick rejects what is called the substitutionary theory of the atonement in which God is said to take on human flesh to serve as a substitute for human sin, understood as a violation of God's law and entailing a penalty that humans themselves cannot pay.[20] This theory of atonement operates under the idea that only if Jesus is God and therefore perfect, but also human and therefore like us, can he be an adequate substitute for human sin. Hick points out that acceptance of this theory requires acceptance of the idea of a literal Adam and Eve who fell into sin and passed original sin to all humanity, thus requiring this kind of sacrifice, and he rejects the idea of an original fall from grace. It also requires the notion that an innocent person can be punished on behalf of the guilty, something he rejects as well. And most importantly to Hick, this theory makes God the one who is unreconciled to humans and fails to understand God as a loving Father who is ready and willing to forgive the penitent, an understanding of God that Hick thinks Jesus himself taught.

In place of the substitutionary theory of atonement, Hick proposes that Christians think in general of salvation as the process of being elevated to a more Godlike condition.[21] On account of his unity with God, Jesus is the exemplar who inspires that transition for all who claim to be Christians. To Hick, Jesus' death was not a substitute for human sin but an outcome of his commitment to unity with God at all costs, which inevitably aroused opposition but was something Jesus was willing to stand for, despite facing death. Such a commitment is an inspiration to followers of Jesus.

Criticisms of Hick: Self-Conscious Inclusivism and Exclusivism

While deeply influential, Hick's pluralist hypothesis and the transformations it implies for Christianity have also been widely critiqued by inclusivists and exclusivists alike. This section examines the critique of Hick from both perspectives. The development of this critique is intended to show modifications in the positions of inclusivism and exclusivism that are prevalent on the contemporary theological scene. This is not meant to suggest that these modifications are possible or meaningful only as critiques of pluralism. They have their own history and independent standing. However, juxtaposing them to Hick's pluralism clarifies them, which is why they are developed at this point.

The main line of critique that inclusivists and exclusivists alike have launched against Hick claims his generalizing theory about the religions falsifies them. Hick's theory rests on two significant generalizations: first, that the main function of all religions is the transformation from ego-centeredness to centeredness in the Real, and second, that the understanding of ultimate reality in all religions is a combination of the universal presence of the Real and some categorical and historical formation. These two generalizations are proposed as the essence of religion in terms of its practical function (human transformation) and theoretical meaning (idea of ultimate reality). All individual religions are understood as particular manifestations of this essence. Hick's critics counter, however, that it is not possible to collapse all of the religions into this essence. In trying to do so, Hick does not understand the religions, but forces them into a mold of his own making.

Two forms of this critique can be distinguished. The first form comes from a modified version of inclusivism. It says Hick's attempt to grasp the essence of religion overlooks the decisive fact that humans are always concretely determined by a certain perspective when examining other religions. Hick proposes to stand above all perspectives and employ a neutral theory to explain all religions. The critics say there is no such place to stand. Everyone can stand only within a particular concrete tradition, and to some degree, everyone—including Hick—always sees other traditions from his or her own point of view. According to the critics' position, this does not require abandoning all theorizing about other religions from one's own religious perspective. Instead, one should recognize that all religions, Christian and non-Christian, are going to try to explain each other from their own point of view. Allowing all such explanations should be part of an ongoing dialogue between the religions, among other things, so the religions' explanations of each other are not merely talking past one another.

What makes this position inclusivist is its claim that all religions can and should attempt to understand other religions, even though such understanding is invariably done from one's own religious perspective. For some who take this perspective, it is perfectly acceptable to make an explicit argument for the superiority of one's own religion.[22] What one must do, however, is be ready to admit one's limitations and acknowl-edge—or even expect—that members of other religions will make the same arguments for the superiority of their religions.

These elements make this form of inclusivism both more self-conscious and more circumscribed in its claims than the inclusivism of Karl Rahner. Rahner worked from an understanding that everyone shares in an experience of God's grace mediated through the different religions and completed in Christianity. He never seems to have ques-tioned seriously the degree to which his understanding of God's grace working through the different religions was shaped by his own Christian assumptions. He never actually engaged the other religions. He took it as an unshakable assumption that the fulfillment of salvation is in Christian-ity and that as the religions encounter one another, non-Christians will recognize the truth of Christianity, and the non-Christian religions will fall away. This more self-conscious version of inclusivism recognizes that people bring the presuppositions of their concrete perspective to bear on their understanding of others. On some level, this type of inclusivism claims that all religions have something to learn from each other, and it promotes dialogue and a deepened understanding between the religions. It is skeptical or reserved about the idea that members of non-Christian religions will invariably see Christianity as the highest truth and convert.

The fact that this version of inclusivism continues to affirm the attempt of the religions to understand each other, even though this is always done from each individual's point of view, means that underly-ing this position is a commitment to the idea that there is some shared religious experience. The religions must have something in common that enables representatives from each one to understand the others and even make the argument that their position is superior to others. This element is precisely what is denied by the second kind of critique of Hick, which is a modified version of exclusivism. It claims there is no common experi-ence or unifying element among the religions. In this view, each religion is fundamentally a different entity with different ideas about ultimate reality and different conceptions about ultimate human destiny. To this position, for example, the Buddhist idea of Enlightenment is not another way of expressing what is essentially the kind of transformation realized in Christian salvation. It is, in fact, a different kind of transformation with a different goal than the Christian one. Similarly, the Hindu idea of ultimate reality, which in some versions is impersonally conceived and called Brahman, is not another way of expressing the same universal Real that is expressed in the Christian idea of the Trinity. It is, in fact, a different understanding of ultimate reality.

For this position, since each religion is a different and incompatible entity, the religions cannot all be true, and salvation cannot occur in all of them in an equal way. At the same time, each religion being different and incompatible opens the possibility that only one religion is true and the only place of salvation. That is why this position, when embraced by Christian believers, is a version of exclusivism. However, it differs from the versions of exclusivism articulated earlier because it is based on a philosophical theory of religion, which makes it more self-conscious and circumscribed in its claims.

This theory and the limitations it implies for thinking about other religions can be best explained by referring to the groundbreaking work of one of its most important proponents, George Lindbeck. Lindbeck claims that to understand religion correctly, one must first understand there is no common religious experience, which is then interpreted in different ways by the different religions. Instead, what comes first is always one's being shaped by the language and culture of a specific religion. That shaping by a language and culture is so deep that it creates the different religious experiences people have in the different religions.[23] The particularities of a religious culture and language create a particular kind of religious experience, rather than a universal religious experience being expressed in different ways in differing religious forms. Whereas Hick claims there is some universal experience of transformation in all religions and Christianity is one particular form of it, Lindbeck claims there is no universal experience of transformation. Instead, the particular message of salvation through Jesus in Christianity creates a particular kind of transformation in someone who hears and is shaped by it that is incompatible with any other experience created by the message of any other religion.

As explained in the section on exclusivism, one of the characteristics of exclusivism is to stress the incompatible difference between Christianity and other religions. Lindbeck's philosophical theory of the religions agrees with exclusivism on this level. However, unlike the versions of exclusivism articulated earlier, Lindbeck's version is based on a philosophical theory that does not allow a Christian believer to make universal claims about other religions, something that was an important part of those versions of exclusivism. Those versions of exclusivism claim, for example, that members of other religions are engaged in projects whereby they try to make themselves righteous instead of admitting their sinfulness and submitting to God's grace in the only place it can be found. The theory espoused by Lindbeck says there is no common experience by which one can make such a judgment of members of other religions. The only thing one can claim about other religions is that distinct religious experiences occur in them as a result of the formation of people by the culture and language of that religion. One can claim the experiences in other religions are different, but one cannot claim they are negative or rebellious versions of the experience realized in Christianity, because this would imply there is some common religious experience that goes awry in those religions, and Lindbeck's theory denies there is a common religious experience.

Critics of this form of exclusivism say it cuts off the possibility of justifying one's religious beliefs (the revelation acceptance problem), since those beliefs are seen as thoroughly created by a particular culture and language and their effects on the believer. The critics say this exclusivism does not lead to greater understanding among the world's religions, but to a hopeless isolation of the religions from one another. Further, this position does not solve the historical contingency problem, but instead appears to magnify it by claiming everyone is and always has been thoroughly shaped by a religious language and tradition such that there is no place outside that shaping to evaluate other traditions or options. Lindbeck himself proposes a postmortem opportunity for members of non-Christian religions to hear the Christian gospel, and earlier the question was raised whether this is an adequate answer to this problem or an attempt to sidestep the problem.[24]

Despite these difficulties, what makes this position attractive is that, on a theoretical level, it seeks to affirm genuine differences between the religions. Where Hick sees unity, it sees difference. Its claim is that difference needs to be acknowledged in order to allow religions to be true to themselves, which is above all what this position seeks to do.

Chapter 7

Christianity and Feminism

The Boston Marathon has been an annual event since 1897, but women were not officially allowed to sign up for the race until 1972. This did not stop a young woman named Kathrine Switzer from sending in an application to run the race in 1967. Instead of using her full first name on the application, she applied as K. V. Switzer and was given a race number that allowed her to run. In a now infamous incident, when one of the race officials was traveling by runners in a car and realized a woman was running the race, he jumped out of the vehicle and physically tried to stop her from running. Switzer's running partners pushed the official away, and she became the first woman to complete the race with an official number.[1]

While the race official's attempt to stop Kathrine Switzer from running is notorious, essentially he was trying to enforce official race policy, albeit with a dubious method. The race policy was supported by a national organization called the Amateur Athletics Union, which barred women from long-distance races. More important than the actions of an overwrought official in a single race was this national and even international policy barring women from marathons. In fact, the women's marathon was not accepted as an Olympic sport until 1984.[2]

To explain the policy that kept women from running marathons, one has to point to certain assumptions people held about who men and women are and how they should act, assumptions that were behind the policy. Changing the policy required a change in attitude not only to see women as capable of the kind of physical exertion required to train for and run a marathon, but also to see it as desirable that women would be this way. Moreover, men were in charge of the organizations that established the policy, so if women wanted the policy to be different, at least initially, they had to convince the men in charge to make the change.

The change in attitude about women's physical capabilities, the corresponding policy change, and ultimately the representation of women on the commission deciding the policy were all goals for which the feminist movement successfully fought. In hindsight, while changing this particular policy was important, it was actually relatively easy to implement. Historically, however, the same combination of elements that kept women from long-distance running has also limited women's participation in other areas of life. In many of these cases, change has been much harder to implement. For example, in the world of business, what held women back was male authority, biased hiring practices, and the attitude that women's proper role is to support men, so women make good full-time housewives or secretaries but not chief executive officers and company presidents. In the world of politics, despite getting the vote in 1920, women were held back by political parties dominated by male authority and the attitude that women are neither smart enough nor tough enough to keep the nation safe and make important decisions about the direction the country should take. In both areas, much progress has been made. Yet as of 2007, women working full-time still made only 77.8 cents for every dollar men made.[3] As of 2008, women accounted for only 15.2 percent of the members of the boards of directors of Fortune 500 companies.[4] The number of women serving in Congress in 2009 was higher than ever at ninety (in 1950, it was ten; in 1970, eleven; and in 1990, thirty-one), but this is only 16.8 percent of total congressional representation.[5]

Not only in the leadership of business and government, but also in the leadership of the church do the influences described limit women's participation. Many churches have official policies backed by male authority and undergirded by ideas about who men and women are and how they should act that keep women from leadership roles. Other churches over the past several decades have transitioned to allow women's leadership at the highest levels, although there are always concerns that while women technically are allowed leadership roles, they are in fact unable to attain them because of ingrained biases. The difference between the groups that allow women's leadership and those that do not is explained by whether the churches have been open to the influence of the contemporary feminist movement.

When feminist ideals about the equal value of women and the right to equal opportunity for women are applied to religious thought, what emerges is feminist theology. While there is an indigenous movement of feminist theology in all the major world religions, the concern of this chapter is Christian feminist theology. As a large-scale endeavor, Christian feminist theology emerged with the feminist movement of the 1960s and 1970s to become what is arguably the most important development in Christian theology in the contemporary period. While not attempting to be comprehensive, this chapter examines some of the major themes and contributions of feminist theology to contemporary Christian thought.

The Why and What of Feminist Theology

Why does Christianity need something that calls itself feminist theology? Does not the very idea of theology with that label indicate a narrowing and a fragmentation of Christian thought? Why not just have theology?

These important questions are often directed against feminist theology, but they are questions to which feminist theologians have developed a sophisticated response. They claim feminist theology is needed because, in the history of Christian thought as a whole, theology has ignored women's experience. By ignoring women's experience, the truth in the Christian tradition has been expressed in a narrow, one-sided, and at times twisted way. Christian feminist theologians disagree on how much transformation is required in the Christian tradition to enable it adequately to account for women's experience, and they disagree on the specific types of transformation needed. However, all Christian feminist theologians understand themselves as reformers within the Christian tradition. They do not call for a new denomination, but they call for concrete changes, as well as changes in ways of thinking, within existing denominations to account for women's experience.

Fully spelling out what it means to account for women's experience in doing theology is complicated and not universally agreed upon by feminist theologians. Still, there is an underlying consensus that in Western history at least, women's experience was oppressed experience. Women were not the only group to be oppressed in this history. At times, other oppressed groups, such as slaves, included both men and women. Also at times, certain women of an elite class were given extraordinary opportunities and gained power and notoriety. On the whole, however, women were oppressed in the sense that their opportunities were limited and they did not have control over their own lives or destinies. It was men who received whatever education or training was available in society, and men were given the opportunities for leadership in society. Men ran the businesses, government, civic groups, education, and religion, and ultimately men were in charge of women in the home. At birth, a girl was under the authority of her father until her father turned her over to the authority of another man in marriage. To lack opportunities to develop and use one's skills and to be deprived of the ability to determine one's destiny means to be oppressed.

Feminists point out that understanding the depths of the problem of oppression requires understanding the psychological element involved in an oppressive situation. The fact that men held the opportunities for power and self-determination was backed by ideas or arguments that made the claim that reality should be this way. It was never acknowledged that men were in charge because they arbitrarily imposed their power on women. Instead, men were in charge because it was claimed they had greater leadership abilities and educational capacity, they were smarter and more rational, or God said they should be in charge. All of these reasons and more, which were often put forward in complicated theoretical constructions, were given to explain why women's position was circumscribed. In this cultural context, not only men but also women often believed these arguments. Internalizing their own inferiority was a psychological condition through which women accepted a system that oppressed them.

A common term feminists have coined to refer to this kind of oppression is *patriarchy*.[6] Patriarchy literally means "rule of the father." It refers both to the concrete authority of men over women and to the ideas used to justify it. The latter in particular is sometimes called ideology. It is the promotion of a worldview that justifies the oppression of one group over another but masks this oppression by arguing this is the way things should be. Because this worldview is often embraced by those who are oppressed, breaking through it requires what is called "consciousness raising" among the oppressed. Women have needed to become aware of their situation as oppression and not accept it as a true worldview, or the way things should be.

These definitions of key terms and the dynamic to which they refer enable a greater understanding both of what feminist theology is and of why feminists think it is needed. Feminist theology done from a Christian context makes an extended Christian argument for the equal value, equal opportunity, and equal right to self-determination for women in all aspects of life. It supports a concrete political agenda that promotes women's equal right and access to leadership in society and the church. It argues against all worldviews that suggest women are inferior or should not be afforded equal opportunity, regarding those worldviews as ideology. It promotes a worldview affirming women's abilities and supports consciousness raising among women to help break through whatever ideas they have internalized that perpetuate their oppression.

Christian feminist theology is needed because of the patriarchy in Western Christian history. This patriarchy is ingrained in the foundational sources of the Christian tradition, including the Bible. It emerges and is solidified in the ongoing interpretation of the Bible and development of theology in the Christian tradition. It is embedded in the historical cultures shaped by Christianity, including the culture of the ancient world, the Middle Ages, early modern cultures whether Protestant or Catholic, and the cultures of modernity resulting from the spread of Christianity from Western Europe across vast reaches of the globe. Because patriarchy is so deeply ingrained historically in Christianity, one cannot simply accept a past text, past interpretations of the text, past beliefs, or a past culture as they are. Instead, an insightful theological interpretation is needed that will expose and root out patriarchy.

As feminist theologians know, however, simply rooting out the negative is not enough. They must also construct something positive and promote a new worldview with a new vision of human fulfillment that leaves patriarchy behind. Insofar as Christian feminist theologians seek to form this new vision from within the Christian tradition, they work from the presupposition that the resources for this vision are already present in Christianity. In other words, feminist theology has a complex understanding of Christianity and Christian history. It affirms that nonpatriarchal elements exist deeply in the Christian tradition, but they are fused with or stand alongside other elements in the tradition that support patriarchy. What feminist theology seeks to do is critique the patriarchal elements while bringing forward and promoting the nonpatriarchal elements understood in a new way. This involves a sifting and sorting of Christian ideas and practices, but it also involves a creative rethinking and re-presenting of Christian beliefs and practices so that patriarchal elements are denied while liberating elements are affirmed.

The remainder of this chapter analyzes feminist theology's critique of patriarchy in the Christian tradition and looks at some proposals for reconstructing Christian beliefs and practices. In particular, this chapter examines feminist theology's view of the Bible, women's leadership, God-language, and understanding of sin and salvation.

Feminist Theology and the Bible

The main current of Christian feminist theology has worked from the insights of the historical-critical study of the Bible. This approach to the Bible is standard in academia and in many denominations, including Roman Catholic and mainline Protestant groups, even while it is controversial in Evangelical and fundamentalist contexts.

The historical-critical approach to the Bible takes into account the human element in the construction of the biblical text without denying the possibility that a word from God comes in and through the humanly constructed text. Broadly speaking, for historical criticism, the human element in the construction of the text includes some key or formative experiences of a people that are subsequently interpreted by the community before the actual writing of the text. In the Old Testament, for example, there is the freedom from slavery in Egypt, and in the New Testament, the encounter with Jesus in his ministry, death, and resurrection appearances. These events are subject to ongoing and creative interpretation over time, at first by word of mouth or by the transmission of stories and preaching in the believing community as it seeks to understand what God is doing at present. In the case of the New Testament, it takes decades, and in some parts of the Old Testament, it takes hundreds of years of this oral interpretation of the events before the text is creatively constructed by an author or authors from the community who seek to understand the past on the basis of an understanding of what God is doing at present.

One of the implications of uncovering this human process behind the text is that, because the text comes out of a particular culture and its ongoing interpretations, invariably some of the time-bound, conditioned, and limited ideas of that culture make their way into the text. For example, historical criticism regards the biblical writers as unaware of the discoveries of contemporary science and understands the writers as informed by an ancient scientific worldview. Similarly, and most importantly for feminist theology, historical criticism regards the biblical writers as unaware of the insights of the contemporary feminist movement and understands the writers as informed by the patriarchal presuppositions of their culture. The writers were attempting faithfully to interpret what God was doing in their own time and place, but their own time and place were infused with the presuppositions of patriarchy that made their way into the text.

The Twofold Approach to the Bible and Its Interpretation

If feminist theologians thought the only thing in the biblical text is patriarchy, they would reject it and leave Christianity. Instead, Christian feminists are committed to the idea that while the text is infused with patriarchy, it also contains a word from God that is liberating for women and transcends the patriarchal limitations and presuppositions of the authors and their contexts. This understanding of the text calls for a twofold method of interpretation involving both a critique of patriarchy and an appropriation of liberating, nonpatriarchal elements from the text.

The renowned feminist New Testament scholar Elisabeth Schüssler Fiorenza coined the term *hermeneutics of suspicion* to refer to the approach to the biblical text that looks to expose and critique patriarchy within it.[7] The term *hermeneutics* refers to a theory of interpretation. A "hermeneutics of suspicion" is a theoretical approach to the biblical text that is suspicious of finding patriarchy within it. In Christian feminist hermeneutics, including that of Schüssler Fiorenza, the hermeneutics of suspicion is always counterpoised with an approach to the text that works through suspicion and critique to an appropriation of the Bible's liberating message. In a recent work, Schüssler Fiorenza calls her full method of interpretation "critical feminist emancipative hermeneutics."[8] This phrase combines the two elements of critique of patriarchy and appropriation of a freeing message.

This twofold method applies not only to the biblical text itself but also to the ongoing interpretation of the text in Christian history. As feminist theologians recognize, insofar as the community that receives the text and regards it as authoritative is also infused with patriarchy, there is yet another opportunity for patriarchal presuppositions to be put into play in the community's approach to the text. In fact, the patriarchy in the ongoing interpretation of the text could even be worse than the patriarchy in the text itself. In any case, the twofold method must be applied not only to the biblical text, but also to its historical interpretation.

Before moving to examine the biblical text, it is important at this point to draw attention to a significant distinction between types of Christian feminists today. There are conservative Christian feminists who claim patriarchy is present only in the interpretation of the biblical text in Christian history and not in the text itself. The Bible, they claim, is inspired by God in such a way that it transcends patriarchy.[9] While this position is outside mainstream feminist theology, which accepts historical criticism of the Bible, it is an increasingly important voice for women's rights in Evangelical Protestant contexts. Whether it will succeed in bringing about concrete changes regarding women's leadership in Evangelical churches that currently prohibit it is one of the most intriguing questions in Christianity today.

Exposing and Critiquing Patriarchy in Text and Interpretation

One of the great contributions of feminist theology to the contemporary understanding of the Bible is its drawing attention to the fact that the patriarchy in the Bible is not just in individual passages or stories but is an overarching framework infecting the text as a whole. Patriarchy is a back-ground presupposition of the biblical authors, or part of their worldview, and this worldview informs the text broadly. In other words, it is not as if the Bible consists of a given number of stories that are dangling like apples on a tree, and a contemporary interpreter can inspect each individual story as one would inspect an individual apple, deciding whether it is patriarchal and must be thrown away, or not patriarchal and can be used. It is much more the case that patriarchy is an infection affecting the entire apple tree and all the apples on it, though some apples are affected more than oth-ers. While all apples are affected, some can still be picked and put to use if one knows the right way to process the apples to get rid of the infection in them. While it is beyond the scope of this chapter to uncover the full range of patriarchy in the biblical text, it is possible to get a sense of that patriarchy by a brief survey of some highlights in the biblical literature.

Patriarchy is present early in the biblical narrative in the creation of woman from the primal man, Adam, in Genesis 2. This reverses the biological order in which men are birthed from women, and although Genesis 1 says both men and women are made in the image of God, it makes a male the primal human and source of both genders. The woman is the first to succumb to the temptations of the serpent in the Garden of Eden in Genesis 3. Her influence on her husband leads to his eating the forbidden fruit, the eating of which means sacrificing immortality and entering a harsh world of pain and toil.[10]

The majority of the book of Genesis (chapters 12–50) contains cycles of stories about the biblical patriarchs Abraham, Isaac, and Jacob. The patriarchs are all heads of their clans, and except for Isaac, they have multiple wives and concubines. A predominant feature of the portrayal of the wives is their ability, or lack thereof, to bear sons for the patriarch. This theme emphasizes women's role in the patriarchal situation and runs throughout the Old Testament. The wives are subject to the author-ity of the patriarch, and lacking power, they are at times presented as scheming in order to get their way (Genesis 16, 27).

The central figure in the narratives of Exodus, Leviticus, Numbers, and Deuteronomy is the lawgiver Moses. Unlike any other figure, he has a direct relationship to God, with whom he is said to speak "face to face" (Exod. 33:11). The 613 commandments of the law given in these books come from a God referred to with male pronouns, to the man Moses, and to the people represented by their male leaders, called "elders" (Exod. 19:7).

The law is directed to men, who are assumed to be the ones in charge in the community and in their households. This comes across perhaps most clearly in the tenth commandment in Exod. 20:17, where men are told, "You shall not covet your neighbor's house; you shall not covet your neighbor's wife, or male or female slave, or ox, or donkey, or anything that belongs to your neighbor." Wives, slaves, and animals are all considered part of a man's house and therefore, technically, his property. The inheritance of property passes through sons except for the temporary situation in which there would be no male heir in a generation.

The law prohibits women from being priests, a role they never serve in the approximately one thousand years in which Israel had a temple in Jerusalem. Among other things, this is because women's menstrual cycle makes them ritually unclean for seven days a month, during which time anyone who touches them or that upon which they lie or sit becomes unclean (Lev. 15:19-24).

When Israel comes into the land, the people are divided by tribes, each of which has male leadership in the form of elders who enforce tribal law. When Israel gains a king, the heir is always a male, as are the leading figures of the government. Like other kings in the ancient Near East, Israelite kings have harems to ensure multiple progeny, including sons.

The New Testament is not a vast story of a people in the same way as the Old. Its focus is on a much briefer period of history concerning Jesus of Nazareth, who comes out of the Jewish context just described, and the early Christian movement that emerges after Jesus' death, resurrection, and ascension.

Women play important roles in the stories about Jesus. They also appear to play important roles in the early Christian movement. Still, when Jesus chooses the twelve disciples who have the most intimate association with his ministry according to the Synoptic Gospels, they are all men. The book of Acts, which records approximately the first thirty years of the history of the Christian movement, focuses almost exclusively on the actions of the male disciples. The central focus of the early part of the book is the apostle Peter, with the latter part focusing on the apostle Paul. Paul, who is responsible by name for thirteen books of the New Testament, says in Gal. 2:9, a letter written probably in the early fifties, that the "acknowledged pillars" of the early church are James (Jesus' brother), Peter, and John (two of the original twelve disciples). Paul also lists important church leaders in a letter to the Corinthians from the midfifties, where he chides the Corinthians for claiming to follow him, Apollos, Peter, or Christ, instead of only Christ. From the beginnings of the movement, a focus on male activity and the centrality of male leadership appear to be the norm.

The patriarchy in the interpretation of the text is also complicated and diverse. Among the elements characterizing it, feminist theologians point to the fact that women of strong character or great faith in the text tend to be overlooked. The history of biblical interpretation and appropriation tends to focus on the "faith of our fathers," further marginalizing the importance of women in the biblical story.

While the positive contributions of women are overlooked, negative portrayals of women from the Bible can become exaggerated. This is especially the case with regard to the first woman, Eve, who is blamed for the human fall into sin. Eve comes to represent the prototypical female, prone to sin because of her weakness and ultimately responsible for the problems humans face in the world.

In contrast to Eve, Mary the mother of Jesus is exalted as the ideal image of womanhood and the one through whom the savior comes. While Mary is the most important female personage in Christian history and theology, feminists point out that hers is a troubling image, tinged with patriarchy. Mary is presented as passive, subject to her male son. Her virtues are limited to sweetness and compassion. Her purity is expressed in her asexuality, with a virginity that is maintained despite the fact that she bore children. Her role is limited to that of a domestic housewife. As a sweet, passive, virgin mother, Mary comes to inscribe the male patriarchal ideal, even though in many ways the Mary of historical Christian image and interpretation is far from what is known of the historical Mary in the biblical text.[11]

ADDITIONAL INFORMATION

How Mary Magdalene Became a Prostitute

Contemporary writers and directors who put the gospel story in cinematic form have invariably presented Mary Magdalene as a prostitute or adulteress. This is true in *The Greatest Story Ever Told*, *Jesus Christ Superstar*, *The Last Temptation of Christ*, *Jesus*, and *The Passion of the Christ*.

Given this reflexive cultural understanding, it is striking to note there is no evidence of Mary Magdalene being a woman of ill repute in the biblical literature, a fact stressed by numerous biblical scholars. In the canonical gospels, Mary appears in four scenes. In

Luke 8:2, she is mentioned as one of the women who followed Jesus during his itinerant teaching and healing ministry in the region of Galilee. Luke says the women who followed Jesus were healed by him, and he says of Mary Magdalene that seven demons had been cast out of her. All four gospels claim Mary Magdalene was present at the crucifixion scene (Matt. 27:56; Mark 15:40; Luke 23:49; John 19:25). The Synoptic Gospels say she witnessed Jesus' burial (Matt. 27:61; Mark 16:47; Luke 23:55). All four gospels present her as a witness to Jesus' resurrection (Matt. 28:1-10; Mark 16:1-8; Luke 24:1-11; John 20:1-18). In Matthew and John, she has an explicit encounter with the risen Christ.

In other noncanonical gospels, Mary Magdalene is often mentioned, but she is never identified as a prostitute or adulteress. She is often presented as engaging in dialogue with Jesus in an intelligent manner, and she appears to have an important status among the disciples. This is true, for example, in the *Gospel of Thomas* (saying 21) and the *Dialogue of the Savior*.[12] In the *Gospel of Mary*, which is attributed to her, she has a vision of the resurrected Christ and is a teacher to the disciples, although some of the disciples do not accept her teaching.

The first clear indication of Mary Magdalene's identification as a woman of ill repute is in a sermon given by Pope Gregory in 591.[13] In the sermon, Gregory combines biblical stories involving different women, two of whom were named Mary. Mary was a common name in first-century Palestine, and many different Marys are mentioned in the biblical text. Gregory fuses two Marys and an unnamed woman into a composite image, which he claims is Mary Magdalene.

In the sermon, Gregory says, "She whom Luke calls the sinful woman, whom John calls Mary, we believe to be the Mary from whom seven devils were ejected according to Mark."[14] The last-named Mary is surely a reference to Mary Magdalene. Gregory is referring to Mark 16:9, one of the additional endings to Mark's gospel. There, Mary Magdalene is named as one from whom Jesus had cast out seven demons, echoing Luke 8:2. Gregory's first reference to the sinful woman in Luke refers to an unnamed woman in Luke 7:37. The only thing said about the woman in this passage is that she is a sinner. The kind of sin is not mentioned. She brings a jar of perfume to a dinner Jesus attends, anoints Jesus' feet with the perfume and her tears, and dries his feet with her hair. After a debate with the hosts over the appropriateness of Jesus' toleration of the woman's act, Jesus says the woman's sins, which were many, have been forgiven (Luke 7:47). In his sermon, Gregory is identifying this unnamed woman with the one "John calls Mary." The reference is to John 12:1-8, where a woman named Mary of Bethany also anoints Jesus' feet with perfume and wipes them with her hair. In the Gospel of John, Mary of Bethany is a character distinct from Mary Magdalene. She has a sister named Martha and a brother, Lazarus. Jesus is sometimes a guest in their house, and when Lazarus dies, Jesus raises him from the dead (John 11). However, since this woman was named Mary and because she performed an act similar to the unnamed sinner of Luke, Gregory is able to identify the unnamed sinner with Mary Magdalene. In one sentence, Gregory conflates Mary Magdalene with Mary of Bethany, who in turn is identified as an unnamed sinner.

Having identified Mary Magdalene as an unnamed sinner, Gregory develops the nature of her sin:

> It is clear that in the past Mary Magdalene, intent on forbidden acts, had applied the ointment to herself, to perfume her flesh. So what she had used on herself, to her shame, she was now offering to God, to her praise. Everything about her that she had used for pleasure, all this she now offered up as a sacrifice. She offered to God every service in her penitence which she had disdained to give God in her guilt.[15]

This passage does not explicitly say Mary Magdalene was a prostitute. It does suggest, however, that the reason she had the perfume to anoint Jesus' feet is that she had used it on herself. She perfumed her own flesh, being intent on forbidden acts of pleasure. Pope Gregory has tagged Mary Magdalene as a woman of ill repute who repented of her sinful past in anointing Jesus. This became the predominant view of Mary Magdalene in Western Christianity.

This interpretation of Mary Magdalene is not validated by the text, but it exposes certain assumptions of the interpreter of the text. In Gregory, those assumptions involve easily identifying as a great sinner one of the few female characters who is named in the gospels, and who plays an important role in the crucifixion and resurrection. They also involve the specification of that sin as sexual sin. As a woman, Mary is identified by her body and her sexuality. She is a temptress of men who appears to enjoy the role, although she gives it up in encountering Jesus. None of Jesus' male disciples either had or acquired the reputation of being repentant sexual sinners. That role was reserved for Mary Magdalene.

Liberating Appropriation of the Text

One direction feminist theologians have embraced to appreciate and appropriate the message of the biblical text is to raise the often over-looked stories of strong, capable, and faithful women. Shining a light on such women can help yield a usable history for women or female models to whom contemporary women can turn for inspiration. As feminist scholar Lynn Japinga points out, in the Old Testament, these women include Miriam, who was a leader of the Israelites along with Moses and Aaron (Numbers 12); Vashti, the queen who refused to dance before a drunken king at his command at the risk of her life and cost of her position (Esther 1); and Jael, who boldly killed the leader of the army of one of Israel's enemies (Judges 4).[16] New Testament scholar Bonnie Thurston shows there are many positive presentations of women in the New Testament. As only one example, she points out that the Gospel of Mark alone contains sixteen references to women, many of which are positive. These include the woman with the flow of blood, who violates social and legal tradition in approaching Jesus (Mark 5:24-34); the Syro-phoenician woman who "restores Jesus to his proper attitude" (7:24-30); and the unnamed woman who anoints Jesus at a banquet and "appears in a prophetic office . . . [as] the first person to understand Jesus as the crucified Messiah" (14:3-9).[17]

While raising the often-overlooked women in the text is important, many feminists find it inadequate in itself, since overwhelmingly the text remains focused on males and presents women in patriarchal contexts under patriarchal assumptions. In this light, another approach to the biblical text taken by feminist theologians is to use insights from the text to reconstruct the history behind the text in which, it is claimed, women played more sig-nificant roles than the ones they are granted in the text itself.

Working from the insight that there is a gap between the events recorded by the text and the writing of the text itself, feminist theologians have sought to show that patriarchal assumptions that exclude the important contributions of women made their way into the formation and writing of the text. This is an especially common approach in New Testament studies, led by the groundbreaking work of Elisabeth Schüssler Fiorenza. She argues that in Jesus' own time, and in the period of the earliest church but before the writing of the gospels (approximately 30–70), women played important roles, including leadership roles in the Christian community.[18] According to this approach, the earliest Christian community was an egalitarian countercultural movement that embraced women's leadership. It understood the kingdom of God about which Jesus spoke to be a kingdom of equals that broke down the oppressive hierarchical structures that were part of Roman society. As time went on, however, and it became clear Jesus' second coming was delayed, the church felt pressure to conform to society. By the end of the first century, the full-blown patriarchal assumptions of Roman society had a deep effect on the writing of many books of the New Testament, including books that prohibit women's leadership. Therefore, it is only by reading between the lines of the books of the New Testament that one can see hints of the significant role women actually played in the early movement.

As an example of this approach, Schüssler Fiorenza points out that in the letters of Paul written in the fifties, Paul mentions women who are important leaders in the church whom he regards as his equals (e.g., Rom. 16:1, 6, 12; Phil. 4:2-3). If some women were prominent enough to be mentioned by Paul, she reasons, there must have been many more female leaders who went unmentioned. She points out, however, that the book of Acts—which tells the story of the early Christian movement and was probably written approximately thirty years after Paul's letters—fails to mention women's leadership in the early church explicitly. She reasons patriarchal biases from the late first century influenced the author of Acts to overlook women's contributions.[19]

Another important approach to the biblical text taken by feminists to appropriate its meaning is to shine a special light on the ways and places in which the text promotes liberation from oppression. This message of liberation is taken to be the Bible's most important message. Religiously speaking, it is God's word within the text.

In appropriating the liberating message from the text, feminists claim that, even though the context of a particular text may not explicitly be about liberation from patriarchy, the theme of liberation from oppression can still be abstracted and applied to liberation from patriarchy. For example, one place in which the theme of liberation from oppression resounds in the biblical text is the Old Testament story of the Israelites' exodus from Egypt. In this story, God frees the suffering and oppressed Israelites in order to bring them into a land of their own, where they are able to control their own destiny. As feminists point out, despite the exodus, Israelite society remained patriarchal. This patriarchy is expressed in many of the stories of the Old Testament and many of the laws it records. This does not mean, however, that God willed this patriarchy. It means the people of the time were not able to realize fully what God had desired in the overcoming of oppression. Christians today see more of the fullness of what God desires in overcoming patriarchy than was seen by the community that experienced the Exodus or the biblical writers who wrote the story. When the Bible presupposes patriarchy or promotes it, this is not to be taken as an expression of God's will. It is to be judged on the basis of the principle that God desires the release from all oppression, including patriarchy.

The feminist theologian Rosemary Radford Ruether calls this message of liberation from oppression in the Bible the Prophetic Principle and claims it should be used to critique patriarchy and other forms of oppression in the biblical text.[20] She refers to this message as prophetic because it is a common theme of the Old Testament prophets to denounce the oppressive abuse of power in the name of the God of justice. The Old Testament prophets also maintained a vision of a new age to come in which oppression is vanquished and God's justice and peace are definitively established.

Many feminists, including Ruether and Schüssler Fiorenza, stress that the historical Jesus taught a message emphasizing liberation from oppression in his prophetic proclamation of the kingdom of God. Imbued with the prophetic tradition from the Old Testament, he had a vision of the kingdom of God as one of justice and peace where oppressive hierarchies were undone. It was a kingdom of equals, where none of the members lorded themselves over any other but all were servants of one another. Moreover, the historical Jesus lived in a way that broke through many of the dominating power structures of his time, and this included treating women as genuine human subjects with dignity.

This understanding of the historical Jesus, as someone announcing God's will in the form of an egalitarian kingdom of justice and peace, has been highly influential in feminist theology. Like other reform movements in the Christian tradition, feminist theologians claim they are not promoting something entirely novel but trying to retrieve the original message of Jesus himself. What is new in feminist theology, and is owing to the adoption of a critical approach to the biblical text, is the claim that the central message of Jesus is at times obscured by the biblical text itself.

Women's Leadership in the Church

While the feminist cultural movement has fought for women's equality in society, feminist theologians have fought for women's equality in the church, including the right of women to attain all positions of leadership. Beginning in the 1960s and 1970s, mainline Protestant denominations in the United States went through the process of either granting ordination to women for the first time or promoting it more thoroughly. Since that time, many of these denominations have experienced growing numbers of women attending seminary and serving in ordained ministry, although full acceptance of these women's ministries in individual churches remains a problem. Several mainline denominations have had women hold the highest position in the denomination.

Evangelical groups differ in their approach to women's leadership. Some Pentecostal groups, including the Assemblies of God, and some holiness groups, including the Salvation Army, have allowed women's ordination from their founding. Other Evangelical groups, such as the Southern Baptists, the largest Protestant denomination in the United States, deny ordination to women. In 2000, the Southern Baptists adopted a revised summary of their faith, part of which states, "While both men and women are gifted for service in the church, the office of pastor is limited to men as qualified by Scripture."[21] This line is telling, as Evangelical and fundamentalist groups that deny ordination to women do so on the basis of an interpretation of biblical passages.

Roman Catholics do not allow women's ordination. Women can take vows and join orders of nuns, but women under vows cannot perform the sacraments, which are reserved for ordained men. Beginning with the latter part of the twentieth century, Catholic churches in the United States have allowed greater participation of women in services and in their daily operation. This has not led to a serious public debate by the church hierarchy regarding women's ordination. The reasons given by the church hierarchy for not allowing women's ordination differ from those of Evangelical Protestants and are examined in a separate section.

Evangelical Protestants, the Bible, and Women's Ordination

At several points in the New Testament, the Bible promotes exclusively male leadership. One of the most important texts in this regard is 1 Tim. 2:11-14. First Timothy is a letter purportedly written by the apostle Paul to his younger assistant, Timothy. Paul gives advice about several matters involving church order, including the following:

> Let a women learn in silence with full submission. I permit no woman to teach or to have authority over a man; she is to keep silent. For Adam was formed first, then Eve; and Adam was not deceived, but the woman was deceived and became a transgressor. Yet she will be saved through childbearing, provided they continue in faith and love and holiness, with modesty.

As pointed out in this chapter's earlier survey of how feminist theology approaches the Bible, mainstream feminism was built upon a critical understanding of the Bible. As such, it was able to affirm that the biblical authors were limited by the cultural understandings of their time and place in much of what they wrote. Feminists have pointed to the centrality of the Bible's theme of liberation from oppression and have claimed that when the biblical writers affirmed patriarchy, they were succumbing to the culture, rather than promoting God's ideal. This approach determines the standard feminist interpretation of 1 Tim. 2:11-14.

Following critical scholarship on the New Testament, feminist scholars affirm that the author of this passage from 1 Timothy was not actually Paul but one of Paul's disciples, writing perhaps forty years after Paul's time. The author was concerned that Christianity fit into the patriarchal structures of late-first-century Roman society, so Christianity would not be seen as a threat to Roman order. The author was also concerned to establish a more unified Christian movement, one that excluded certain beliefs that may have been promoted by some women in certain churches. As a result, he limited church authority to men, justifying it by claiming the Adam and Eve story shows women are more prone to deception than men, thus disqualifying women as leaders. For feminists, this is patriarchy in action, limiting power to men alone and backing it by ideology, with a supposed reason rooted in women's inferiority.

While mainline Protestant churches have embraced this kind of interpretation, it has been more difficult for many Evangelical Protestant churches, which take a more literal interpretation of the Bible. For biblical literalists, the biblical writers were not negatively influenced by their culture but stood above cultural influences to speak God's word to their culture.

Some biblical literalists who are feminists or sympathetic to the feminist cause have put forward interpretations of this passage that affirm it was meant to address particular problems in the church to which Paul was writing and not meant to be a valid rule for the church for all time.[22] This argument has had a difficult time gaining significant traction, and whether it will prove persuasive in conservative Protestant circles remains to be seen.

While conservative Protestants base their exclusion of women's leadership on the Bible, many also give reasons for this exclusion. In other words, it is one thing to say women should not lead "because the Bible says so," and it is another thing to explain why the Bible says what it does. Many conservative Protestants go beyond simply saying the Bible does not allow women's leadership and give reasons rooted in nature or the character of reality as to why women should not lead.

Broadly speaking, one can imagine two possible reasons why men alone should lead. One reason is that the choice is purely arbitrary. In any group, only some can lead. Arbitrarily, God excluded women and chose men for the sake of convenience and good order. The problem with this reason is that it does not seem to make good sense. Should not those chosen to lead be those with the greatest leadership abilities?

That leaves the second possible reason why men alone should lead: because men are naturally better at it. This reason is rooted in an understanding of men and women as having different natures or natural abilities, with one of men's natural abilities being leadership and all it entails. Having a nature oriented toward leadership would mean having an excess of certain virtues such as strength and fortitude, but also an excess of right reasoning ability, or the ability to make the correct decisions demanded of a leader. If men have these abilities naturally in a way that exceeds women, then it makes sense they should be leaders. If women do not have these abilities in the degree men do, they should not lead. Women's nature must be understood as suitable for fulfilling supportive roles under male leadership.

The view of men and women as having different roles, with men leading and women being supportive, and the assumption that different roles imply different natures are together called the "complementarian" view of gender in conservative Protestant contexts. A burgeoning literature has risen to support it, including a quarterly journal called the *Journal for Biblical Manhood and Womanhood*.[23] Feminists regard this project as ideology. They claim that men and women have no distinctive natures that can be discriminated between the genders, and people are only socialized to think so, or they claim men and women may have distinctive natures or tendencies, but these distinctions do not run along the lines of dominant/submissive and thereby justify male leadership.

Roman Catholics and Women's Ordination

The question of women's ordination is different in the Roman Catholic Church than in Protestant churches because of the different structure of the Catholic Church. Protestant churches in the United States make decisions either locally, in individual congregations, or through an independent national structure. The Roman Catholic Church is international, with more than a billion adherents in multiple countries and cultures. The Catholic Church in the United States cannot make a decision about an important issue like women's ordination independent of the decision of the church as a whole. While Protestant denominations differ in their governance structure, they all affirm some version of representation of ministers and laypeople in making national decisions. The Roman Catholic Church is hierarchical, with important decisions being made by the church leaders in Rome, including the pope and the teaching office called the Congregation for the Doctrine of the Faith, along with church councils, if and when they are called.

With the rise of the feminist movement in Western Europe and the United States, the issue of women's ordination has inevitably risen in Catholic contexts. Contemporary popes have addressed the issue, including most recently Pope John Paul II in a 1994 letter to the bishops of the church, titled "On Reserving Priestly Ordination to Men Alone."[24] In this letter, John Paul II reaffirms reasons from scripture and tradition to conclude why men alone are to be ordained. The main scriptural reason given is "the example recorded in the Sacred Scriptures of Christ choosing his Apostles only from among men." In Catholic theology, one of the bases of the authority of church leaders is rooted in Jesus choosing particular apostles to whom he gave authority to represent him and carry out his ministry. After Jesus' ascension, those apostles established churches and handed on their authority, granted from Jesus, to their successors.[25] This pattern proceeds through history to the present leaders, who represent Christ in their leadership of the church and whose authority is claimed to be rooted ultimately in Jesus' own decision and will. Pope John Paul II stresses that when Jesus chose apostles, he chose only men. The apostles and their successors have consistently done the same in order to be faithful to Jesus' will and actions. The church today must continue that pattern. John Paul II concludes the letter by saying, "I declare that the Church has no authority whatsoever to confer priestly ordination on women and that this judgment is to be definitively held by all the Church's faithful."[26]

The Catholic feminist argument against this position claims that the reason Jesus chose only male apostles was conventional. In his time and culture, Jesus had to choose only men to carry out his ministry because women were not respected and would not have been given a voice. Women were not able to speak in official contexts such as synagogues; women were not free to travel, and it was not safe for them to travel. These and other culturally relative reasons were behind Jesus' decision. Women claim they can represent Christ as well as men. Representing Christ does not mean sharing in his maleness, just as it does not mean sharing in his Jewishness. Instead, it means sharing in his ongoing ministry, and women can do that as well as men.

John Paul II was certainly aware of these arguments. In the letter, he makes a point to say that when Christ chose only men, "Christ's way of acting did not proceed from sociological or cultural motives peculiar to his time." Instead, he "acted in a completely free and sovereign manner."[27] In rejecting this response, feminists see the same ideological danger that is present in the Evangelical Protestant interpretation of scripture. They fear the church's claim that Christ chose only men to lead, so they should as well, is ideology seeking to reinforce the idea that men are better leaders than women.

Language for God

One of the most controversial aspects of feminist theology is the claim that Christianity has a history of using almost exclusively male language for God and that this language is ideological and reinforces patriarchy. The idea that the Bible and church tradition use male God-language almost exclusively is not a difficult or controversial case to make. Consider, as one example, the beginning of the Gloria, a traditional praise hymn to God that is sung or said weekly near the beginning of many Christian services:

Glory to God in the highest and peace to his people on earth. Lord God, Heavenly King, Almighty God and Father. We worship you. We give you thanks. We praise you for your glory.

The first line refers to God with the male pronoun *his*. In the second line, God is called Lord, King, and Father, all male images for God. Significantly, God's power or Almightiness is connected with fatherhood.

Significance of Male God-Language

The feminist claim is that when male language is used to symbolize God and women are excluded from such symbolism, men are regarded as more valuable than women, and men's position as "rightful" leaders over women is stressed, even if it is in an unconscious way. To explain how exclusively male language for God values men over women, it is important to recognize that all human images of God are based on establishing some sense of likeness between something in human experience and God, who transcends human experience. Calling God a fortress implies taking something from human experience—a strong place of protection from an outside enemy or threat—and saying God is like that. While the fortress image may be benign, feminists claim that using only male language for God, excluding female language, reinforces the idea that men are in some sense like God but women are not. Men have some value that makes them able to be compared to God, the source of all value, while women do not have such value. As feminist philosopher and theologian Mary Daly put it in her succinct hyperbolic quip, "If God is male, then the male is God."[28]

In any image of God, it is important to delineate what aspect of the thing from human experience is being compared to God. Calling God a fortress compares the aspect of strength and protection from an enemy to God. In much male God-language, the aspect of male leadership is being compared to God. In monotheism, God is traditionally conceived as all-powerful and ultimately in control of the history and destiny of the cosmos, and this is imaged with the language of male leadership. Look again at the lines from the Gloria. In the first line, God is regarded as above "his people on earth." In the second line, male leadership images are used to express the relationship between God and "his" people. God is called Lord, implying that "his" people are "his" servants. God is called Heavenly King, implying that "his" people are subjects in "his" realm. God is called "Almighty God and Father," implying that "his" people are subservient members of "his" family. In every case, male leadership is used to express God's relationship to people.

For feminists, when the language of male leadership is used to express God's ruling relationship to the world, this reinforces the idea that males are to be rulers in the world. Male rule in the world and male language for God as ruler are symbiotic.

Many Christian feminists want to break this symbiosis by transforming the language Christians use for God. It is an extremely touchy subject, however, to propose changing God-language. For one thing, those who affirm male leadership would see no reason to make any changes in God-language, since they would claim the language is doing what it is supposed to do, which is represent God as ruler of all through analogy with male leadership. Others point to the fact that this language is deeply ingrained in the Bible and church tradition. The language of male leadership is the language Jesus used when he called God "Father." It is part of the historic Christian creeds and traditional liturgy. To change it would seem to veer dangerously from Jesus himself and the two-thousand-year history of the church.

Still others point out how uncomfortable it is to change the language for God, especially if one proposes to replace male God-language with female God-language. For those who grew up with male God-language, it is the channel through which they relate to God. To change the language appears to break the channel of relationship. Consider again the lines from the Gloria. In their current form, they sound normal and provide the opportunity for people to praise God. Could people still use this language to praise God if it were changed to female God-language?

> Glory to God in the highest and peace to her people on earth. Lady God, Heavenly Queen, Almighty God and Mother. We worship you. We give you thanks. We praise you for your glory.

These are thorny questions that many individuals and denominations are facing today. In confronting these issues, feminists have made the case that transforming Christian God-language can be seen as coherent with biblical teaching and insights of the theological tradition. They have stressed how the transformation from exclusively male God-language can be valuable and positive both theologically and spiritually. They have pointed out that while many people are uncomfortable with a change from exclusively male God-language, many others are already uncomfortable with the old language and seek a change. They are longing to find a fresh language to speak about their relationship to God. Feminist theologians regard this longing as the inner working of the Holy Spirit among God's people.

Feminist Arguments for Change from Exclusively Male God-Language

For feminist theologians to argue for change from exclusively male God-language, they must do more than simply critique this language as reinforcing patriarchy. They must show that the use of alternative language for God is coherent with some of the deepest insights of the biblical and theological tradition. The feminist theologian Elizabeth Johnson has made just such an argument in her important book *She Who Is: The Mystery of God in Feminist Theological Discourse*. This section examines some of the central points of her argument.

One of the main theological principles to which Johnson refers in arguing to change exclusively male God-language is the prohibition against idolatry and the mystery of God.[29] The biblical and theological traditions affirm God is a mystery who transcends all human mental categories and language. If this is the case, to argue God can only be imaged or spoken of in male language violates God's mysterious unknowability and makes an idol out of that language. To insist on using exclusively male language for God is, in essence, to insist one knows what God is. It is to close down the transcendent mystery of God in order to affirm a particular set of terms as describing God. When any language claims to describe God literally, it becomes an idol. When this happens, Johnson says, "Divine mystery is cramped into a fixed, petrified image. Simultaneously, the religious impulse is imprisoned, leading to inhibition of the growth of human beings by the prevention of further seeking and finding."[30]

Raising the prohibition of idolatry and mystery of God opens the possibility of using something other than exclusively male God-language. With this possibility established, Johnson points to positive elements in the biblical and theological tradition that justify the use of female language and symbols for God.

Johnson analyzes three important biblical symbols for God that use female imagery: Spirit/Shekinah, Wisdom/Sophia, and Mother. Regarding Spirit, among many elements, she points out that in the Hebrew Bible, the Spirit mirrors women's activities of creating, sustaining, and renewing life, and in the New Testament, in John 3:4-6, Jesus likens the work of the Spirit to bringing forth new life through childbirth.[31] She points out that Wisdom/Sophia, who is explicitly identified as female, "is the most developed personification of God's presence and activity in the Hebrew Scriptures."[32] Sophia appears in Proverbs 1, 8, and 9 and is developed further in Hebrew intertestamental literature, according to Johnson, as "a female personification of God's own being in creative and saving involvement with the world." The gospel writers, especially Matthew and John, understand Jesus as embodying the role of Sophia in providing the path of life.[33] In multiple biblical texts, God is symbolized as mother, "conceiving, being pregnant, going into labor, delivering, midwifing, carrying, nursing."[34] These texts include Deut. 32:18; Isa. 42:14; and Psalm 22.

Johnson develops three themes from the Christian theological tradition that provide justification for female imagery of God. These are divine incomprehensibility, analogy, and many names for God. She points to the many biblical and theological expressions of God's transcendence and unknowability, a theme echoed through the centuries in theologians such as Augustine, Aquinas, and Karl Rahner. This theme breaks down the exclusivity and literalness of male language for God.[35] In classical theology, the doctrine of analogy affirms that because of God's transcendence, human beings cannot speak literally of God. God can only be known through analogy from created things. Analogy for God is validated because God must in some sense be like what God creates. The doctrine of analogy helps criticize the literalizing of exclusively male God-language, while it points to the possibility of using female language.[36] Finally, because God cannot be known literally but only by analogy, the classical theological tradition affirms the use of many names for God. This safeguards the divine mystery and otherness, since no single name, image, or concept can grasp God. As Johnson says, it also "opens up space for the renewal of God-language," a renewal sought by contemporary feminists.[37]

Difficult questions surround the project of carrying out the transformation of God-language. While individuals can freely use alternatives to exclusively male God-language in private prayer, more difficult issues arise in finding acceptable language for public use and official liturgy. Some argue for replacing all male pronouns for God with the term *God*. Others claim this makes God seem impersonal, and argue for alternating between male and female pronouns to refer to God, or even using only female pronouns to counter the centuries-old tradition of using only male pronouns.

Many feminists point out that while using more explicitly female images for God is positive, the explicitly female images chosen should not be stereotypical ones. In other words, what should be avoided is exclusively referring to God in male terms when speaking of God's power and authority, and exclusively referring to God in female terms when speaking of God's nurturing care. In some cases, male and female terms for God can be combined rather than alternated. God can be called the Divine Parent instead of alternating between Divine Father and Mother.

In general, feminists think many of the old symbols based on hierarchies from a past culture, including Lord and King, should be excised or at least seriously minimized, rather than being replaced with female equivalents. Part of feminists' attempt to refresh our language about God is the claim that old language based on hierarchical and oppressive cultural patterns should be replaced by new language rooted in egalitarian cultural ideals.

While controversial in many ways, the promotion of gender-neutral or gender-free language for God has opened for many a new and relevant way of approaching the God of the Bible and the God of Jesus. This innovation is something that many women and men find refreshing and fulfilling.

ADDITIONAL INFORMATION

The Bible and Inclusive Language

In 1983, the National Council of Churches, an interdenominational organization of mostly mainline Protestant churches, published the first volume of *An Inclusive Language Lectionary*. A lectionary is a set of biblical readings used by churches that follow an established liturgy, including many mainline Protestant churches, the Roman Catholic Church, and the Eastern Orthodox Church. The readings are standardized and include lessons to be read each week from the Old Testament, Psalms, New Testament epistles, and New Testament gospels. Over the course of three years of lectionary readings, approximately 95 percent of the New Testament and 60 percent of the Old Testament are covered.[38] The first volume of *An Inclusive Language Lectionary* covered the first year of readings and was the result of three years of work on the readings by a committee of scholarly experts. In successive years, the group continued its work, and the entire three-year lectionary was published.

The publication of these works was groundbreaking. The use of inclusive language in them involved the use of inclusive language not only for people, but also for Christ and God.

In Hebrew and Greek, the languages of the Old and New Testaments, male terms are typically used when referring to all humanity. Traditional English does this as well. Human beings are called "men" or "mankind." When substituted with a pronoun, the masculine "he" or "him" is used. The preferred term of endearment for a group of men and women is "brethren." Previous Bible translations followed the pattern of changing the Hebrew and Greek to the masculine equivalent in English. *An Inclusive Language Lectionary* broke this pattern. The claim by the committee that put out the text was that the Bible intended its pronouncements to be for both men and women, and this was essentially expressed improperly in the language of the day with masculine language. The committee resolved this problem with inclusive language. For example, instead of the traditional translation of Matt. 5:16, "Let your light so shine before men," the new lectionary translates the verse "Let your light so shine before others." When Paul began a statement to one of his churches with the affectionate term *brothers*, it was translated often as "sisters and brothers" or with another non-gender-specific reference.[39]

Changing the language used to refer to human beings in a Bible translation was significant, but not nearly as significant or controversial as changing the language for Christ and God. The committee that put together the lectionary acknowledged the fact that Jesus was a male human being, and when he was referred to as a historical person in the text, they used male pronouns. However, they also sought to make the theological point that in God becoming human, what was decisive was not Jesus' maleness, but Jesus' humanness. Because of this, they sought language to express the humanness rather than the maleness in the titles applied to Jesus as the Christ. So, for example, rather than speaking of the "son of God," they used "child of God"; instead of "son of man," they used "human one."[40] They put notes in the text alerting the reader to the changes.

The committee also revised exclusively masculine language for God in the Bible. This included changing the title Lord to either God or Sovereign. They changed the title Father to "[*Mother and*] Father," placing the additional terms in italics and brackets.

John 1:14-18, a familiar passage for many Christians, gives a sense of these changes in the following quotation from the second volume of *An Inclusive Language Lectionary*:

And the Word became flesh and dwelt among us, full of grace and truth; we have beheld the Word's glory, glory as of the only Child^ from [God], the Father [and Mother*]. (John bore witness to the Child, and cried, "This was the person of whom I said, 'The one who comes after me ranks before me, for that one was before me.'") And from the fullness of the Child have we all received grace upon grace. For the law was given through Moses; grace and truth came through Jesus Christ. No one has ever seen God; the only Child^ who is in the bosom of [God] the [Mother and*] Father, that one has made God known.

^RSV Son. See Appendix.

*Addition to the text. See "Metaphor" and "God the Father and Mother" in the Appendix.

It appears many church members were not ready for these changes. The proposals remained controversial, and *An Inclusive Language Lectionary* was never widely adopted. It did, however, pave the way for some changes in major Bible translations that came in the ensuing years.

In 1989, the National Council of Churches published a revised English translation of the Bible. The previous translation, for which it holds the copyright, is called the Revised Standard Version. It had last been updated in 1971. This revised translation, called the New Revised Standard Version, uses inclusive language to refer to human beings. In general, it has been welcomed in mainline Protestant and scholarly contexts. The New Revised Standard Version does not change terms for Christ or God.[41]

In 1978, a new English translation of the Bible was published, called the New International Version. This translation was begun and supported mostly by Evangelical Protestants, including the National Association of Evangelicals, an interdenominational Evangelical organization.[42] The translation enjoyed wide popularity in Evangelical contexts in the 1980s and 1990s. In 2005, a revised version of this translation was published, called Today's New International Version. The new version uses inclusive language for human beings, but not for Christ or God. Its reception in Evangelical contexts was controversial. As a result of this controversy, a revision of the New International Version of the Bible is scheduled for 2011. The committee working on the revision has not made a public commitment about whether it will use inclusive language for human beings.[43]

Sin and Salvation

Another major contribution of feminist theology to contemporary Christian reflection is the critique and reconstruction of the correlated concepts of sin and salvation. While there is no single feminist view on these issues, this section examines important themes, significant voices, and key developments.

Sin as Self-Negation, Layered Oppression, and Structural Reality

Three important contributions of feminist theology that expand the Christian understanding of sin can be delineated. First, sin involves not only pride but also self-negation. Second, sin not only involves oppression due to gender but also consists of interwoven layers of oppression. Finally, sin not only involves individual acts but also is a social and structural reality.

In 1960, the early feminist thinker Valerie Saiving wrote an article examining the work of important contemporary Christian theologians to show they identified "sin with self-assertion and love with selflessness."[44] She claimed this pattern is ingrained in the Christian theological tradition, where sin has been most fundamentally understood as pride, or the attempt to make oneself the center of the universe in a kind of self-assertion that devalues others. Overcoming the tendency toward this kind of sin involves self-giving responsiveness to others, or relating to others in a completely self-giving way. Saiving claimed this dynamic of sin and the personal transformation required in response to it are rooted much more in men's experience than in women's experience. For Saiving, the more fundamental problem faced by women has been "underdevelopment or negation of the self."[45]

This analysis has had a deep resonance in feminist theology. A generation of feminists have claimed that, whatever its cause, the most fundamental problem for many women is not pride or improper self-assertion, but improper self-negation. In improper self-assertion, one makes oneself the center at the expense of others. In improper self-negation, one suppresses, denigrates, or denies one's unique capacities and abilities, never allowing them to develop, but allows oneself to be swallowed by others. If the answer to improper self-assertion is self-giving love, the answer to improper self-negation must be becoming a self. It is the development of one's potential so the actualized self stands in relation to others as the full being it is.

This insightful analysis has led to an important expansion of the Christian ideas of sin and salvation to include not only pride and its opposite, but self-negation and its opposite. While self-negation may tend to be more of a problem for women than for men, feminists including Rosemary Radford Ruether have called attention to the fact that both types of sin can be a problem for both genders. Ruether also points out that people in different social contexts may engage in both of these forms of sin simultaneously.[46] An upper-class woman may be compelled to negate herself in relation to her husband while simultaneously being improperly self-assertive in relation to those of a lower class or different race.

This last insight about the interlocking character of human lives in gender, class, and race relationships, along with relationships involving diverse sexual orientation, is the second major contribution of feminist theology to the Christian understanding of sin. Becoming sensitive to the layered character of sin in human social relationships has been an important development in feminist theology itself. As a significant widespread movement, feminist theology began with the feminist movement of the 1960s and 1970s among predominantly white middle- and upper-class women of the developed world. They identified and analyzed the gender oppression they faced but did not always focus on oppression due to race, class, and sexual orientation that existed in the broader society and of which they were often a part.

As feminist theology has matured, its focus on ending one kind of oppression has expanded to include explicit analysis and critique of all forms of oppression. This has involved an increasing sensitivity to the layers of oppression different women often face. A woman can be doubly, triply, or quadruply oppressed because she is a woman, an ethnic minority, a minority in terms of sexual orientation, or a member of the developing world who faces economic exploitation. In all these cases, the interlocking layers of oppression call for unique analyses, unique kinds of consciousness raising regarding each type of oppression, and differing kinds of solutions to the variety of problems. To make this analysis and call for ending all oppression requires hearing many different voices that can shed light on the nuances of the struggle and possible solutions.

The emergence of a variety of voices testifying to interlocking layers of oppression in feminist theology is often called the "third wave" in feminism.[47] It has emerged with particular significance from the 1980s to the present, with important theological movements, including Womanist theology (theology done by African American women), Mujerista theology (theology done by Hispanic women), and Asian feminist theology, all gaining a significant voice.

From its beginnings, the touchstone of feminist theology was its analysis of gender oppression. Any analysis of oppression invariably understands sin as social and structural rather than merely a matter of individual acts. This is the third major contribution of feminist theology to the Christian understanding of sin.[48] Understanding sin as structural and social means grasping the idea that oppressive patterns are ingrained in the social fabric itself. So ingrained are these patterns that, in an ongoing way, the regular functioning of society reinforces oppression. The reinforcing of oppression can be deceptive or hidden, because individuals within society can still act in what appears a completely moral or decent way on an individual level while reinforcing oppression.

Perhaps the best way to explain sin as structural is through a hypothetical example. Imagine a white wealthy couple who live in a high-end suburb and employ a minority woman to clean their home. On a personal level, they treat the minority woman with the utmost decency. They call her by name, give her tips, and rave about the good work she does and how thankful they are for it. At the same time, what they overlook in their relationship are the factors that have allowed the couple to be where they are and the woman to be where she is. While it is not always the case, it can be supposed for the example that the couple had a privileged upbringing: they went to good schools and had the support to pursue careers and make the kinds of connections that eventually led to high incomes. It can also be supposed that the maid had a significantly different upbringing: she attended poor schools and lacked the material and emotional support to develop her skills into a white-collar profession, so she ended up cleaning houses as a last resort. The privileges of the couple and the struggles of the maid are structural, transcending the question of whether individuals in society treat other individuals in a decent or moral way. The ability of the couple to actualize their potential and live a life of privilege, and the inability of the maid to do so, is significantly rooted in the way the social fabric is constructed. The answer to this kind of situation is not to tell the privileged couple to treat the maid better, since they are already treating her well on an individual level. The answer must mean to change the structural conditions of society so that people like the maid have equal opportunity materially and emotionally to develop their skills.

For many feminists, including Rosemary Radford Ruether, the structural character of sin identified as oppressive relationships is what is meant by the Christian doctrine of original sin.[49] Original sin is not the act of our primal parents that transmits damnation to everyone through the centuries, being passed on through the act of sexual intercourse, as Augustine thought. Original sin manifests as the oppressive structure of society into which everyone is born—oppressed and oppressors alike—and to which everyone is socialized in the process of his or her upbringing. This is sin that is bigger than any individual acts or decisions but determines and constrains the structure of relationships in society. The response to it must be action for social change.

Salvation

In an important sense, the features of salvation in feminist theology have already been examined in the discussion of its distinctive emphasis on sin. If sin is not only pride but also self-negation, then salvation must mean becoming a self. If sin is not only gendered oppression but also multiple layers of oppression, then salvation must mean liberation from all types of oppression. If sin is not only individual acts but also structural fact, then salvation must mean social change to rid society of its oppressive structures. These are all important features in feminist ethics. At the same time, however, what needs to be examined is how the feminist analysis of sin affects the distinctive Christian understanding of salvation in Jesus Christ.

Like other issues, the issue of redemption through Jesus Christ is complicated in Christian feminist theology, and there is no single response to it. However, there is a strong vein of critique and reconstruction. The critique is directed foremost toward what is called in the history of Christian theology "substitutionary atonement." In this view of salvation, humans are separated from God because of their sins. God is wrathful toward humanity and requires a blood sacrifice. Out of love, God becomes incarnate in Jesus, and the innocent son of God substitutes for guilty humans on the cross, paying the price for their sin. What humans need to do is confess they are sinners and accept what God has done for them, either in a direct encounter or by ongoing participation in the sacraments of the church. Feminists critique four aspects of substitutionary atonement: (1) its primary idea of sin; (2) its presupposition of a wrathful God demanding a sacrifice; (3) its validation of innocent suffering; and (4) its affirmation that salvation comes simply through acceptance rather than action.[50]

The primary idea of sin in substitutionary atonement is that the inherited guilt of original sin manifests itself in individual moral sins that God condemns. As seen earlier in the passage from 1 Timothy 2, from the time of the New Testament, women have been held responsible for all sin and their options for leadership negated because of Eve. Feminists strongly reject the idea of women being held accountable for original sin and regarded as inferior because of it. They also critique the understanding of sin as primarily individual moral acts. While not denying that sin exists on the level of individual moral failings, they stress the importance of understanding sin as self-negation and structural oppression.

Many feminists think the idea of a wrathful God who demands a blood sacrifice is a negative image, and they reject it. They claim the image comes from the social context of the controlling patriarchal father who demands subjection to his rules at any cost, even demanding a death, to maintain his control. Feminists say Jesus taught about a forgiving God in parables like the story of the Prodigal Son. God is not alienated from humans and does not require a sacrifice to atone for human failings. God has open arms and is always ready and willing to forgive those who earnestly repent.

Substitutionary atonement stresses that Jesus is an innocent and passive lamb led to the slaughter as part of God's plan. In the theological tradition, this passive suffering of the innocent is elevated and validated as a redemptive act and often held forward as a model to be imitated. This concerns feminists, who say all too often women are innocent victims of oppression, and the encouragement to imitate Jesus' innocent suffering is used to encourage women to stay in conditions of suffering or oppression rather than fight against them.

In substitutionary atonement, salvation comes simply through admitting one's individual sins and accepting what God has done for one. As a consequence, a better moral character is to be formed in the person over time. Some feminists claim this makes people passive in relation to social oppression. Admitting individual sins vis-à-vis some authority justifies that authority and its structures, overlooking the fact that the authority and its structures may have deep-seated oppression within them. The promotion of the need for a better moral character for women often affirms keeping them in their place, regarding it as sinful if they complain about their inferior condition and take action to change it.

In general, feminists have not looked to Jesus as a substitute for original sin and individual moral sin, but as a visionary model and activist who critiqued the oppressions of his time. He spoke of a kingdom of God that reversed the oppressive structures in his society. As feminists point out, to direct one's vision to a "kingdom" is to look at the problem of sin in a deeper way than the level of individual moral failings. It is to recognize injustice as structural oppression of the powerful against the powerless in the kingdoms of this world, to have an alternative vision, and to call for its enactment. Redemption is not something Jesus does for us so much as it is something of which Jesus had an empowering vision. It is not the appeasement of a wrathful God. It is the realization of a just society. The vision Jesus had of such a society, even while he lived in an unjust society, is an important step toward that realization.

Not only Jesus' vision, however, but also his action was decisive. He broke the oppressive religious and cultural taboos of his day by treating sinners, outcasts, and women with dignity and respect. He called others to act as if the kingdom of God were present now. He courageously denounced the religious and secular authorities that perpetuated oppression in Jewish and Roman society, even though it meant the arousal of opposition against him and ultimately the possibility of death. In the spirit of the Hebrew prophets, he spoke judgment against the powerful, even though he was powerless and faced the threat of death.

For many feminists, the reason for the saving power of Jesus' death on the cross is not that it appeased God's wrath. Rather, it is an example of what happens to someone who courageously stands up to powerful oppressors. Jesus is a model not because he embraced innocent suffering. The kind of suffering he faced should be avoided if possible. He is a model in revealing the injustice of the world and taking courageous action against it.

The purpose for which leaders of oppressive systems kill those who challenge them is to end their movement and make their group fall apart. That is what the religious and political powers tried to do to Jesus' movement. What the resurrection reveals, however, is that the movement did not fall apart, despite the cross. The resurrection is the rising to life again of the message and vision of Jesus against those who tried to stomp it out. It means God's power against oppressive powers continues undefeated and is in those who take up the mantle of Jesus' message and example.

Chapter 8

Christianity and Homosexuality

The struggle for homosexual recognition and homosexual rights is one of the defining issues of our time. Merely a few decades ago, homosexuality was mostly an underground phenomenon. For the most part, gays and lesbians kept their orientation hidden. Today, gays and lesbians have come out of the closet and into the public arena. There are gay, lesbian, bisexual, transgendered support groups on most college and university campuses and in many high schools. The issue of alternative sexual orientation is discussed widely in the media, and many popular television shows have at least one gay or lesbian character. Gay pride parades are a regular occurrence in cities large and small. Significant numbers of gays and lesbians are open about their orientation and live in all kinds of communities with this openness. Legal recognition of homosexual relationships, along with the benefits such recognition brings, is an ongoing political debate. Significant numbers of employers grant the same benefits to homosexual couples as to heterosexual couples.

Not surprisingly, the recent openness about homosexuality in society has had a deep impact on the church. In some denominations, it is the most divisive issue they currently face, as gays and lesbians and their supporters face off against critics, each trying to lead the church in their direction. Part of what makes the issue so divisive is that there does not appear to be a solid middle ground for each side to work toward. There is a natural and even logical divide between those who think the homosexual orientation is a good part of God's creation so homosexual relationships should be accepted by the church, and those who think the homosexual orientation is some sort of perversion or disorder and acting on it is sinful.

Those who think the homosexual orientation is a good part of God's creation seek open support for homosexual relationships, arguing that the church should ordain gay and lesbian ministers and perform gay and lesbian marriages. They are offended at the idea gays and lesbians should be told something is wrong with them, a form of prejudice they regard as the moral equivalent of racism. They think it is not good enough to say we love and accept gays and lesbians as people but regard their orientation as distorted and homosexual relationships as sinful. On the contrary, to call their orientation sinful is itself a sin. It is an offense to the identity and dignity of gay and lesbian people, and Christians above all should stand up for the identity and dignity of those who are marginalized by society, representing God's inclusive love for all.

Those who think the homosexual orientation is a perversion or disorder worry that the church has lost its way. They argue that the church should not sell out to society but bear witness to society God's truth about human sexuality, a truth that does not change with the times. This truth affirms exclusive heterosexuality as God's norm for God's creation. If the church fails to call a sin a sin, it offends God, jeopardizes people's happiness in this life, and potentially even threatens people's standing in the afterlife.

Emotions can and do at times run high on this issue. The polarization of sides has led certain church bodies to feel the threat of schism. Amid the controversy, many denominations have made a commitment to study the issue seriously, and much good scholarship has been done on it. Some of that scholarship is examined in this essay. Beyond the particulars of the scholarship, however, this is a good issue for examining the way different denominations make decisions. How does a church decide about a controversial issue like this? To what sources of authority does a denomination turn for guidance in making a decision? How does a church evaluate and weigh those sources of authority? Are there inherent problems with the way certain traditions understand their sources of authority? These are just some of the questions engaged in examining this issue.

Sources of Authority according to the Main Christian Groups

The three groups of Christianity in the United States with the greatest number of adherents are Roman Catholicism, Evangelical Protestantism, and mainline Protestantism. Each of these groups engages the issue of homosexuality differently because of differences in the groups' structures and approaches to sources of authority. A source of authority is something to which the church turns for guidance about a belief or practice. The following section briefly examines homosexuality and Roman Catholicism, before turning to this issue for Protestant groups.

Roman Catholicism, the Church Hierarchy, and Homosexuality

Typically, the Roman Catholic Church acknowledges the Bible, tradition, and reason as sources of authority. In any decision, ideally, all three of these elements should be in harmony, since it is affirmed that all three are gifts from God that are given to guide the church.

Tradition may be the most complex source to explain. It refers to important content deemed to be derived from the Bible, such as the ideas affirmed in the Nicene Creed and other important church councils. It also refers to patterns of thinking or approaches to issues typical of Catholic theological reflection that have long-standing value and significance in the history of the church. In fact, the idea that scripture, tradition, and reason are all sources of authority that work together to guide the church is itself part of church tradition. While certain elements of the tradition are considered unchanging (again, such as the affirmations of the Nicene Creed), other elements are not. Catholic thinking typically maintains openness to creative reformulations of the tradition, but such reformulations need to be shown to be in accord with the deeply rooted patterns of thinking within the tradition.

Tradition is important for the Roman Catholic Church's argument against homosexuality because a significant part of that argument is rooted in the church's traditional teaching about human sexuality. This teaching has both commonalities with and differences from typical Protestant teachings on sexuality. One of the main differences is the strong and consistent emphasis against birth control in Roman Catholic thought.

Another major way the Roman Catholic Church differs from Protestant churches is that the Roman Catholic Church is a hierarchical body in which authority is vested in church leaders, including the pope in Rome, to make decisions to guide the faithful. The church has an official teaching arm, called the Congregation for the Doctrine of the Faith. Working with the pope, it has the power to make official position statements about controversial issues. The individual teachings of the Congregation for the Doctrine of the Faith are not considered infallible. In Roman Catholic belief, the pope alone can make infallible statements about faith and morals and can do so only in the special situation where infallibility is invoked. However, the Congregation for the Doctrine of the Faith has the authority to make statements that are to inform the conscience of believers. The Congregation for the Doctrine of the Faith also has practical authority. It can and at times it has silenced Catholic theologians who write content considered to be at odds with official teaching. The Congregation for the Doctrine of the Faith also can determine and has determined church policy, informing congregations not to support groups or engage in activities deemed to be at odds with official teachings.

Before becoming the current pope, Benedict XVI was a cardinal who was the head, or prefect, of the Congregation for the Doctrine of the Faith. He played an important role in clarifying the church's position on homosexuality. In 1986, he wrote a letter to the church's bishops, articulating official teaching on the issue and engaging the bishops to enforce this teaching.[1] The letter was approved by Pope John Paul II.

In the letter, Cardinal Ratzinger stresses how the church has taken a traditional stand against homosexual acts based on the consistent teaching of the Bible, which affirms exclusive heterosexuality as God's will for creation. He acknowledges there is such a thing as a homosexual orientation and calls it an "objective disorder." He explains that having this orientation is not itself a sin, but since the orientation is "a more or less strong tendency ordered toward an intrinsic moral evil," it is a disorder.[2] Acting on the orientation and engaging in homosexual sex is a moral evil or sin. Those with the orientation are to remain chaste.

Ratzinger explains the reason homosexual sex is a moral evil is that it defeats God's intention for sex, which involves what he calls a "rich symbolism" and also "goals" or purposes.[3] The symbolism is rooted in the fact that what it means to be made in God's image is to be made male and female, the two complementary sexes forming a union that represents "the inner unity of the Creator." By this understanding, when a man and woman have intercourse—something that is to be done only in the context of marriage—the unity realized there is a symbolic representation of God's inner unity. Further, in giving themselves to each other in sexual activity, men and women fulfill the purpose of sex. This purpose involves both the emotional and physical unity experienced by the partners and the cooperation with God in bringing forth new life. In Catholic thinking, these two goals are so intimately intertwined that they cannot be separated. If a couple uses birth control and has intercourse that is not open to the possibility of life, they are not truly giving themselves to each other. In that case, they cannot experience true union either, but are engaging in self-indulgence.

By this understanding of the meaning of sex, homosexual sex defeats both the symbolism and goals of sexual activity. It does not reflect the unity and creativity of God, and it does not fulfill the goal of sex, because new life is not a possibility. Since unity and the possibility of life must both be present for a sex act to be properly self-giving, Ratzinger says homosexual sex cannot be self-giving but is "essentially self-indulgent."[4]

Critics of the church's position point out that the two goals of sex—the unity the couple experiences in the act and the possibility of life—are separable. When a heterosexual couple uses birth control and has intercourse, the use of birth control does not automatically make the act self-indulgent and illegitimate. The partners can still experience emotional and physical unity and self-giving. Whether the act is self-indulgent depends on other factors rooted in the actions and attitude of the participants. If sex can involve an emotional and physical unity that is self-giving, and is distinguishable from the need for sex always to be open to the possibility of life, then, many argue, homosexual sex could potentially be legitimate. It could be an expression of the unity of the couple.

This analysis shows that the Roman Catholic Church's position on the meaning of sex would have to be transformed in order for the church to regard homosexuality as a legitimate sexual alternative. Thus far, the church has been unwilling to consider changing its teaching. In fact, in the same letter to the church's bishops in which Ratzinger calls the homosexual orientation a disorder and acting on it a sin, he makes it clear that no support should be given by Roman Catholic churches to groups that contradict this teaching, nor should such groups be allowed to use church facilities.[5] With these statements, he urges the closing of the doors of the church to groups who support a different position or who want to debate the issue. There has been no softening of this stand in the Roman Catholic hierarchy since this time.

Sources of Authority in Evangelical and Mainline Protestant Groups

It is common to divide Protestantism in America between mainline and Evangelical groups. While any broad distinction like this invariably overlooks much complexity, this distinction is telling for understanding the issue of homosexuality and the church because this issue is contentious only in mainline Protestantism at the present time. The reason it has deeply affected only mainline groups and not Evangelical groups is related to the different sources of authority each group acknowledges and the way each group evaluates those sources of authority.

Mainline Protestant denominations are groups that have a long presence in this country, with many denominations having their origins in the Protestant Reformation of the sixteenth century. Generally, they are open to culture and developments in contemporary thought, including contemporary science, the arts, and literature. While they differ as to their specific type of church organization, they tend to have a strong national structure with individual congregations tending to think of themselves as being connected to a larger national and even international movement that establishes guidelines for liturgy, theology, and practice. The main denominations in this group are United Methodist, United Church of Christ, Presbyterian, Episcopalian, Evangelical Lutheran Church in America, American Baptist, and Disciples of Christ.

Many Evangelical groups began in this country. They often have significant difficulties with aspects of modern culture and tend to be more critical of developments in contemporary thought than mainline churches are. While some groups have significant national organizations, many do not, valuing the autonomy of the local congregation above all else. The main denominations in this group are most Baptist groups (including the Southern Baptists, the largest Protestant denomination in the country), Pentecostal groups such as the Assemblies of God, Holiness groups including the Church of God and Church of the Nazarene, and a host of independent or loosely affiliated churches.

Generally speaking, mainline churches acknowledge the Bible, tradition, and reason as sources of authority.[6] Like Roman Catholics, mainline thinkers affirm that these three sources are valuable gifts from God and ideally should be in harmony. Each denomination puts this combination of sources together in its own way, and within each denomination are wide disagreements about how the sources are to be used. Still, there is a general pattern in using the sources of authority that helps to describe how mainline denominations approach the issue of homosexuality, and it is this general pattern we present and analyze.

On the issue of homosexuality, what especially leads mainline denominations to a different approach from that taken by Evangelicals is the use of reason as a source of authority. The openness to reason takes two main forms. First, mainline thinkers affirm that human reason, working in culture as a whole but also in rigorous academic scholarship, is able to discover new truths about reality and right patterns of human behavior. New scientific discoveries about the nature of the cosmos, as well as new insights about human culture and who we are as human beings, are constantly unfolding. On the question of homosexuality, many mainline thinkers are led to ask what ethicists, psychologists, sociologists, and scientists are saying. They ask whether people today are discovering something new and important for which the church needs to account when it promotes its ideals for human sexuality.

Second, mainline thinkers affirm that new knowledge about the world and human beings can lead to criticism of the Bible and elements of the tradition. Generations of scholarship in mainline seminaries and in the academy have shown that the biblical writers were limited and conditioned to some degree by their contexts. They had an ancient view of the cosmos that is no longer scientifically viable, and they often supported political systems and social structures, such as monarchies, slavery, and the inferiority of women, that Westerners today find offensive. Many mainline thinkers ask whether the Bible's statements about homosexuality should be criticized on the basis of contemporary knowledge.

Criticizing the Bible on some level does not mean rejecting the Bible as a whole. For all mainline thinkers, the Bible is still a source of authority, but it functions as a complex source. Not everything the Bible promotes is taken to be authoritative, because some things the Bible affirms are owing to the cultural limitations of the biblical writers. Still, mainline thinkers are committed to the idea there is a word from God in the Bible. Uncovering that word requires the critical interaction of contemporary reason with major biblical themes. It is in this interaction that a word from God for the contemporary situation can emerge. Each mainstream denomination interrogates the text and articulates the word from God it finds in the text according to the traditional pattern of thinking characteristic of that denomination.

The approach to the Bible characteristic of mainstream traditions can be called a "critical-thematic" approach. The approach gives due weight to contemporary reason, recognizes the way tradition forms and informs the approach to the Bible, and seeks a word from God deeply in the themes of the Bible, rather than in everything the culturally bound authors affirm. Religiously speaking, mainline thinkers claim it is in the interaction of Scripture, tradition, and reason that the church opens itself to the Spirit of God or to being sensitive to hearing and promoting what God wants for the church in this and each new generation.

Evangelicals tend to criticize the idea that reason and tradition are legitimate sources of authority. In their understanding, the Bible is the sole source of authority, and they tend to interpret the Bible in more of a direct and literal sense. They claim God so guided the biblical writers that what they wrote was God's will for all time. The biblical writers stood above the limitations and conditioning of their culture in speaking God's word to it. The Bible is without error in what it affirms, and Christians should submit to what it says. The Southern Baptists are a good example of this approach. The first statement of their creed begins, "The Holy Bible was written by men divinely inspired." It continues, "[The Bible] has God for its author, salvation for its end, and truth, without any mixture of error, for its matter."[7]

Given this view of the Bible, no other source of authority such as reason is allowed to turn and criticize the Bible or show the cultural limitations of the biblical authors. Evangelicals commonly claim that criticizing any part of the Bible is heading down a dangerous slippery slope in which the church rebels against God's word and sets up its own human words as truth.

Mainline thinkers respond that we must take human reason more seriously, even if it means criticizing the Bible at times on some level. To fail to do so is to fall into destructive conflicts. It destroys the integrity of the human subject to insist that people ignore contemporary knowledge or, what is worse, hold beliefs against contemporary knowledge when that knowledge is backed by sound evidence. Human reason is a gift from God that should be valued, treasured, and put to use in determining what God wants from us, and human reason shows us that the biblical writers were limited and influenced by their culture.

Furthermore, mainline thinkers point out that while the Evangelical position may sound good on the surface, in fact, Evangelicals never hold it consistently. Those who say the Bible is inerrant are committed to the idea the Bible has a single coherent message and whatever constructive commands it gives should be followed. However, inerrantists never follow everything the Bible says. They always selectively choose to follow some things and ignore others. An example often cited is the fact the Bible at times gives support for slavery, while Evangelicals say slavery is wrong. How can one claim all of the Bible is to be read and interpreted literally yet be against slavery?

Finally, mainline thinkers point out it is naive for Evangelicals to claim to be above tradition. Knowingly or not, like everyone, Evangelicals always approach the Bible from a perspective that informs what they see in it and what they do not see in it, or what they overlook. This means tradition has an influence. No one ever sees the Bible raw or grasps it fully for what it is. The fact that there are so many denominations, all with somewhat different traditions yet all claiming to be based on the Bible, shows that the Bible itself contains a variety of emphases. Evangelical theology's approach to the Bible is only one approach, representing a particular tradition or way of seeing the Bible.

While these large-scale debates will not be easily or readily resolved, they explain the different approaches of the groups to the issue of homosexuality. Evangelical groups tend to limit their serious questioning to asking what the Bible says on the issue. Insofar as they can uncover a positive message in the Bible, they claim it is God's word and will for all time. Mainline groups are much more likely to weigh the various sources of authority in a complicated fashion and ask what God wants the church to do now, given what is said by the various sources. At present, mainline churches are split about how to weigh the sources and what they say, which is why they are facing tension about this issue.

The rest of this chapter analyzes the debate about this issue that is taking place in mainline churches. The next section examines explicit references to homosexuality in the Bible, looking at some of the various ways mainline thinkers interpret and appropriate these passages. Following this is an examination of the way reason and larger biblical themes are used by mainline thinkers in making arguments for or against the full acceptance of gays and lesbians in the church.

Biblical Passages on Homosexuality

Many contemporary interpreters of the Bible have pointed out there was no word for homosexuality in Hebrew or Greek, the languages of the Old and New Testaments. In fact, the term *homosexual* was coined only in the early part of the twentieth century, in German, and was then translated into English. The word arises in the contemporary period to give expression to the developing concept of a homosexual orientation, or the idea that a relatively small percentage of the population is oriented in sexual drive to members of the same sex, rather than members of the opposite sex.[8]

As many mainline thinkers point out, this is an important factor to consider when examining the specific passages on homosexuality in the Bible. It means that not only did the biblical writers lack the word to refer to people oriented in their sexual drive to members of the same sex; they also lacked the concept meant by the word. Their lack of knowledge about the homosexual orientation raises questions regarding what the writers had in mind when they referred to homosexual sex acts. People today generally think those who engage in homosexual sex do so because of their sexual orientation. The biblical writers did not have recourse to that commonplace understanding.

Old Testament

Three biblical passages in the Old Testament speak directly to homosexual activity. One of the most famous is the story in Gen. 19:1-29 of
the men of Sodom who wanted to rape two male angels who had come
to visit Lot, who lived in Sodom. Many biblical scholars dismiss this passage as being irrelevant to the contemporary debate about homosexuality,
since what is explicitly critiqued in this story is homosexual rape. The
men of Sodom wanted to violate Lot's guests sexually instead of receiving
them with hospitality into their village. Those who dismiss this passage
say one cannot build a case that homosexual sex as such is to be condemned from a story whose primary focus is the critique of homosexual
rape. It would be like building a case for condemning heterosexual sex on
the basis of a story that critiques heterosexual rape. They also point out
that, in other parts of the Bible, including Ezek. 16:49 and Matt. 10:12-
15, Sodom is condemned not for homosexual acts but for the failure
to show hospitality to strangers. Hospitality was an important aspect of
social ethics in the culture of ancient Israel, and the Bible's interpretation of itself suggests this was the fault or sin of Sodom.

Other interpreters say this story is important as part of a larger biblical theme critiquing homosexual acts. Since homosexual acts are condemned elsewhere in the Bible, this story should be read as reinforcing
that condemnation.

Two legal passages in the Old Testament deal explicitly with gay sex:

- Lev. 18:22: "You shall not lie with a male as with a woman; it is
  an abomination."
- Lev. 20:13: "If a man lies with a male as with a woman, both
  of them have committed an abomination; they shall be put to
  death; their blood is upon them."

These passages are part of what is commonly called the Holiness Code,
a series of laws in Leviticus 17–26. The Holiness Code consists of a
compilation of several legal traditions that developed over a long period
of time in ancient Israel and were put into their present form in the sixth
century B.C.E.[9] While the material in the code is diverse, it contains two
codes of sexual ethics from which these individual verses come (18:6-30;
20:10-21). Leviticus 19:2 summarizes the overall intent of the code, saying, "You shall be holy, for I the LORD your God am holy."

It is notable that only male homosexual sex is mentioned and condemned in the code. There are no references to lesbian sex in the Old

Testament. Presumably, this is because the law is directed to men, so male concerns figure most prominently in it. Men are presumed to be in charge of the family and the community, so the law primarily regulates their behavior. Overlooking lesbian sex, even if only to condemn it, may also be owing to the lack of accounting for female sexuality in the biblical context.

Advocates for acceptance of homosexuality commonly point out that there are many laws in the Holiness Code contemporary Christians do not accept today, and they ask why the laws condemning male homosexual sex should be accepted. A glance at only one of the chapters in the code, Leviticus 19, reveals a cacophony of laws, many of which are rejected today, and others that are accepted. Among other things, this chapter says not to reap to the edges of fields or completely strip bare vineyards, so the poor and alien can have something to eat (vv. 9-10). It says not to let different kinds of animals breed together, not to sow fields with two kinds of seed, and not to wear a garment made of two kinds of cloth (19). It provides a means of atonement for a man who sleeps with one of his female slaves when the slave is to be given to another man (20-22). It forbids rounding off the hair on the temple, marring the beard, or making scars or tattoos on one's flesh (27-28). It is common for Christians today to reject all of these laws as being valid, at least in their strict or literal form.

At the same time, Leviticus 19 says not to steal, lie, or swear falsely in God's name (vv. 11-12). It commands one not to look down upon the deaf or make life difficult for the blind (14). It says to treat others equally, whether they are poor or of great means (15). It insists on the use of fair weights when doing business (35-36). It contains the commandment Jesus quoted, to "love your neighbor as yourself" (18). Commonly, Christians would regard all these laws as valid today. Part of what makes reading a code like this so fascinating is that it is a journey into another world with its alien practices, even while it includes elements recognizable and affirmed in the contemporary world.

It is important to discern a principle by which it can be claimed laws in the code are either valid or invalid over time and across cultures. While this effort is complicated, generally speaking, universal moral laws meet this criterion.[10] These laws would include individual behaviors, such as being honest, and principles of social justice, such as treating the poor fairly. The way universal moral laws are enacted in the code involves cultural peculiarities and may be different for the ancient Israelites than for us. Still, one can often see an abstract law at work despite the cultural peculiarities. For example, in the biblical law commanding the use of accurate scales, one can recognize the universal moral principle to be honest. Contemporary society may not emphasize using accurate scales, since most business today is not done by weighing merchandise on scales. What could be emphasized, however, are requirements such as honest accounting practices and fair invoices.

While universal moral laws are binding, mainline Christians disagree about whether the prohibition against homosexual sex is a universal moral law. For many mainline Christians and scholars, even if the biblical writers thought the prohibition was a universal moral law, it is not decisive for the church today. They claim people today can see the limitations of the biblical authors regarding many of the laws they promoted, and the biblical writers did not know about a homosexual orientation. Contemporary culture has gone through a transformation by which contemporary people are aware of a homosexual orientation and know it is not harmful or a disorder. For these Christians, this cultural transformation is decisive in informing them that the prohibition against gay sex is not a universal moral law but an expression of the cultural limitations of the biblical authors.

Other mainline scholars are not satisfied with the claim that contemporary knowledge negates this prohibition of gay sex. They make the argument that the Bible should inform people today more deeply about human sexuality, and they seek to show how this prohibition against gay sex is part of a larger biblical condemnation of homosexual sex and the affirmation of an exclusive heterosexual order of creation. They connect this prohibition with other biblical stories and themes, including the creation stories in Genesis, where God's order of creation includes an exclusive male/female sexuality. In these stories and other references to sexuality in the Bible, heterosexuality is exclusively affirmed, and homosexual acts univocally condemned.[11] Such unequivocal teaching must represent God's word and not be owing to the limitations of the biblical writers.

Still other mainline scholars interpret the Levitical prohibitions against gay sex as a purity law. They claim that, as a purity law, it is irrelevant to the contemporary discussion about homosexuality. Those affirming this interpretation point out that the Old Testament writers never discriminated between the kinds of laws they promoted. They simply sanctified all the relevant laws of the community, which included religious laws, moral laws, and purity laws. Christians today need to discriminate among types of laws, however, because purity laws do not apply to them.[12]

Purity laws do not have to do with what is right or wrong, but with what makes one ritually clean or unclean. They relate not to moral decision making, but to contact with some thing or process that puts one in a ritually unclean state. As an example, in ancient Israel, bodily discharges, such as the ejaculation of semen for men and menstruation for women, were thought to make one unclean (Lev. 15:16-24). They were not morally wrong, although one could violate moral rules at least in the context in which ejaculation of semen occurred that would make it morally wrong. Their ordinary prescribed use or regular function made one unclean, and having become unclean, one needed to undergo a purification ritual to become clean again.

These interpreters point out that, in ancient Israel, part of being pure meant being a full or complete representation of one's kind. This is why the ancient Israelites refused to mix kinds of things—for example, interbreeding animals, sowing two kinds of seed in a field, or combining types of clothing (Lev. 19:19). Wrongly combining kinds of things made them impure because each thing was no longer a pure representation of its kind. In this context, male homosexual sex is understood as making one impure because it wrongly combines the male and female kinds. The man who is being penetrated in the sex act is taking the role of the woman and so is no longer a pure representation of his kind. To these interpreters, the basis for considering male homosexual sex impure was related to the Israelites' cultural ideas about purity, which Christians today no longer accept. Since it is not a moral law, the condemnation is not valid.

New Testament

The New Testament makes three references to homosexuality, and all three are in the Pauline literature: 1 Cor. 6:9; 1 Tim. 1:10; and Rom. 1:26-27.

The passages in 1 Corinthians and 1 Timothy are similar. Both include homosexual sex in a list of condemned behaviors. The 1 Corinthians passage uses two Greek terms to describe homosexual sex, *malakoi* and *arsenokoitai*, while 1 Timothy uses only the term *arsenokoitai*. Contemporary scholars are not certain about the meaning of these terms, since there was no word in the Greek used by the biblical writers for homosexuality. The word *malakoi* literally means "soft ones." The word *arsenokoitai* literally means "male bed," and bed often functioned as a euphemism for sex. In 1 Corinthians, Paul is making some distinction with the use of the two terms, and there has been much speculation about exactly what that distinction is. A plausible interpretation held by many interpreters is that *malakoi* refers to the passive partner or the one being penetrated in male homosexual sex, while *arsenokoitai* refers to the active partner or the one penetrating.[13] In any case, the context in which these terms occur suggests Paul regarded homosexual sex as a moral issue and not a purity issue, since the other types of behavior condemned in the passage are moral acts.

Paul gives no reasons for his condemnation in 1 Corinthians but spells out his thinking in more detail in Romans 1, the most important passage in the Christian Bible on homosexuality:

> For this reason God gave them up to degrading passions. Their women exchanged natural intercourse for unnatural, and in the same way also the men, giving up natural intercourse with women, were consumed with passion for one another. Men committed shameless acts with men and received in their own persons the due penalty for their error. (Rom. 1:26-27)

The passage is part of a larger context in which Paul is describing the human descent into sin (1:18—3:20). In the immediate context, Paul is discussing Gentile sin. He says the reason God gave people up to degrading passions (at the beginning of verse 26) was idolatry. Although the true God's invisible power and nature were known through creation, so all people should have known this God, people did not give honor and thanks to God but became confused and worshipped idols. In turn, God handed people over to their own wickedness, so moral perversity followed from idolatry. One of the moral perversions mentioned is homosexual sex (vv. 26-27). A host of other perverse acts and attitudes is listed in verses 28-32.

This is the only time in the Bible that lesbian sex is mentioned. Both female and male homosexual sex acts are described as involving an "exchange" of what is "natural" for what is "unnatural." In giving up what is natural, men in particular are described as being "consumed" with passion for other men.

Tremendous scholarly efforts have been put into interpreting what Paul meant in describing homosexual sex as involving an exchange of what is natural for what is unnatural. Some scholars, led by an interpretation initially put forward by John Boswell, think that since Paul did not have the idea of a homosexual orientation, Paul regarded it as "natural" for everyone to have heterosexual desires and engage in heterosexual sex. The perversion he is describing in this passage is a condition where heterosexuals override their heterosexuality to engage in homosexual sex. This is what Paul regarded as unnatural. By implication, however, Paul's critique does not include those of a homosexual orientation who engage in homosexual sex, since that would be natural for them.[14]

This position has been critiqued in many ways. One of the most profound critiques comes from Richard Hays. Hays says Boswell is incorrect in presupposing that what Paul is critiquing in this passage is heterosexuals making a perverse conscious decision to override their heterosexual desires and engage in homosexual sex. Rather than critiquing perverse conscious decisions per se, Paul is describing the general descent of humanity into sin. This general descent into sin transcends the perverse conscious decisions of any specific individuals. Specific, perverse, conscious decisions of individuals are not the descent into sin, but manifestations of the descent into sin. Understood in this way, homosexual sex is critiqued by Paul because it is a striking example of the larger, more decisive, entrapping character of sin into which humans have fallen. To Hays, Paul knows from the Genesis creation stories that exclusive heterosexuality is "natural" for human sexuality.[15]

Other interpreters claim Paul must have been influenced in his views by the general cultural attitude toward homosexuality of his time. These interpreters have tried to shed light on that cultural attitude by studying first-century Greco-Roman ideas about homosexuality, as well as the ideas prevalent in Paul's Jewish subculture.

Some scholars have noted that pederasty was a common form of homosexual activity in Greco-Roman culture. Pederasty involves a grown man having intercourse with a prepubescent boy. While it was accepted in certain contexts in Greco-Roman culture, it was universally condemned by Jews. In the Roman Empire, the boy was often a slave or someone forced into prostitution for survival. The claim is made that Paul, in calling homosexual sex unnatural, could be echoing the Jewish condemnation of pederasty.[16]

While it may be that Paul had pederasty in mind in the 1 Corinthians passage, where he condemns the active and passive partners in a male sexual relationship, it is difficult to see how it fits the entirety of the Romans passage, since it refers to lesbian sex as well. Still, as many interpreters point out, it is important to recognize that Paul did not have the model of a loving, committed, monogamous homosexual relationship in mind when he thought of homosexual sex, since this kind of relationship did not exist in his Jewish subculture or the larger Greco-Roman culture. As Victor Paul Furnish notes, in that culture, homosexual sex was considered inherently lustful. It was not something that could be imagined as a normal part of a committed and caring relationship.[17] In Romans, Paul describes homosexual sex, for men at least, as a matter of being "consumed" with passion.

Other scholars have pointed out that both in Paul's Jewish subculture and in the larger Greco-Roman culture, it was assumed that "natural" sex involved an active and a passive partner, with a man playing the active role and a woman the passive.[18] Paul's Jewish subculture was more aggressive than the larger Greco-Roman culture in condemning homosexual acts as a whole. It remains the case, however, that even in the Greco-Roman context, a free male was considered to have something wrong with him if he played the passive role in sex, which was to be reserved for women, slaves, and young boys. Presumably, taking the active role in sex had to do with an expression of male power. Paul could have had this in mind with his condemnation of homosexual sex as unnatural. Lesbian sex is unnatural because it involves a woman taking the dominant, active role that is supposed to express male power, and gay sex is unnatural because it involves a man taking the passive role and abnegating his power.

The debate over the meaning of this passage will no doubt continue to evolve as scholars continue to attempt to understand the attitudes toward homosexuality in the New Testament context and ask about the influence of these attitudes on Paul. Nevertheless, the two sides of interpretation are generally clear. Many mainline Christians and thinkers claim Paul did not know about the homosexual orientation and was no doubt influenced by negative stereotypes and harmful practices that were part of his culture when he claimed homosexual acts were an exchange of the natural for the unnatural. From that perspective, the church should not make its decision about homosexuality on the basis of Paul's condemnation of homosexual acts. Other mainline Christians and thinkers claim Paul condemns homosexual sex as a manifestation of sin. Paul's condemnation is part of a larger biblical theme that supports exclusive heterosexuality. The church should hear and respect that theme as God's word for today.

Arguments from Human Reason and Scriptural Themes

This final section examines arguments for and against the full acceptance of homosexuals in the church from the perspective of human reason. It also looks at the way those on each side of this issue use biblical themes to support their positions. It is important to analyze the role of human reason before examining biblical themes, because those who support the full acceptance of homosexuals in the church do so in large measure on the basis of developments in human reason. Their appropriation of biblical themes to support their position occurs in the context of these developments.[19]

Human Reason

The arguments from reason regarding homosexuality involve a variety of ethical theories, along with evidence from the social sciences. While differing incompatible ethical theories are often used, this section summarizes a natural-law theory and virtue ethic.

For some ethical reasoning, the ideal of a full human life excludes the possibility of homosexuality and homosexual relationships. In this view, the social and personal ideal for humans involves strong families of opposite-gendered couples in lifelong marriage commitments who bear and raise the next generation. Values are learned and transmitted in the long-term relationships of the parents and the interaction with each other and their children in bringing up the next generation. The biological fact of the compatibility of male and female sexual organs is seen as the basis in nature for the ethical ideal of exclusive heterosexuality. It is often argued that opposite-sex attraction and opposite-sex coupling is based on the fact that each gender has an essential nature. Mutual attractiveness between the genders is not only because of biological differences, but also because of differences in male and female natures that make them compatible with each other. Males and females must embody their natures in order to be fully human. If a marital relationship does not include both genders, or if the members in the relationship do not embody their male or female nature, the relationship cannot be humanly ideal. A homosexual identity and homosexual relationships are critiqued on this basis. Same-gender attractiveness implies some gender confusion in individuals and, inevitably, some problem with the coupling of homosexuals.

Those who argue for the full acceptance of homosexuality stress that an exclusively heterosexual proscription of an ideal human life is too narrow. They claim there is no essential nature given to each gender to embody. There are only individuals with their distinct characters. Same-sex attractiveness or same-sex relationships do not involve confusion or failure to embody a certain nature. In all populations, a certain small percentage of people have same-sex attraction. For those with same-sex attraction, a full ideal human life is found in a homosexual relationship where values can be learned and, if desired, ways can be found to involve the next generation and pass on those values. Human beings are all individuals. Individuals attracted to the same sex, like those attracted to the opposite sex, can find others with whom they are compatible and with whom they can lead meaningful and fulfilling human lives in committed relationships.

Those who argue for the full acceptance of homosexuals often use evidence from the social sciences to buttress their position. In the 1960s and 1970s, the mental health community underwent a paradigm shift with regard to homosexuality. This shift involved a reversal of what had been the accepted understanding of homosexuality. Before the 1970s, homosexuality was regarded as a disorder, so people with same-sex desires were encouraged to seek treatment for it. Various experimental techniques were proposed to heal the disorder, under the assumption that some medical or behavioral technology could be discovered that would be effective. From the 1970s forward, the social-scientific paradigm has shifted to understand homosexuality as a benign sexual variation. In a public expression of this understanding, homosexuality was removed in 1973 from the list of disorders published by the American Psychological Association. Since it is not a disorder, people should not seek treatment for it. In fact, it is understood that the failure to accept one's orientation is what causes psychological harm. Homosexuality is a stable condition that is not caused by willful acts and is not subject to change.[20]

The major piece of evidence that led to this paradigm shift was the claim by researchers that there was no connection between homosexuality and psychological illness.[21] It could not be shown that homosexuality as such is a disturbing psychological condition that needs treatment. Homosexuals were and are as capable as heterosexuals of living creative lives and entering into meaningful, fulfilling relationships. For the mental health community, this meant homosexuality is not to be regarded as a sickness but as a benign sexual variation.

While the position on homosexuality affirmed by the mental health community has become stronger and more widespread since its initial acceptance in the 1970s, it has also been subject to controversy and criticism. Certainly not all mental health experts think homosexuality is benign. Some point to data that show increased problems of gays and lesbians, like shorter life spans or a greater tendency to mental or physical illness. This serves to buttress arguments that the homosexual orientation represents a disordered and, in some sense, troubled condition.

While it is hard to quantify, the experience of gays and lesbians has also been an important factor in many people's views of homosexuality. As gays and lesbians have come out of the closet, they have shown they do not have intellectual or moral impairments but contribute to the life of society at all levels—in business, academics, athletics, politics, community formation, and the arts. They have shown they do not have religious impairments, but are capable of the same kind of spiritual expression as heterosexuals.

Those who argue against the full acceptance of homosexuals acknowledge that gays and lesbians may not be disordered in all aspects of their lives. However, they say, gays and lesbians are still disordered in their sexuality. A person may be intellectually sound and even morally or spiritually upright in many ways but still have the particular problem of being blind to the disordered nature of his or her sexuality.

Those who argue for the full acceptance of homosexuals in the church embrace the relatively new insights of reason and experience that affirm the benign character of homosexuality. They think if the church would just listen, it would hear God's word speaking to it in these insights. They affirm that God's creation is more diverse than almost all previous human cultures understood. The fact there is variety and diversity in God's creation should add to our appreciation of it. There are positive purposes and contributions that gay and lesbian people can make to society and the church—contributions that are part of God's plan for humankind—and the church should open to this.

Those who are against the full acceptance of homosexuals in the church are not persuaded by the new cultural insights about homosexuality. Some say that, at best, the insights of reason and experience with regard to homosexuality are not definitive. The church should not change its traditional stand on the basis of the ambiguous evidence of reason and experience when the Bible and tradition speak clearly against changing that stand. Others go beyond this and claim reason and experience show that the violation of God's order for human sexuality invariably causes harm on some level.

ADDITIONAL INFORMATION

Mainline Protestant Denominations and the Affirmation of Homosexuality

Several mainline Protestant denominations affirm the full accept-ance of homosexuals in church life, with some of them only recently and tentatively making a shift to this position. Uncovering the official positions of these denominations and what they mean can be difficult, since each church has a different organizational and decision-making structure, and the decisions made on the issue of homosexuality are constantly in flux. Still, examining these denomi-nations' positions is valuable because it shows how difficult it is for a church body to hold a position on this controversial issue in a way that pleases all of its constituents.

The United Church of Christ is the mainline denomination that has officially supported gays and lesbians for the longest time. The denomination began a formal study of the issue of human sexuality in the 1970s. By the mid-1980s, the General Synod of the church, the national body that makes formal policy positions, was encourag-ing congregations to accept gay, lesbian, and bisexual people without discrimination. Individual congregations who were willing to do this formally were called "open and affirming."[22] In 1991, the General Synod passed a resolution accepting gay, lesbian, and bisexual peo-ple as ministers.[23] In 2005, the General Synod officially endorsed homosexual marriage.[24]

The decisions of the United Church of Christ have not come without controversy. Constantly, the denomination has urged educa-tion along with the development of its policies. The denominational structure of the United Church of Christ allows individual congrega-tions considerable autonomy. Owing to this, it is possible for indi-vidual congregations to disagree with the decisions of the General Synod on issues like homosexuality and still remain in communion with the larger church.

The issue of homosexuality in the Episcopal Church burst onto the public scene in the summer of 2003, when the General Con-vention of the church confirmed the election of Gene Robinson as bishop. The General Convention, which meets every three years, is the national body that determines policies for the Episcopal Church. Gene Robinson is a gay man in a long-term relationship with another man. The Episcopal Church is split into regional dioceses, and a bishop oversees each diocese. The Diocese of New Hampshire had previously voted to make Robinson its bishop, but he needed to be confirmed at the General Convention.

The events leading to the vote drew considerable media attention, and there was some contentious debate from church members throughout the meeting of the General Convention. A majority vote of two different bodies was required to confirm Robinson. One body, consisting of laypeople and priests, voted 128 to 63 to confirm Robinson. The other body, consisting of the church's bishops, voted 62 to 45 to confirm.[25] Thus, while the vote was not razor thin, it shows there was considerable disagreement over the issue within the church. At the same convention, the delegates voted that individual parishes could perform a rite blessing same-sex unions.[26]

The issue of homosexuality remained contentious in the Episcopal Church after the 2003 Convention—in fact, so much so that the church began to feel the threat of schism. Individual parishes and dioceses that were against the 2003 decision began organizing to form an Anglican communion that would be separate from the Episcopal Church. A number of parishes and dioceses left the Episcopal Church. Instead of being led by a bishop in the U.S. church, they made agreements to be led by more conservative African bishops. In 2009, the Anglican Church in North America was formed. It consists of individual parishes and dioceses in the United States and Canada that have withdrawn from the larger church body primarily because of the issue of homosexuality.[27] It claims to include "some 100,000 Anglicans in 700 parishes and 28 dioceses."[28] They seek recognition as an official part of the worldwide Anglican Communion, or acknowledgment as a sister church in the worldwide group of churches with a historical connection to the Church of England. While the Anglican Church in North America has engineered a split, in 2010, the Episcopal Church approved the ordination as bishop of Mary Glasspool in the Diocese of Los Angeles. She is the second openly gay bishop to be ordained by the church, and the first since Gene Robinson in 2003.[29]

Every other year, the Evangelical Lutheran Church of America holds a Churchwide Assembly in which delegates vote on church policies and positions. In 2009, the Churchwide Assembly made two important decisions on homosexuality and the church.

In the first decision, the assembly approved what is called a "social teaching statement" on human sexuality. According to the ELCA's Web site, social teaching statements "address significant issues that affect the common good . . . [seeking] to bring God's justice not only in the world but in the church."[30] The statement on human sexuality was the result of years of study and debate in the church.

While the statement on human sexuality is lengthy, the most contentious part is its relatively brief statement regarding homosexuality. This section clearly states that in the ELCA, "consensus does not exist concerning how to regard same-gender committed relationships, even after many years of thoughtful, respectful, and faithful study and conversation."[31] It continues by articulating four main positions that the church recognizes as being held by those within it with "conviction and integrity." At one extreme are those who regard same-gender sexual acts as sinful and reject same-gender sexual relationships as a good for society, with celibacy being promoted as an alternative. At the other extreme are those who promote the acceptance of same-gender relationships for individuals and society, affirming that those relationships are to be held to the same standards of lifelong monogamous commitment as heterosexual marriage. In between are two more moderate positions: (1) those holding to a more limited acceptance of same-gender relationships while contending that, since they reflect the brokenness of creation, they should not be publicly recognized; and (2) those holding to a more thoroughgoing acceptance of same-gender relationships that should receive public recognition but not be equated with heterosexual marriage.[32]

Recognizing the lack of consensus in the church body on these issues, the church affirmed the need for "profound respect for the conscience-bound belief of the neighbor."[33] While this decision was not a clear victory for either side, it represents a policy shift for the ELCA, insofar as the church officially acknowledged for the first time that those who affirm the full acceptance of homosexual relationships for individuals and society embrace a conscience-bound position that is to be respected in the church. Interestingly, a two-thirds vote of conference delegates was required for the statement to pass. The statement received exactly the requisite number of votes: 676 in favor to 338 opposed.[34]

At the same assembly, the ELCA voted to allow congregations to "recognize, support and hold publicly accountable life-long, monogamous, same-gender relationships." The church also voted to commit itself to "finding a way for people in such publicly accountable, lifelong, monogamous, same-gender relationships to serve as rostered leaders of this church."[35] These decisions opened the way for the churches of the ELCA to bless same-sex relationships or marry same-sex couples, and for homosexuals in committed relationships to serve as ministers or staff members of the church. With each decision, the church sought to acknowledge the reality of dissent and disagreement of individuals and congregations. For some churches, that acknowledgment was not enough and they left the denomination as a response. Whether this church, or any other, can continue to be united through these disagreements remains a serious question.

Biblical Themes

Those who support the full acceptance of homosexuals propose an interpretation of biblical themes to support their position. Dan Via offers one such sophisticated interpretation that is summarized in this section.[36] Via's interpretation is supplemented by that of feminist theology.

Via points out that the biblical tradition does not negate but affirms bodily existence, including human sexuality. The Bible regards sexuality as a good thing and an essential element of human identity.

Via claims the Bible itself gives warrant for opening to the insights of human reason on moral questions, including the question of sexual orientation. Contained in the Bible is what is called the "wisdom tradition," which affirms that wise people can see evidence of God and God's purposes in creation.[37] This justifies listening to contemporary scientific evidence regarding the benign character of a homosexual orientation.

Listening to this evidence leads to the understanding that homosexuals, like heterosexuals, are embraced as part of God's creation in their bodiliness and sexuality. Their same-sex desires give them an alternative destiny from heterosexuals, but it is a destiny with integrity in which they are called to make choices to fulfill their own sexuality responsibly. The Gospel of John in particular stresses how God wants abundant life for all. Given the biblical understanding of the human as bodily and sexual, such life invariably includes sexual life. It is not adequate to tell gays and lesbians to remain celibate, for that excludes them from the abundant life God wishes for all. In Pauline thought, a special emphasis is placed on the idea that Christians have experienced God's love for them in Christ and are called to show this love to their neighbors. According to Paul, love promotes the good of the other. To promote the good of gays and lesbians means to help them realize the abundant life in community God wants for them.

As to the question of whether there can be a new revelation that overturns the explicit biblical prohibitions against homosexual acts, Via says ongoing revelation is present in the Bible itself. In the history of the Old Testament, there is continual discovery and reinterpretation of the tradition so that God's word is understood anew. The New Testament is a reinterpretation of the Old Testament that hears God's word anew. Via says, "This reinterpretive process that produced the Bible must continue in the life of the Christian community."[38] He also points to the fact that in the Gospel of John, Jesus claims that after he leaves, the Spirit will come and lead the disciples into all truth. This means there is more truth in Jesus' message yet to be discovered by the church.

In addition to arguments like those given by Via, many feminists in particular interpret the biblical themes against the social oppression of one group by another as applying analogously to the status of gays and lesbians. Feminist theology effectively appropriates the general biblical message critiquing social oppression even though the explicit biblical context does not refer to gender oppression. Many feminists argue the same can and should be done to critique the oppression of homosexuals. They identify with gay and lesbian people who are told they are somehow inferior or have something wrong with them that does not allow them to affirm who they are or be leaders in the church. Overcoming psychological and social oppression wherever they exist brings wholeness to God's creation.

Those opposed to the full acceptance of homosexuality in the church remain unconvinced by these biblical interpretations. They agree with Via that we are sexual beings and our sexuality is good, but they claim the exclusive order of heterosexuality is deeply inscribed in the Bible. From the creation story forward, heterosexuality is promoted as the norm. The prohibitions against homosexual sex must be understood in light of this deeply rooted biblical affirmation that the only true means of human sexual fulfillment is heterosexual. For these people, the way to show love to gays and lesbians is to awaken them to the troubling nature of their condition in God's eyes. Of course, this must be done carefully and with sensitivity. They claim gays and lesbians should not be regarded as an oppressed group seeking liberation in the same way as women. God created males and females in God's image with the intention they live in fulfilled sexual relationships together. Pointing out the fact that gays and lesbians violate God's intention for human sexuality is not oppression but a path toward healing.

It appears likely that U.S. culture and many of the churches within it will continue to struggle with this issue into the indefinite future. Many people on either side appear to be inflexible, and for those who undergo a change of mind and heart, this usually occurs only over the course of a considerable length of time and as a result of a variety of influences. What this will mean for individuals and church bodies wrestling with this issue is left to be determined in the future.

Chapter 9

Christianity and the Natural Environment

Although it is sometimes overlooked, one of the most dramatic changes on earth in the past few centuries is the growth of the human population. According to estimates presented by the U.S. Census Bureau, in 1000 B.C.E., the time of the biblical King David, there were perhaps 50 million people on earth.[1] In Jesus' day, there were perhaps 300 million. That figure remained approximately the same one thousand years later. Sometime between 1800 and 1850, the number of humans on earth had more than tripled, as humans passed the 1 billion mark. Over approximately the next century, the population doubled again, with humans passing the 2 billion mark sometime between 1900 and 1950. At the beginning of 2009, there were approximately 6.7 billion people on earth, over three times as many people as in 1900. The Census Bureau predicts a slowing growth rate but estimates the human population will exceed 9 billion by 2050.[2]

The recent population explosion is owing to several factors. Paramount among them are advances in science and technology. Advances in medicine have helped eradicate diseases, decrease infant mortality, and increase life spans. Advances in agriculture have made possible food provisions for greatly increasing numbers of people. Modern mechanization and industrialization have made possible a more extensive and effective use of natural resources in order to provide not only shelter and clothing for greater numbers of people, but luxury items on a scale never before imagined.

The growth of the human population and the advances in science and technology that enabled it have been so successful that, starting in the latter half of the twentieth century, for the first time in human history, humans started asking seriously whether human power and influence would harmfully disrupt the natural systems on which human life depends. Before this time, it was unquestionably assumed the natural world was so much bigger than humans, and human influence comparatively so small, that natural systems would continue to operate unchanged and provide for humans into the indefinite future.[3] The

natural resources humans need for their continued sustenance and live-
lihood would always be sufficiently available. The weather patterns that
bring the heat and the cold, the sunshine and the rain, would continue
unchanged. Untapped wilderness and the variety of species it contains
would exist in sufficient plentitude to flourish beyond the realm of
human cultivation and claim.

As humanity moves deeper into the twenty-first century, it seems
clear there are no guarantees for these assumptions. While there is
serious analysis and debate about just how many people the earth
can sustainably support, an increasing number of people today are
conscious of the human potential to influence harmfully the entire
biosphere—that is, the totality of living systems on the planet upon
which human life depends.[4] The vast majority of scientists think global
warming is a reality and is caused by human activity. This warming has
already begun to change ecosystems. Deforestation, due to the ongoing claim of land by humans, continues to change the terrain of vast
stretches of continents. The advance and impact of human cultivation
and the human claim to natural resources have led to a shrinking of
wilderness and subsequent extinction of species in numbers matched
in the past only by times of dramatic climate change, such as the transformation into an ice age.

Many people today also have an increased awareness of the finitude
and limitations of the natural resources upon which human life and the
modern Western lifestyle depend. Even if the current consumption of
fossil fuels did not cause global warming, a world that will soon have 7
billion people cannot continue that level of consumption indefinitely,
much less continue its trend of dramatically increasing consumption.
Fossil fuels are a finite resource. In certain places of the globe, having
enough water to sustain the current population is an increasingly serious
and tenuous issue. A world with 6.7 billion people produces an enormous amount of waste every day, and piling garbage higher and broader
in more landfills is not a viable long-term option. If humans want clean
air and water, and wild places to refresh their souls and stimulate their
imaginations, humans need to set limits on their claim to the natural
world. As environmentalists point out, if humans want to survive and
flourish as a species into the indefinite future, they need to learn to live
sustainably so that the natural systems on which human life depends
flourish along with humans. The failure to learn to live sustainably will
mean that eventually the environment will exact a chilling price on
human lives and human societies.

Awareness of humans' dependence on the natural world and the harm humans are doing to it has spawned a burgeoning environmental movement. This movement includes representatives from a wide variety of philosophical and religious traditions, including great numbers of Christians, upon whom it has been incumbent to demonstrate how their Christian beliefs cohere with and motivate environmental activism. Numerous contemporary theologians have made a priority of showing that Christianity is, or can be interpreted as, pro-environment. This has been done in a context in which, at times, questions have been raised against Christianity about whether in fact it is responsible for the environmental crisis in the first place. After all, Western civilization, a civilization profoundly shaped by Christianity, is where modern science and its technical application arose. These factors made possible the industrial revolution, during which the use and abuse of the natural world occurred in a manner and degree never before known in human history.

Is Christianity, or some interpretation of it, responsible for the environmental crisis? Can Christianity, or some interpretation of it, provide at least part of the basis for global environmental activism and healing? These important questions are being asked and answered with urgency today by many Christians and non-Christians alike. This chapter traces some of the criticisms directed against Christianity by those who hold the Christian worldview responsible for environmental harm. It also examines some responses given by Christian theologians who understand their faith as promoting the restoration and well-being of the natural world.

The Anti-environmental Charge against Christianity

In 1967, when the contemporary environmental movement was in its infancy, Lynn White, a scholar who specialized in medieval history, wrote an important article that is still widely read and cited. In it, he argues that the worldview of Christianity is largely responsible for what he called "our ecological crisis."[5] White identifies aspects of a Christian worldview that have been responsible for environmental harm, while also offering interpretations of Christianity that can address the ecological crisis in a positive way. Since White's article, many of the charges he pressed against Christianity have been repeated, developed, and expanded by critics both inside and outside of Christianity. Others have debated seriously whether White and the critics who followed him represent Christianity properly, or whether they point the finger at the wrong culprit: Was Christianity responsible for the worldview that eventuated in environmental harm, or was it Enlightenment thought, which emerged on Christian soil but had its own distinct emphases? Historians continue to grapple with this question, and a simple either/or answer may be inadequate to the complexities involved. In any case, however, the charge of anti-environmentalism against Christianity continues to be affirmed in many quarters.

The charge against Christianity can be summarized with three interlocking parts. The first part claims that Christianity, following Judaism, definitively separates God from the world and with this turns the world into an object of human use. Many of the nature religions replaced by Judaism and Christianity experienced the divine or the sacred in and through the natural world. Natural cycles, including the emergence of spring and the fecundity of the earth, were thought to express the Gods' sexuality or rejuvenation from a period of inactivity. Natural features such as mountains, streams, fields, and forests were regarded as filled with a numinous divine aura. Animals and birds, with their unique capacities that differentiate them from humans, were regarded as capable of representing the divine, and worship was often directed to their images.

Judaism, and subsequently Christianity, denied that God is sexual and outlawed carved images of God. God was understood to stand apart from creation as an independent being who both created and controlled the processes of creation. God alone is sacred, not the creation, nor elements or processes within it. According to this critique, when the natural world ceased to mediate the divine, it could and, in fact, did become an object of human use. No longer bearing the divine presence, the natural world was open to being shaped for human purposes according to the human will, an understanding that eventually led to abuse of the natural world in the long arc of Western history. When a mountain no longer mediated the presence of the High God, it could become understood as a storehouse of minerals for human use.

The second part of the charge against Christianity is that it inordinately separates humans from the rest of the natural world, elevating them above it. Sometimes this charge is summarized with the term *anthropocentrism*. According to it, in the created order, human beings alone are regarded as having intrinsic value. Everything else has only instrumental value insofar as it is intended to serve human ends.[6] Correspondingly, humans are understood not so much as a part of nature, but as standing above nature. They have the capacity and the God-given right to grasp and use the natural world for their own ends. Humans have the distinct vocation to tame the wild world of nature, even while they are not considered substantially to be part of the natural world they are to tame.

Among other ways, critics justify this charge by pointing to the biblical creation story, where it is stated humans alone among all the creation are made "in the image of God" (Gen. 1:27). This is interpreted to mean they are uniquely the crown of creation, its driving purpose, and are differentiated from everything else in creation. Twice in the same story, humans are told to "have dominion" over fish, birds, and all animals, domestic and wild (Gen. 1:26, 28). Humans are also told to "fill the earth and subdue it" (Gen. 1:28), implying the right to control or perhaps even dominate other living things on earth.

Another aspect of this charge is the claim that what is deemed important in the biblical narrative is distinctly human history and human destiny. The biblical story is a sweeping drama whose overwhelming concern is human relations and the human future. The natural world is overlooked, playing the role of insignificant background object. The natural world provides the means for human flourishing and human destiny, but in itself is not of intrinsic concern.

The final part of the charge against Christianity claims Christianity is so exclusively concerned with human salvation and the afterlife that it negates concern for the natural world and its inhabitants and cycles. Rather than finding God in nature, Christianity affirms that God is known in historical actions for God's people. The meaning of these historical actions is ultimately human salvation. While human salvation is the goal of history, it is ultimately understood as something above and beyond history. Owing to the influence of Greek thought in particular, Christian salvation is often envisioned in otherworldly terms. Following the Greek anthropology, humans alone out of all creatures are thought to have an immortal soul that either ascends to heavenly bliss or descends to eternal punishment at death. Nothing of the teeming but merely finite life on earth can ultimately have significance compared with the decisive question of the eternal destiny of the human soul.

These three elements—the separation of God from the world, the elevation of humans as the only thing with intrinsic value in the world and as separate from the natural world with the vocation to subdue it, and the overwhelming concern with human salvation and the human afterlife—constitute the anti-environmental case against Christianity. Generally speaking, those making this charge do not claim Christians in the past or at present have directly called for the destruction of the natural world. Rather, the charge is that the Christian worldview has provided a context where the natural world has been devalued or deemed insignificant. In this context, the natural world justifiably could be—and, in fact, was—turned into an object merely to serve human ends. While this context may have been there for a long time, essentially it did not matter for most of the sweep of human history, because the number of humans on earth and their power over the natural world was limited. Only in the contemporary period, with the dramatic increase in human population and human power, has the issue of environmental harm been raised to the level of a crisis.

Some regard these charges against Christianity to be accurate enough and serious enough that Christianity itself should be abandoned for alternative religions that are compatible with promoting the healing of the natural world. Many Christians, however, have a different response. They regard Christianity as compatible with caring for and restoring the natural environment if the message of Christianity is rightly interpreted. Some Christians claim only a minor rethinking or reinterpretation of Christianity is called for in light of the charges against it in order to show how Christian beliefs and practices are compatible with environmental care and healing. Certain elements in Christianity that may have been suppressed, or may not have been emphasized, need to be brought to the fore. Other Christians have called for a more thoroughgoing rethinking of Christian ideas or emphases in order to make Christianity compatible with environmental care and restoration.

The rest of this chapter examines three kinds of responses given by Christians to show that Christianity supports environmental care and healing. The first response is the most modest in terms of the rethinking of Christianity it envisions, while the final one is the most radical.

Stewardship of Creation

One of the most common responses Christians make against the charge of anti-environmentalism is the claim that Christianity promotes the stewardship of creation.[7] The idea that Christians are to be stewards of creation is often presented as the biblical position. Although the word *stewards* or *stewardship* in regard to creation is not found in the Bible, it is claimed this idea represents the intent of the larger biblical message.

A "steward" is someone who manages someone else's property and who is supposed to take care of that property in the way the owner desires. When Christians are regarded as stewards of creation, it implies the creation is God's property. God made the creation, and God owns it, not humans. Numerous passages in the biblical text affirm this, including the proclamation in Ps. 24:1 that says, "The earth is the LORD's," as well as the legal passage in Lev. 25:23 where God is presented as claiming, "The land is mine; with me you are but aliens and tenants."

While God owns the creation, God has put it in the human trust. Among other places, this is shown by the creation story in Genesis 1, where God tells humans they have "dominion," or rule, over the creation, and they are to "subdue" it. What is stressed by the proponents of the stewardship model is that the rule God intends of humans over creation is not a negative rule of domination and control, but a positive rule of care for the well-being of creation.[8] Much analysis of the biblical text has been done on this point to show that the rule God intends between humans is never a rule of domination or control, but one that seeks the good of the other. The ruler is even called to be self-sacrificing for the sake of the other, and the model of Jesus as servant or self-sacrificing ruler is promoted as representative of God's idea of true rule. For proponents of the stewardship model, this idea should apply to the human rule of the natural world. Humans are to exercise a rule that cares about the good of creation.

Proponents of the stewardship model often turn to the biblical text, and especially the Old Testament law, to give examples of the benign rule humans are to show over the natural world. In the Ten Commandments, provision is made not only for humans to rest one day out of seven, but also for domestic animals to rest (Exod. 20:10). Exodus 23:12 explicitly says one of the reasons for resting on the Sabbath is "so that your ox and your donkey may have relief." The law also provides for the fertility and right use of the land by specifying that the land should not be farmed but lie fallow every seven years (Exod. 23:10-11; Lev. 25:1-7). There is even provision for the wild animals, which are to be allowed to eat from the land that is lying fallow (Exod. 23:10; Lev. 25:7). Broadly speaking, proponents of the stewardship model interpret these and other biblical passages as advocating a caring stewardship according to God's desires. This stewardship promotes the flourishing and health of creation, and involves sustainable practices with regard to the use of creation and its resources.

The stewardship model understands the relation between God, humans, and the creation to be such that God remains transcendent and separate from creation, while humans are given the distinctive vocation to take care of God's creation. The model makes harm of the creation an act of disobedience against God, its rightful owner. Thus, divine sanction is attached not merely to relationships of justice between humans, but also to relationships of justice between humans and the natural world.

Despite the popularity of the stewardship model, it has not escaped criticism. One critique of the model claims that its predominant focus on the use of the natural world is troubling. A steward is someone who manages someone else's property. The strength of the stewardship model is that it makes clear that the creation is God's and not humans' to do with as they will. The model stresses the importance of right manage-ment, right rule, or right use of the natural world. The model belies any simple-minded criticism of Christianity, which would claim that because Christianity promotes the use of the natural world, it must be harmful. Instead, the model focuses on the difference between wrong or abusive use of the natural world and proper or sustainable use.

At the same time, however, the model is ambiguous on the question of whether the human relation to the natural world should be anything but use. Proponents of the model certainly can and do make the case that in the biblical vision, the human relation to the natural world involves more than just use. It involves the promotion of the flourishing of wild-ness as such, not just the turning of wildness into something that can be put to human use. Still, the fact that the stewardship model has an economic basis in managing property means it is something of a stretch of the model to regard it as promoting the flourishing of wildness as such, apart from human use. In Jesus' parable in Matt. 25:14-30, a wealthy man entrusts part of his wealth to stewards. The stewards who invest the master's money, putting it to right use, are praised. The steward who hides the master's money and does nothing with it is criticized. In this case, being a steward implies being active in using that with which one is entrusted, rather than letting it be for itself.

This critique brings out the potential limits of the stewardship model when it operates as the foundational model to express the relation between God, humans, and the natural world. The stewardship model is in fact an analogy. It takes an economic relationship between humans and property and applies this relationship analogously to the relationship between God, humans, and the natural world. Like all good analogies, it is meant to express something important. This analogy expresses the need for the proper use of the natural world. At the same time, all analo-gies have limits, and this must be true of the stewardship analogy as well. One of those limits appears to be the inability to express in a significant way a relationship to the natural world apart from use.

When it functions as a foundational model, the stewardship model implies a separation of God from the world, which is God's property. It also implies the special status of humans in relation to the creation, for humans are to take care of it and use it rightly. Some critics take issue with these elements of the model as well. In particular, many critique the fact that the model's emphasis on humans taking care of the natural world implies a fundamental difference between humans and the rest of the natural world. In saying humans are to take care of the natural world, where in this model is the affirmation that humans are also a part of the natural world? Clearly, humans are biological creatures with physical needs who share many things in common with animals and the rest of creation. The model does not account for this identity of humans and other creatures. In fact, theoretically speaking, given the fact that the stewardship model only stresses that humans are put in charge of the natural world, humans could be angels or other supernatural beings, according to the model.

An alternative model proposed by some Christian thinkers that expresses the identity of humans and the rest of the natural world is the idea that humans are brothers and sisters to animals and other living things. In this model or analogy, God is the parent, and humans, along with other creatures, are God's children. This model is able to express the identity of humans with other creatures and also to show how, as parent, God wants all of God's children to flourish. The natural world is not simply something humans are to use properly as God directs. Instead, the Divine Parent has a relationship with all creatures, all of whom are God's children, and for whom God independently desires their flourishing.

At least some Christians think this alternative can be a healthy balance to the exclusive focus of the stewardship model. As many environmentalists point out, one of the problems today with the development of our technological society and modern lifestyle is that humans have lost a vital or sympathetic contact with the natural world and its inhabitants. By itself at least, the stewardship model appears to reinforce this lack of contact. A model stressing humanity's shared siblinghood with other creatures can open up a channel for experiencing contact with nonhuman creatures anew.

Owing primarily to criticism of the stewardship model, many Christians and Christian groups no longer use the model explicitly or predominantly. In pro-environment Christian contexts, it is common for Christians to use the more generic language of "caring for creation" or "creation care," rather than stewardship of creation, to express the Christian attitude to the natural environment.

Salvation History, Eschatology, and Ecology

Another response of some eco-theologians to the anti-environmental charge against Christianity is to reaffirm Christian salvation history, or God's cosmic plan of salvation, in a fresh way. This reaffirmation stresses that the Christian understanding of salvation, properly understood, does not involve the escape of disembodied human souls from their bodies, nor is it limited to the salvation of humans alone. Salvation involves the renewal and transformation of the entire cosmos, including the nonhuman world. According to this approach, because Christians perceive God's purpose in salvation as the transformation of all things, including the nonhuman world, the meaning and value of the nonhuman world are emphasized in a way that has environmental or ecological implications.

Numerous theologians represent this approach. This section will examine two, the Roman Catholic theologian Denis Edwards (1943–) and the Lutheran theologian Paul Santmire (1935–).

The Transformation of Nonhuman Creation: Denis Edwards

Edwards's ecological theology is multifaceted, but central to it is an adaptation of the understanding of salvation history expounded by the German Jesuit Karl Rahner (1904–1984).[9] Drawing on an important stream of interpretation in Christian history, Rahner stressed that the salvation or redemption accomplished in Jesus Christ must be understood as coherent with and the fulfillment of God's purpose in creating. In other words, for Rahner, it is not the case that God had a certain plan in making the creation but human sin defeated that plan. Upon the defeat of the original plan, God enacted an alternative plan that involved becoming incarnate in Jesus to save human beings from their sin. Instead, for Rahner, God had a single plan for all of creation from the beginning that God in fact carried out and is carrying out in history despite the reality of human sin.

The plan of God from the beginning involves God making created reality outside of God's self in order to give God's self to it and transform it and bring it back to God. The point in history where the culmination of God's giving of God's self to creation occurs is in the incarnation of God in Jesus of Nazareth. Here, God gives God's self completely to creation in the Word of God becoming flesh. In the resurrection of Jesus, God takes up the created reality into God's own life. The material reality of the human Jesus is permanently transformed and taken up into God. This is called "deification," and it is God's ultimate plan for creation and the goal of creation. All along, God made created reality outside God's self in order to become incarnate in it and bring this created reality back to God's self.

While the resurrection of Jesus occurs in the middle of history, it is the beginning of what will come for all of creation when it reaches its fulfillment. Edwards says, for Rahner, the resurrection is a change "in the deepest level of things in the universe." It is "the beginning of the divinization of the world itself."[10]

Since the cosmos itself will be taken back into God, it is not just human souls that are saved and transformed, and not even just human bodies that are saved and transformed. All of creation—which means all matter, life, and spirit—shares in salvation or the deification that God will bring to all things in and through the incarnation and resurrection of Jesus.

Edwards stresses with Rahner that humans are not able to understand fully what this deification means on this side of the consummation of creation. Summarizing Rahner, Edwards says, "What we know, on the basis of the promise of God given in the resurrection, is that we will be brought to our fulfillment by being taken into the unfathomable loving mystery of God—and, Rahner says, 'that is enough.'"[11]

While the future of consummation cannot be pictured in a concrete way, it involves the fulfillment of all creation. Edwards claims, however, that while Rahner affirms this fulfillment for all creation, he tends to overlook what it may mean for living creatures other than humans. If all creation is to be transformed and fulfilled, all living creatures, individually and as a whole, must somehow be taken up and transformed in God's ultimate plan for creation.[12] Edwards proposes to develop this affirmation in a way that is not done explicitly by Rahner.

Edwards reasons that each individual creature and all living things as a whole must reach their fulfillment in a way that is appropriate to the being of that thing. He suggests this fulfillment must be more than the fact that each individual living thing is taken up into God's memory.[13] Simply being remembered by God does not adequately express the reality of the transformation and consummation of creation. More than this, every sparrow, bug, slug, bear, and whale must be taken up by God into an ultimate fulfillment that is appropriate for what it is. Edwards claims humans cannot know what this means concretely. Christians can affirm, however, because of Jesus' resurrection, that all creation, and therefore all creatures, will reach their fulfillment in God.

What this means ecologically, for a Christian theologian like Edwards, is that no living thing ever simply appears, dies, and is forgotten. All life is ultimately significant because all life somehow shares in

God's final transformative fulfillment of reality. For Edwards, this breaks down a narrow anthropocentric worldview that would focus only on human well-being and the human future, regarding nonhuman creation merely as a backdrop for human fulfillment and only of instrumental value for human use. In all its teeming variety and diversity, creation is made by God, loved by God, and will come to its fulfillment in God. That variety and diversity must be respected and valued in its independent relation to God and role in God's plan for the cosmos, rather than as an insignificant object of human manipulation and use.

Overcoming Christianity's Ecological Ambiguity: Paul Santmire

Paul Santmire has written two important works on Christianity and ecology. The first work, *The Travail of Nature*, is a study of tensions in Christian thought regarding Christianity's ecological message. The second work, *Nature Reborn*, is a constructive attempt to display how those tensions can be overcome.

In the first work, Santmire acknowledges the environmental critique of Christianity, especially the claim of critics that Christianity is fundamentally and troublingly anthropocentric. Santmire claims, however, that this critique is only partly true. He thinks there is an inherent ambiguity in Christian theology itself, such that some expressions of Christian theology are harmfully or dangerously anthropocentric, while others are not.[14]

Santmire seeks to display this tension in Christianity by analyzing New Testament texts and significant thinkers in the Christian tradition. He claims Christian thinkers give expression to one of what he calls two main "theological motifs." A theological motif is a pattern of thinking or fundamental way of expressing the relation between God, humans, and the nonhuman world. This pattern of thinking lies behind various theological systems and expressions.[15]

One main theological motif, according to Santmire, is the spiritual motif. As with all motifs, its inspiration comes from some formative experience that serves as the imaginative background out of which it is constructed. Santmire claims the experience behind this motif is the imaginative ascent of a mountain in order to transcend the mundane realm below. This motif stresses a spiritual journey upward, taking one beyond and out of this world.

The other main theological motif is, in Santmire's terms, the ecological motif. Its inspiration comes from the imaginative journey or migration to a good land overflowing with diversity and abundance of life. Instead of this motif taking one beyond and out of this realm, it expresses a landed journey where the traveler is always a part of the natural world in which the journey is undertaken. Santmire says, "In the thought world of the metaphor of migration to a good land, one can never lose one's rootedness in the world of nature."[16]

Santmire claims these two motifs stand in considerable tension with each other, and because of this, a theological system will ultimately give expression to one or the other. It is true that individual theologians may give lip service to both motifs, but ultimately, because of the tension between them, one motif or the other will predominate in a particular system.

To Santmire, the ecological critics of Christianity have latched onto the spiritual motif and regarded it as the only expression of Christian theology. They are correct in seeing this motif as deeply rooted in the Christian tradition and correct in critiquing it as anti-environmental. However, they have overlooked the ecological motif, which is just as central in Christian thought and provides material for a fruitful response to the environmental crisis in the contemporary period.

Throughout the text, Santmire analyzes the way these two motifs come to expression in a variety of important biblical authors and classical Christian theologians. For example, regarding the New Testament, he argues that the Gospel of John and the book of Hebrews are fundamentally determined by the spiritual motif, while the historical Jesus, Paul, and the pseudonymous author of Colossians and Ephesians are shaped by the ecological motif.[17] Similarly, he thinks the church father Irenaeus gives expression to the ecological motif, while the church father Origen expresses the spiritual motif.[18]

In the spiritual motif, according to Santmire, creation and redemption are "asymmetrical."[19] This means that in the worldview of this motif, while God is regarded as creator and often there is an emphasis on the great variety and diversity within creation, the goal of creation is the spiritual redemption of humans apart from the rest of creation. However, in the ecological motif, creation and redemption are "symmetrical." God makes a world with variety and diversity in it in order to redeem it all. As Santmire says, referring to the final vision of this motif, "All things finally shall be consummated in glory by God, when every creature shall enjoy the glorious liberty of the children of God."[20]

Santmire's second book, *Nature Reborn*, develops the ecological motif for contemporary theology.[21] At the heart of this text are three chapters that propose overcoming some expression of anthropocentrism. First, he proposes a way of reading the biblical literature that goes "beyond anthro-pocentric interpretations."[22] In this way of reading the Bible, one looks for "meanings that point to the future and the fullness thereof."[23] This fundamentally means seeing the interpretive center of the biblical story as promoting deliverance from a negative state into "the land of fecundity and justice."[24] This land is the place where God's blessings abound in their fullness, not just for humans, but for all creation. Santmire reads the Old Testament narrative and the creation story, along with the New Testament gospels, epistles, and book of Revelation, from the perspec-tive of this central theme and its ongoing historical development.

Second, Santmire proposes transcending "evolutionary anthropo-centrism," which means telling the story of the evolution of life from a Christian theological perspective that affirms the value and legitimacy of the abundance and diversity of all life, not just human life. The meaning of the evolutionary process according to this story is not that lower levels of matter and biological life are understood to have instrumental value only insofar as they give rise to higher levels of mind. Instead, as Sant-mire says, "each stage of cosmic evolutionary history has its own divinely established, eternal value throughout the course of its history: since every creature, and indeed all creatures together, are one day to be consum-mated in God, not just the so-called spiritual creatures."[25]

Considering the cosmic process as a whole, Santmire says, God makes "an infinitely variegated, multidimensional cosmos, in order to mirror his infinite being in that finite cosmos."[26] The great diversity of creation reflects "God's own infinite life."[27] Furthermore, God's fullness overflows into all that God makes. The presence of God in all, working patiently and without coercion, elicits "a succession of stages or phases of genesis" that today is understood by scientists as evolutionary history, the movement from matter to life to mind.[28] Like Edwards, Santmire stresses that God's intention from the beginning was to become incarnate in Jesus to deify the entire cosmos, even while he stresses the importance of the incarnation as restoring human brokenness through the cross.

Finally, Santmire proposes overcoming "anthropocentric personal-ism" in the human relation to the nonhuman world.[29] According to Sant-mire, this requires development of a distinct category of understanding that gives full expression to the human relation with the nonhuman world. This category cannot have exactly the same characteristics as a person-to-person relation, since that relation is characterized by mutual interaction and by language. The nonhuman world cannot speak and thereby mutually commune with humans in the same way humans do with each other. At the same time, the category for expressing the human relation with the nonhuman world cannot turn natural objects merely into things to be manipulated and used by humans. Even though humans can and must manipulate and use things of the natural world to survive, conceiving all human relations on this level is reductionist. It sacrifices elements that are given in the human relation with nature.

Drawing on the Bible and other classical theologians, Santmire suggests that the distinctive human relationship to the natural world can have a presence and immediacy similar to the relation with other humans. One can have a genuine encounter with the fullness of an individual object, like a squirrel or a tree, or a unity of objects together in a natural landscape. In either case, one immediately encounters the full being of the object as it gives itself to one. Individual natural objects have their own interiority, even though this is not at the same level as that of a human. The natural world also displays beauty in unity and diversity. In encountering a natural object, the subject can express wonder that grabs "a person's total attention."[30] This wonder includes openness to the natural object, a willingness to appreciate it for what it is, and a sense of gratitude for it, since one does not possess it, but it belongs to God. The wonder can be accompanied by both repulsion and delight. Through the encounter with the object comes a "sense for the divine presence." Santmire claims this involves being "captivated by [the object's] openness to the infinite, by its openness to a dimension that lies behind and permeates its givenness, its spontaneity, and its beauty."[31]

This latter emphasis, on seeing the infinite in the finite through encounter with things of the natural world, is an important element in Santmire's ecological Christian vision, although it tends not to stand at the forefront of that vision. What is at the forefront of his vision, as with Edwards, is an understanding of salvation history in terms of movement or development toward some ultimately ideal future. The emphasis on encountering the infinite in the finite here and now comes to the fore more explicitly in the final type of Christian ecological vision examined in this chapter, creation spirituality.

Creation Spirituality

Creation spirituality is a term for an eclectic movement that has generally responded to the environmental critique of Christianity by deeply embracing it. In embracing the critique, it has called for a re-envisioning of Christianity that is more thoroughgoing than the other positions examined in this chapter. This re-envisioning involves the appropriation of elements within the Christian tradition. Of particular importance is the idea of the goodness of creation, and often there is an emphasis on the idea that God's glory, spirit, wisdom, or word can be encountered in and through the elements of the natural world. Proponents of creation spirituality often favor classical Christian theologians who emphasize the presence of God in nature.

While re-envisioning Christianity, representatives of this position have also tended to show considerable openness to non-Christian religions and their approaches to the natural world. In particular, the religious worldview of indigenous people is often regarded as ideal and taken to be harmonious with what is perceived as the best or most worthwhile elements of the Christian tradition. On the whole, indigenous people have tended to understand themselves as radically a part of the natural world. They are an extension of the whole and stand in an interdependent relationship with the natural world and its objects, rather than standing utterly distinct and over against the natural world. Indigenous people have tended to be animistic, seeing nature as infused with a divine or sacred presence. They have also tended to deemphasize the historical for the sake of finding the divine within ever-recurring natural cycles. All of these elements are embraced in some degree or another by the proponents of creation spirituality. This embrace has led to creative but also controversial interpretations of Christianity.

This section examines two types of creation spirituality, one promoted by Matthew Fox (1940–) and one by Thomas Berry and Brian Swimme. It is relatively easy to see Fox's re-envisioning of Christianity because he deals deeply and directly with the Christian biblical and theological tradition. This is not the case with Berry and Swimme, who display broader concerns in their work, and precisely what their work means for Christianity remains ambiguous. Despite this, they make a unique contribution to creation spirituality that is worth examining.

Original Blessing and the Cosmic Christ: Matthew Fox

Matthew Fox was a member of the Dominican Order and ordained a Roman Catholic priest in the 1960s. His teaching on creation spirituality was regarded as controversial by the Roman Church and led to his being silenced by the church. Eventually, in response to the controversy, he left the Roman Church. Currently, he is an Episcopal priest.

Fox uses language creatively, and his works are often highly sugges-
tive though lacking in systematic rigor—qualities that make him difficult
to interpret. Still, two of his early major theological works articulate the
interpretation of Christianity he most thoroughly opposes and outline the
major elements in creation spirituality he promotes.

The understanding of Christianity Fox consistently criticizes is what
he calls a "fall/redemption model of spirituality."[32] What Fox means by a
spiritual model is a comprehensive worldview that contains an understanding of the relationship between God, humans, and nonhuman creation,
along with implied modes of action for human life. While Fox identifies
a number of thinkers with the fall/redemption worldview, he targets its
primary source as the Western theologian Augustine of Hippo.

Fox claims Augustine gave the Western church its doctrine of original sin.[33] In Fox's interpretation, original sin means humans enter into
the world as "blotches on existence."[34] Rather than blessings who are
loved by God, humans are contemptible creatures who are guilty and in
a state of rejection by God. Having a sinful nature, humans cannot trust
themselves or anything having to do with their bodies, particularly their
bodily passions. Bodily passions, especially sexual ones, are sinful and are
to be repressed.[35] Humans cannot trust creation, which is also regarded
as fallen, and they cannot trust God, who rejects them.

In a desperate situation, alienated from God and themselves, humans
turn inward, focusing on their individual sinfulness and guilt. They seek
to find salvation individually, in the interior relationship with God, overlooking their situatedness in a bounteous and beautiful creation and thus
overlooking the possibility of finding God in and through the creation.
They seek an otherworldly salvation in an afterlife, having sought control
or negation of their desires in this life, and having rejected the created
world.[36] In short, for Fox, the fall/redemption theology affirms what was
summarized earlier in this chapter as the main points of the environmental critique against Christianity. It separates God from the world;
separates humans from the rest of nature, affirming an interior focus on
the status of one's soul; and claims that the meaning of human life is to
be found in an otherworldly salvation.

Fox's remedy is to reject fall/redemption spirituality, with its affirmation of original sin, for "creation spirituality," with its affirmation of what
he calls "original blessing" (also the title of the first of his books examined
in this section). The worldview of original blessing says humans are not
born as blotches on creation but as blessings who are part of a bounteous

creation and are loved by a God they can trust and whose being overflows into that creation.

Original blessing is a celebratory worldview, and Fox goes to great lengths to show this.[37] It celebrates the passions, rather than denying them. It celebrates the earth and its fecundity, including all of the natural cycles. Rather than turning inward for an introspective spirituality focusing on guilt and sin, it turns outward to creative living that is in touch with the deep sources of creativity in the universe.[38]

Turning to an outward spirituality that expresses itself in creative living is a vital element in Fox's vision. God is the source of creativity and is present in the interdependence, order, beauty, and fecundity of the natural world. In turning outward for their spirituality, humans open to creation with an attitude of trust. In this openness, they touch the source of creativity, which issues forth in distinctive creative living. This creative living, for Fox, always includes justice. It includes the creation of modes of living that are compassionate and caring because it includes an understanding of the interdependence of all things, including all people in the human community. However, creative living is never sterile and static. Like the creation itself, which is always bursting forth with new life, so Fox envisions creation spirituality bringing forth ever new and distinctive forms of creative living.

While Fox draws on a variety of sources from the Bible and Christian theology to express his vision of original blessing, most often and most vigorously he draws on medieval Christian mystics for an inspiring historical tradition.[39] For Fox, mystics like Hildegard of Bingen (1098–1179), Mechtild of Magdeburg (1210–1280), Meister Eckhart (1260–1329), and Julian of Norwich (1342–1415) were especially in touch with the unity and interdependence of all things and were able to penetrate to an awareness of God in creation. They realized intuitively and immediately the divinity within themselves and all things. Having touched this, they called for lives of creative living.

Fox presents Jesus as a prophet who lived a life of creativity and calls others to realize that life themselves. At one point, Fox says, "[Jesus' way is] the way of the Creator, the way of Eros and life. It is a way of abundant blessing and overwhelming fertility, unimaginable greenness, one might say."[40] To Fox, in announcing the coming of the kingdom of God in his ministry, Jesus was not anticipating that God would intervene from outside to fix things in the future. Instead, Jesus was declaring that everyone has royalty or divinity within him- or herself, and Jesus regarded it as his mission to bring out that divinity in everyone.[41] Jesus lived and promoted a spirituality of original blessing that calls for an awareness of God now in one's life and one's living. As Fox summarizes the worldview of original blessing, it emphasizes "making the future (heaven) happen now," and that "Eternal life is now."[42]

The second theological work articulating Fox's creation spirituality is called *The Coming of the Cosmic Christ*. Many of the themes in *Original Blessing* recur, but this work contains a more explicit understanding of how specifically Christian categories can be used to interpret environmental devastation and promote environmental healing. What Fox means by the "cosmic Christ" is complex and layered. In its most general sense, however, it refers to the universal presence of God in the universe. It is God as known and experienced in creation as the source of order, but also of beauty and creativity, of love and ecstasy, of overwhelming fecundity and interrelatedness, of healing and reunion. This principle is recognized in the Old Testament in a variety of ways, including the divine Wisdom that permeates creation. Fox thinks Jesus preached it in his ministry but was also regarded by his followers as the incarnation of this cosmic principle. The New Testament proclaims the risen Christ as exalted above all other cosmic powers that would threaten the order, healing, and unity he brings. The cosmic Christ was grasped and understood by the early church fathers of the East and the medieval Christian mystics of the West.[43]

The cosmic Christ is a universal principle, and as such, it is recognized outside the Judeo-Christian tradition. Fox makes the point that indigenous people in particular lived by the intuition of the cosmic Christ and so lived in a world filled with the divine and permeated with blessing.[44] In the contemporary period, for Fox, intuition of the cosmic Christ embodies the possibility of healing. The coming of the cosmic Christ means the coming of a universal recognition of the divine within the natural world. This recognition alone contains the true hope of environmental restoration. Healing the environment would also involve healing human relationships and would lead to the transformation of religion.

Fox claims that in the past, Christianity was interpreted in ways that enabled it to fit the needs of the context. The contemporary context is that of an injured earth, and Christianity must be able to speak in images relevant to it. To this end, Fox suggests appropriating the Jesus story in a way that speaks to environmental harm and healing. Fox's proposal is that Jesus be symbolized as "Mother Earth" who is "crucified yet rising daily."[45] Like Jesus, Mother Earth is "innocent of any crime." Through eons, she has blessed all creatures. Despite this, humans crucify her with environmental harm. Yet the crucifixion is not the final word for Jesus or Mother Earth. As Jesus rises to new life, so Mother Earth rises daily and continues to shower her blessings. This symbolism, Fox says, "holds the capacity to launch a global spirituality of untold dimensions appropriate for the third millennium [of Christianity]."[46]

What Fox appears to affirm with this suggestion is that identifying Jesus with Mother Earth can be a way at least for Christians to discover anew their place in the cosmos. Currently, according to Fox, the universe is understood by modern people as a mechanical object, as no more than a set of moving parts that can be understood by mathematical calculations. This vision of the universe does not allow humans a meaningful spiritual place. But a vision that connects the familiar story of Jesus' death and resurrection with the suffering and rising of Mother Earth can provide such a place. Humans live and share in responsibility for the harm of earth, yet they are buoyed by the new life the earth brings forth.

This particular suggestion of Fox's has not been embraced by Christian groups in a significant way. Still, Fox's work as a whole remains significant as an important attempt to reinterpret Christianity to meet the charge of environmental harm primarily by resolutely affirming the presence and availability of God in and through the natural world. For Fox, the world is open to the divine presence that pulsates through it. The path to healing the earth and the human community comes by opening to this presence. Fox is adamant that one does not need to go outside Christianity to find a religion that affirms the accessibility of God's presence in the natural world. While his interpretations of the biblical and theological tradition can seem forced and one-sided, nevertheless, he fearlessly engages the tradition from the perspective of his distinctive vision.

The Universe Story: Thomas Berry and Brian Swimme

Thomas Berry (1915–2009) and Brian Swimme (1950–) came to write about ecological concerns from different places. Berry was a Catholic priest who spent most of his intellectual career studying and teaching non-Christian religions. Swimme is a physicist who was trained in mathematical cosmology. Each has had a long-standing interest in history, cosmology, religion, and the natural environment. They collaborated for approximately a decade, and from this collaboration came a work called *The Universe Story*. The book is not an explicitly Christian response to environmental concerns. It emerged, however, in a largely Christian context by thinkers influenced by Christianity. The direction taken by the text has implications for Christian reflection, so it is analyzed in this section.

What Berry and Swimme attempt to do in the text is tell the thirteen-billion-year history of the universe in one continuous and harmonious story. As they acknowledge in the book, this had not previously been done.[47] Previously, natural scientists—and, in particular, physicists and biologists—were often separately concerned with telling the story of the development of the material and organic universe. This includes an understanding of physical events from the big bang to the creation of the conditions for organic life on earth, and the profusion of organic life on earth in all its variety and interdependence by means of evolution through natural selection. Conversely, those working in the humanities and social sciences were concerned with telling the human story. This includes the development of economic and political systems, philosophical and religious worldviews, and the plethora of cultural patterns and psychological conditions that shape and have shaped human life on earth from its origins. These projects have never been brought together into a single story that would constitute the story of the universe.

Berry and Swimme were convinced the information was available to initiate this project, even though much of the information was tentative, so what could be said about the universe story was invariably provisional and would need to be open to change in the future. More than addressing whether the project could be done, however, they repeatedly claim in the book that the project needed to be undertaken. Throughout the text, two main reasons are given why this is the case.

First is the fact that new developments in our understanding of the universe call for a presentation of information about the universe in narrative form. The authors argue that in prior centuries, the universe was fundamentally understood by all human cultures as a "cosmos."[48] They mean by this that the universe was an orderly place of ever-renewing cycles of death and new life perceived primarily through seasonal changes. Through its cyclical changes, the universe was simply "there in some stable manner."[49]

This understanding of the universe changed in the twentieth century. For the first time, the universe itself was understood not simply as cosmos, but as "cosmogenesis."[50] By this term, Berry and Swimme mean a "continuing sequence of irreversible transformations" occurring according to the universe's own "self-shaping process."[51] Only in the contemporary period have people realized deeply that it is not the case that the universe simply "is." In fact, the universe "becomes." Within the universe are inner principles of development that have shaped and are shaping what comes into being in the flow of irreversible time. Whatever comes into being at any point in the ongoing process of the universe is always and invariably dependent upon past developments. Organic reality can come into being only after the process of billions of years of formation and organization of material reality that makes the emergence of the organic possible. Similarly, self-conscious beings can emerge only through hundreds of millions of years of organic developments. Whatever comes to be in this process is unique, distinctive, and irreplaceable. It was not there before and will not necessarily always be involved in cyclical renewal. Whatever emerges in the process of the universe not only depends upon past developments but also continues to exist in an interdependent way with the reality out of which it emerges.

If the universe and its objects all come to be in time through some irreversible and interdependent process, then the form of telling about this coming-to-be must be sequential narrative or story. Thus, Swimme and Berry propose to tell the universe story. Their goal is to include not only material and organic developments but also the coming of the human who, with the power of self-consciousness, is able to reflect on the coming-to-be of the universe itself. Human emergence as the tellers of the story must have a coherent place within the story.

The second reason the story needs to be told is that the authors believe telling this story fulfills an important spiritual and ethical need for contemporary people. In the past, humans have understood their place in the universe by telling the story of the universe, often (although not exclusively) in the form of creation myths. Such stories have "given meaning to life and to existence itself." They have served as the human's "fundamental referent as regards modes of personal and community conduct."[52] Through the telling of such stories, human beings know who they are, where they belong in the universe, and how their societies and their social organization fit into the larger scheme of things.

Berry and Swimme think humans have lost a comprehensive orienting story today. As a result, contemporary humans have "a distorted mode of human presence upon the Earth."[53] The interdependence of humans with all other material and organic systems is lost. Lacking the sense of interconnection, humans have developed a "commercial-industrial mystique" that determines their relation to the natural world.[54] This mystique is actually a new kind of myth where the earth is understood as an object to be controlled and used. Science and technology make possible this control, and trust is placed in them to provide the solutions to any possible problems that may emerge through the execution of this control. Economic growth and increasing consumption are unquestioned goods.[55] This myth or mystique needs to be replaced by the new myth of the universe story.

Berry and Swimme affirm that the universe story is derived from empirical insights of science about the universe and from humanistic studies of culture. As such, it is a universal story rather than the tribal story of a select group of people or the revealed beliefs of a particular religion. As they say, it is "scientific in its data, mythic in its form."[56] It is the story of the emergence of all things, and as such, it is to function in some sense as an orienting story for all people.

While their story is grounded in scientific and cultural knowledge, the authors make it clear that as part of its mythical character, the universe story is meant to evoke a religious sensibility. Telling the one-directional story of the development and interdependence of all things in the universe and on earth brings forth a "sense of the sacred."[57] The "mysterious self-organizing power" present in the universe from the beginning that produces cosmogenesis in the temporal sequence evokes a "sense of awe."[58] With regard to the process of cosmogenesis, the authors claim humans are to "enter into the process, to honor the process, to accept the process as a sacred context for existence and meaning."[59] They propose that humans find ways to celebrate the transitions of cosmogenesis that involve "the sense of the sacred."[60] This emphasis in particular makes their work an exercise in creation spirituality.

As the authors express it, the sense of the sacredness of the cosmos that comes through the telling of the story is not to "suppress" other religious stories. It is to provide "a more comprehensive context in which all these earlier stories discover in themselves a new validity and a more expansive role."[61] The authors do not develop how other religions might understand themselves in light of this new context, nor do they entertain the question of whether the universe story by itself could be an adequate religious expression for at least some people.

The telling of the universe story by Berry and Swimme has a creative flair. Over half of the book is devoted to the story of the emergence and organization of material and organic life. A tremendous amount of knowledge is synthesized from the sciences and human culture to present the story in a readable format for nonexperts. As expected, vast expanses of history are often covered rapidly by means of significant generalizations.

At each turn, the scientific, religious, philosophical, economic, political, social, and cultural history they describe can be questioned. At the same time, the authors display fearlessness, steadfastness, and considerable erudition in telling the story.

As a work of creation spirituality, *The Universe Story* is unique. Unlike the writings of Edwards or Santmire, it does not involve retelling Christian salvation history in a way that brings the importance of the natural environment to the forefront. There is no focus on the entire universe as somehow being brought to an ultimate fulfillment by God. Instead, *The Universe Story* treats Christianity as one religion among many. Christianity emerges in history with distinctive features and makes its unique contribution to human life and culture. The sacredness of the universe Berry and Swimme seek to articulate is not in its future consummation but in its awe-inspiring capacity to produce through a temporal process astonishing variety and beauty in its material, organic, and human forms of being. The creation spirituality of *The Universe Story* is also unlike that of Matthew Fox. Predominantly, Fox seeks to evoke a mystical experience that perceives the divine in the universe in the here and now. Fox's vision is most fundamentally of an atemporal presence of the divine. Conversely, the overwhelming stress of *The Universe Story* is the sense of sacredness that things bear because of their unique becoming. For Berry and Swimme, sacredness is evoked in the one-directional movement of the universe by means of which unique and irreplaceable forms of being emerge.

It is Berry and Swimme's hope that the cultural absorption of the universe story will lead to an era they call the "ecozoic."[62] They understand this as an era in which the primary concern of human activity and the primary criterion of ethical decision making are what benefits the entire planet, all of its natural features and their manifold expressions, and all of its forms of life. Ultimately, this ethical outcome should emerge from embracing the story.

Discussion Questions and Further Reading

Chapter 1—Setting the Stage

DISCUSSION QUESTIONS

1. Do contemporary Western people have a common worldview on issues like the origin and destiny of the cosmos, the origin of life on earth, the place of humans in the cosmos, and the reason for sin and suffering? Is it culturally important to have a common worldview on these issues?

2. What did Deists believe? What does Christianity have in common with Deism? What aspects of Deism might Christians find troubling or deficient?

3. Do you agree that critical and autonomous reason are characteristic features of the worldview of contemporary people? What are cultural examples of critical and autonomous reason? Is the emergence of critical and autonomous reason positive, problematic, or some combination of the two?

4. What are the main hypotheses of historical criticism of the Bible? What questions or challenges does historical criticism raise for Christianity? Should Christians take these questions or challenges seriously, or regard them as an aberration to be rejected on the basis of faith? What role does accepting Christian truths on faith play in responding to the questions and challenges of historical criticism?

FURTHER READING

Anderson, Bernhard, Steven Bishop, and Judith Newman. *Understanding the Old Testament*. 5th ed. Upper Saddle River N.J.: Prentice Hall, 2006. An excellent introduction to the Old Testament literature that applies the tools and insights of historical criticism.

Baird, William. "New Testament Criticism," in *The Anchor Bible Dictionary*, vol. 1, edited by David Noel Freedman. New York: Doubleday, 1992. A concise and informative history and typology of critical approaches to the New Testament literature.

Brown, Raymond. *An Introduction to the New Testament*. New Haven: Yale University Press, 1997. An excellent introduction to the New Testament literature that applies the tools and insights of historical criticism.

Ehrman, Bart D. *The New Testament: A Historical Introduction to the Early Christian Writings*. 4th ed. Oxford: Oxford University Press, 2007. An introduction to the New Testament literature that is especially helpful for clearly articulating a variety of methods used for understanding the New Testament.

Gay, Peter. *The Enlightenment: A Comprehensive Anthology*. New York: Simon and Schuster, 1973. A massive and important text that includes selections from key Enlightenment thinkers.

Gay, Peter. *The Enlightenment: The Rise of Modern Paganism*. New York: W. W. Norton, 1995. *The Enlightenment: The Science of Freedom*. New York: W. W. Norton, 1996. These two volumes are classic works on the Enlightenment by one of its greatest historians.

Hayes, John, "Biblical Interpretation, History of," in *The New Interpreters Dictionary of the Bible*, vol. 1. Edited by Katherine Doob Sakenfeld. Nashville: Abingdon, 2006. A concise and informative examination of approaches to biblical interpretation, including the emergence of critical methods in the modern period.

Jacob, Margaret. *The Enlightenment: A Brief History with Documents*. Boston: Bedford; New York: St. Martins, 2000. An accessible approach to the Enlightenment that includes readings with historical interpretation and analysis.

Kant, Immanuel. *What Is Enlightenment?* in *Foundations of the Metaphysics of Morals and What is Enlightenment*. New York: Macmillan, 1990. A classic, brief, and accessible primary source on the Enlightenment and its meaning by one of its leading proponents.

Locke, John. *The Reasonableness of Christianity*. Washington D.C.: Regnery Gateway, 1965. A seminal Enlightenment thinker, who is not a Deist, argues for the reasonableness of Christian beliefs.

O'Neill, J. C. "Biblical Criticism," in *The Anchor Bible Dictionary*, vol. 1. Edited by David Noel Freedman. New York: Doubleday, 1992. A concise overview of the history of biblical criticism focusing on developments in the modern period.

Paine, Thomas, *The Age of Reason*, Part 1. New York: Macmillan, 1989. A classic and accessible work of Deism from the American context.

Chapter 2—Surveying the Field

DISCUSSION QUESTIONS

1. Does biblical literalism lead to conflicts between faith and the insights of contemporary reason? If so, are these conflicts troubling or are they mostly unimportant?

2. Are theological literalists too willing to sacrifice important elements of the Christian faith to modern thought, or are they too traditional in their interpretation of Christianity?

3. Have theological reinterpreters sacrificed essential elements of Christian belief? Can the Christian church embrace those who hold some variation of this position?

4. How do biblical literalists, theological literalists, and theological reinterpreters each justify their theological positions? How important is it for Christians to have rational justifications for their beliefs? Are universally valid justifications possible for all Christian beliefs?

5. How much is a person's theological position determined by where the person was born and the person's religious upbringing? What kinds of factors may lead someone to diverge from the theological position of his or her upbringing? Are those factors always rational?

FURTHER READING

Bultmann, Rudolph. *New Testament and Mythology and Other Basic Writings.* Edited and translated by Schubert Ogden. Philadelphia: Fortress Press, 1984. Bultmann's controversial essay "New Testament and Mythology" is essential reading for anyone seeking to understand the meaning of modern thought for contemporary theology.

Erickson, Millard. *Christian Theology.* 2nd ed. Grand Rapids: Baker Academic, 1998. A substantial work of theology dealing with all of the major themes and promoting a biblical literalist point of view.

Grenz, Stanley. *Theology for the Community of God.* Grand Rapids: Eerdmanns; Vancouver: Regent College, 2000. A significant work of theology covering the main themes from an evangelical perspective.

Livingston, James C. *Modern Christian Thought: The Enlightenment and the Nineteenth Century,* vol. 1. 2nd ed. Upper Saddle River, N.J.: Prentice Hall, 1997; and Livingston, James C. et al, *Modern Christian Thought: The Twentieth Century,* vol. 2. 2nd ed. Upper Saddle River, N.J.: Prentice Hall, 2000. Two important works covering Christian thought from the age of Enlightenment through the advent of post-modernism.

McGrath, Alistair. *Christian Theology: An Introduction.* 5th ed. West Sussex, U.K.: Wiley-Blackwell, 2011. An important introduction to Christian theology that includes significant analyses of important theologians in the history of Christian thought and seeks to integrate and discuss Protestant, Catholic, and Orthodox points of view.

Migliorie, Daniel. *Faith Seeking Understanding*. 2nd ed. Grand Rapids: Eerd-mans, 2004. A sophisticated survey of major theological themes from a contem-porary Reformed Protestant perspective.

Placher, William, ed. *Essentials of Christian Theology*. Louisville: Westminster John Knox, 2003. A text that places into dialogue leading theologians from mainstream Protestantism, evangelical Protestantism, and Roman Catholicism on key theological questions.

Spong, John Shelby. *A New Christianity for a New World*. San Francisco: Harp-erCollins, 2001. Written by an Episcopal bishop who argues for the importance of reinterpreting Christian theology in this accessible volume.

Tillich, Paul. *Systematic Theology*. 3 vols. Chicago: University of Chicago Press, 1951–1963. A groundbreaking theological work written to provide Christian answers to the questions arising from modern thought.

Chapter 3—God and Cosmology

DISCUSSION QUESTIONS

1. Why are there no proofs for God's existence in the Bible? Is this a shortfall or a strength of the biblical tradition?

2. What would be the implications for Christian theology if there were a definitive, universal, rational proof for the traditional God of monotheism? What would be the implications for Christian theology if there were no definitive, universal, rational proof for the traditional God of monotheism? Are the proofs for God's existence convincing enough that if someone denies God's existence they can be regarded as rebelling against God?

3. Why do Karl Barth and Paul Tillich reject proofs for God's existence as the basis of their theologies? Whose theological approach is more convincing? How would they critique each other?

4. What are the similarities and differences in the conception of the relationship between God and the universe in Deism, interventionist theism, and panenthe-ism? Is it possible to think of God as real without applying categories of the human mind to God?

5. What terms do Christians commonly use to refer to God? Are these terms literal or metaphorical? Are some terms more obviously metaphorical than oth-ers? How can God be transcendent and unknowable, and how can it also be the case that human language meaningfully applies to God?

FURTHER READING

Clayton, Philip, and Arthur Peacocke, eds. *In Whom We Live and Move and Have Our Being: Panentheistic Reflections on God's Presence in a Scientific World*. Grand Rapids: Eerdmans, 2004. An in-depth look at the meaning of panentheism today by a diverse group of scientists and theologians.

Gilkey, Langdon. "God" in *Christian Theology: An Introduction to its Traditions and Tasks*. Minneapolis: Fortress Press, 1994. An introduction to classical and contemporary issues in Christian reflection about God.

Hick, John. *Philosophy of Religion*. 4th ed. Upper Saddle River. N.J.: Prentice Hall, 1989. An analysis of the main themes in the philosophy of religion, including debates about arguments for the existence of God.

Hick, John, ed., *Classical and Contemporary Readings in the Philosophy of Religion*. 3rd ed. Upper Saddle River, N.J.: Prentice Hall, 1989. A selection of primary sources in the philosophy of religion containing works of both historical and contemporary significance.

McFague, Sallie. *Models of God: Theology for an Ecological Nuclear Age*. Minneapolis: Fortress Press, 1987. A notable work in which the ecofeminist Sallie McFague explores the meaning of referring to God as mother, lover, and friend.

McGrath, Alistair, *Christian Theology: An Introduction*. 5th ed. West Sussex, U.K.: Wiley-Blackwell, 2011. A significant work of theology that contains a major section exploring both classical and contemporary issues regarding the doctrine of God.

Pojman, Louis, and Michael Rea, eds. *Philosophy of Religion: An Anthology*. 5th ed. Belmont: Wadsworth, 2007. An anthology covering significant works in the history of the philosophy of religion.

Rowe, William. *Philosophy of Religion*. 4th ed. Belmont: Wadsworth, 2006. An analysis of the main themes in the philosophy of religion, including debates about arguments for the existence of God.

Tillich, Paul. *The Courage to Be*. New Haven and London: Yale University Press, 1952; and *Dynamics of Faith*. New York: Harper and Row, 1957; *Systematic Theology*, vol. 1. Chicago: University of Chicago Press, 1951. Paul Tillich's ideas about religion, culture, God, and God's relation to the universe are developed in distinctive ways in each work.

Chapter 4—Christ and History

DISCUSSION QUESTIONS

1. In what ways are the following types of literature both like and unlike the New Testament Gospels: a newspaper report, a history book, a novel, a biography, a fictional account based on a true story?

2. What are the implications if the early church, over time, developed the idea of Jesus' identity and the meaning of his death and resurrection rather than receiving these things fully formed from Jesus himself? What does this mean regarding Jesus and the nature of his consciousness? What does it mean for affirming or proving the truth of the early church's position?

3. What did many early church leaders regard as threatening about the emergence of a Gnostic interpretation of Christianity?

4. Was the historical Jesus the teacher of a refined morality, an apocalyptic prophet, or a teacher of subversive wisdom? Should theology be based on a scholarly reconstruction of the historical Jesus?

5. Is it problematic that there are a variety of Christologies in the contemporary context, or is it one of Christianity's strengths that it can be interpreted in a number of different ways?

FURTHER READING

Boff, Leonardo. *Jesus Christ Liberator: A Critical Christology for Our Times*. New York: Orbis, 1978; and Boff, Leonardo, and Clodovis Boff. *Introducing Liberation Theology*. New York: Orbis, 2002. The first listed work of Leonardo Boff is a classic work on Christology from a liberation perspective. The second work, written with his brother Clodovis, is an excellent general introduction to the themes and goals of liberation theology.

Bultmann, Rudolph. *New Testament and Mythology and Other Basic Writings*. Edited and translated by Schubert Ogden. Philadelphia: Fortress Press, 1984. Contains the essentials of existentialist theology.

Crossan, John Dominic. *The Historical Jesus: The Life of a Mediterranean Jewish Peasant*. New York: HarperCollins, 1991; and *Jesus: A Revolutionary Biography*. New York: HarperCollins, 1994. The first listed work of Crossan is a scholarly text in which he promotes a nonapocalyptic portrayal of the historical Jesus. The second work is a shortened and more accessible restatement of the main ideas in the first work.

Ehrman, Bart D., ed. *Lost Scriptures: Books that Did Not Make It into the New Testament*. Oxford: Oxford University Press, 2003; and *Lost Christianities: The Battles for Scripture and the Faiths We Never Knew*. Oxford: Oxford University Press, 2005. The first listed work is a good selection of primary sources from the first and second century of the Christian movement that did not make it into the New Testament. The second work is an accessible reconstruction of the history of the early Christian movement, emphasizing the diversity it contained in its first few centuries.

Funk, Robert, et al., eds. *The Five Gospels: What Did Jesus Really Say?* New York: Polebridge, 1993; and *The Acts of Jesus: What Did Jesus Really Do?* New York: Polebridge, 1998. These two works represent the findings of "The Jesus Seminar," a group of scholars who met regularly in the 1990s to examine the New Testament Gospels and the Gospel of Thomas. They voted on the authenticity of the recorded sayings and deeds of Jesus. Their findings, commentary, and a new translation of the Gospels are in these volumes.

González, Justo. *A History of Christian Thought: From the Beginnings to the Council of Chalcedon*, vol. 1. Rev. ed. Nashville: Abingdon, 1987. A classic work on the history of Christian ideas by one of the great historians of the church.

Kasser, Rodolphe, et al, eds. *The Gospel of Judas.* 2nd ed. Washington D.C.: National Geographic, 2008. A translation of the newly discovered Gospel purported to have been written by Jesus' disciple Judas.

Moltmann, Jürgen. *Theology of Hope.* New York: Harper and Row, 1967; and *The Crucified God.* New York: Harper and Row, 1974. Two classic works of the theology of hope by one of the great Protestant theologians of the contemporary period.

Pagels, Elaine. *The Gnostic Gospels.* New York: Vintage, 1979. A classic work on Gnosticism in the early Christian movement and the combination of politics and theology that led to its eradication.

Sanders, E. P. *The Historical Figure of Jesus.* New York: Penguin, 1996. A contemporary work on the historical Jesus by a significant scholar that argues for an apocalyptic portrayal of Jesus.

White, Michael L. *From Jesus to Christianity: How Four Generations of Visionaries and Storytellers Created the New Testament and Christian Faith.* San Francisco: HarperCollins, 2004. A detailed reconstruction of the theological variety, along with the social and political issues, faced by the Christian movement in its first 150 years.

Chapter 5—Heaven, Hell, and Anthropology

DISCUSSION QUESTIONS

1. Since there are different views of the afterlife in biblical literature, should one expect different views in Christianity today? Is Christian belief compatible with denial of a vital afterlife?

2. What elements of Plato's understanding of the afterlife are compatible with the Hebrew understanding, and what elements are incompatible with the Hebrew view? Was it positive or problematic when classical Christian eschatology adopted elements of the Platonic view?

3. What elements of Christian theology need to be reconceptualized in light of the contemporary understanding that human beings emerged through a long evolutionary process? Does this new understanding require a radical rethinking of Christian doctrines or merely minor revisions to Christian ideas?

4. Does belief in the divine restoration of all things at the end of time motivate action in the present for social justice and environmental healing, or does such a belief hamper motivation for social justice and environmental healing?

5. What are the crucial differences between Hick's theodicy and process theodicy? How could one decide the issue between them whether an all-powerful God intentionally made the universe with evil and suffering in it or whether a limited God is perfecting an imperfect and unfinished universe?

FURTHER READING

Braaten, Carl E., and Robert W. Jenson, eds. *The Last Things: Biblical and Theological Perspectives on Eschatology*. Grand Rapids: Eerdmans, 2002. An extended argument by several contemporary theologians for the importance of eschatology for contemporary theology.

Cobb, John, and David Ray Griffin. *Process Theology: An Introductory Exposition*. Philadelphia: Westminster, 1976. An accessible introduction to the approach and main themes of process theology.

Griffin, David Ray. *God, Power, and Evil: A Process Theodicy*. Philadelphia: Westminster, 1976; and *Evil Revisited: Responses and Reconsiderations*. New York: SUNY Press, 1991. Two important works on theodicy and the afterlife from a process perspective by a contemporary process theologian.

Hick, John. *Evil and the God of Love*. Rev. ed. New York: Harper & Row, 1978; and *Death and Eternal Life*. London: Collins, 1976. Works containing Hick's ground-breaking theodicy and his understanding of the afterlife.

McGrath, Alistair, ed. *The Christian Theology Reader*. Oxford: Blackwell, 1995. An excellent introduction to the main themes of Christian theology through primary source readings. Text includes readings from Augustine on sin and salvation, as well as a section on eschatology.

Walls, Jerry, ed. *The Oxford Handbook of Eschatology*. New York: Oxford University Press, 2008. A significant volume that covers a wide spectrum of issues on eschatology by contemporary theologians who represent a variety of perspectives.

Chapter 6—Christianity and Other Religions

DISCUSSION QUESTIONS

1. Why does monotheism tend to be exclusive of other religions? Is this a strength of monotheism or a troubling aspect that needs to be overcome?

2. Are the historical contingency problem and the revelation acceptance problem more significant issues in the contemporary context than in other eras of Christian history?

3. Is unshakable certainty about the truth of Christianity an important part of Christian faith, or does it potentially show a narrow-minded and insecure expression of that faith?

4. How important is it for a contemporary Christian to familiarize her- or himself with the history and beliefs of the major non-Christian world religions?

5. Are the positions of exclusivism, inclusivism, and pluralism adequately judged by how well they answer or respond to the historical contingency and revelation acceptance problems? If the adequacy of the response to these problems functions as the main criterion for the validity of one's theology, have these problems gained an undeserved significance?

6. Does any religious theory that proposes to understand all of the world religions invariably falsify and distort the particularities of those religions? How can one understand other religions if not through some comprehensive and universalizing theory of religion?

FURTHER READING

Hedges, Paul, and Alan Race eds. *Christian Approaches to Other Faiths*. London: SCM, 2008. An analysis of Christianity and other religions by contemporary theologians that both uses and transcends the categories of exclusivism, inclusivism, and pluralism.

Hick, John. *An Interpretation of Religion*. New Haven: Yale University Press, 1989; and *A Christian Theology of Religions*. Louisville: Westminster John Knox, 1995. Significant works by Hick that present both his pluralist hypothesis and his conception of what pluralism means for Christianity.

Hick, John, and Brian Hebblethwaite, eds. *Christianity and Other Religions: Selected Readings*. Rev. ed. Oxford: Oneworld, 2001. An excellent introduction to the thinking of several major Protestant and Roman Catholic theologians on the issue of the relationship between Christianity and other religions.

Knitter, Paul. *Introducing Theologies of Religion*. Maryknoll N.Y.: Orbis, 2002. An excellent, accessible introduction to contemporary theological perspectives on the relationship between Christianity and other religions. The volume critiques the categories of exculsivism, inclusivism, and pluralism for others deemed better suited for the complexities of the situation.

Lindbeck, George. *The Nature of Doctrine*. Philadelphia: Westminster, 1984. A brief yet groundbreaking work in which Lindbeck articulates his understanding of the meaning of religion for the contemporary context.

McFague, Sallie. *A New Climate for Theology: God, the World, and Global Warming*. Minneapolis: Fortress Press, 2008.

Ockholm, Dennis L., and Timothy R. Phillips, eds. *Four Views of Salvation in a Pluralistic World*. Grand Rapids: Zondervan, 1996. An engaging text that involves a presentation and dialogue between John Hick and three evangelical theologians on the relationship between Christianity and other religions.

Wallace, Mark I. *Green Christianity: Five Ways to a Sustainable Future*. Minneapolis: Fortress Press, 2010.

Chapter 7—Christianity and Feminism

DISCUSSION QUESTIONS

1. What is feminism? Does the term have a negative connotation in the contemporary context? Are feminism and feminist theology still needed?

2. Is it possible to critique the Bible for its patriarchy and still revere the Bible as containing God's word? How can those who are willing to critique patriarchy in the Bible avoid the charge that they only affirm what they want to affirm in the Bible and they avoid those things they simply do not like?

3. Name three of the most prominent women in the Bible and Christian tradition. Are they good role models for female Christians today? Do contemporary Christian women need historical female role models?

4. Does the use of exclusively male God-language reinforce patriarchy? Is this a significant enough issue that churches should consciously transform the language they use for God in worship? What are the alternatives to exclusively male God-language?

5. Are the feminist proposals for expanding the Christian understanding of sin an important development of this doctrine, or do they sidestep and avoid the central Christian understanding of sin?

6. Is the understanding of salvation in Christian feminist theology significant enough and rooted deeply enough in the Christian tradition to serve as the paradigmatic understanding of salvation for Christianity today?

FURTHER READING

An, Choi Hee, and Katheryn Pfisterer Darr. *Engaging the Bible*. Minneapolis: Fortress Press, 2006. A fascinating look at a number of different approaches taken toward the biblical literature by contemporary feminists who come from a variety of cultural perspectives.

Christ, Carol, and Judith Plaskow, eds. *Womenspirit Rising: A Feminist Reader in Religion*. San Francisco: HarperCollins, 1979; and *Weaving the Visions: New Patterns in Feminist Spirituality*. San Francisco: HarperOne, 1989. Two significant readers in feminist theology that contain many classic authors and breakthrough ideas. Both include but are not limited to Christian feminist theology.

Clifford, Anne. *Introducing Feminist Theology*. Maryknoll, N.Y.: Orbis, 2001. A good introduction to the main themes of Christian feminist theology.

Groothuis, Rebecca Merrill. *Good News for Women*. Grand Rapids: Baker, 1997. An evangelical approach to the biblical text that denies delimiting patriarchy within it.

Isasi-Diaz, Ada Maria. *Mujerista Theology*. Maryknoll, N.Y.: Orbis, 1996. An important work of Christian feminist theology from the perspective of Latin American women.

Japinga, Lyn. *Feminism and Christianity: An Essential Guide*. Nashville: Abingdon, 1999. An accessible introduction to the main themes of Christian feminist theology that includes revealing and provocative insights about feminism and contemporary culture.

Johnson, Elizabeth. *She Who Is: The Mystery of God in Feminist Theological Discourse*. 10th anniv. ed. New York: Crossroad, 2002. An important work in Christian feminist theology. especially in its engagement of the issue of language for God in the biblical and theological tradition.

Ruether, Rosemary. *Sexism and God-Talk*. Boston: Beacon, 1983; and *Introducing Redemption in Christian Feminism*. Sheffield: Sheffield Academic, 1998. The first work is a classic in the field of Christian feminist theology that examines an extraordinary range of biblical, historical, and theological issues in a sophisticated way from a feminist perspective. The second work summarizes and develops the critical and constructive approach of feminist theology regarding the Christian idea of redemption through Jesus Christ.

Schüssler Fiorenza, Elisabeth. *In Memory of Her: A Feminist Theological Reconstruction of Christian Origins*. New York: Crossroad, 1983. A groundbreaking work of feminist biblical analysis that argues for the increasing presence of patriarchy in the early Christian movement impacting the construction of the biblical text.

Williams, Delores. *Sisters in the Wilderness: The Challenge of Womanist God-Talk*. Maryknoll N.Y.: Orbis, 1993. An important work in Christian feminist theology from the perspective of African American women.

Chapter 8—Christianity and Homosexuality

DISCUSSION QUESTIONS

1. How are the issues regarding the place and role of homosexuals in the church similar and different from the issues regarding the place and role of women in the church?

2. In an ideal situation, how do the sources of authority function together to guide the church? Are the three sources of authority always effective in the decisions of denominations regarding contemporary issues, or are some denominations correct in denying the legitimacy of sources of authority other than the Bible?

3. How do those who take a critical-thematic approach to the Bible avoid the charge that they are judging the Bible by their own standards and overlooking those things in the Bible they simply do not like?

4. Are the Levitical prohibitions against gay sex best understood as moral laws or purity laws?

5. What did Paul mean when he said in Romans that homosexual sex involves an exchange of the natural for the unnatural? What does the interpretation of this passage mean for the church today?

6. Where should one turn for valid insights from contemporary reason about homosexuality? Are the insights of contemporary reason regarding homosexuality secure enough to outweigh traditional Christian teaching and specific biblical passages on this issue?

FURTHER READING

Grenz, Stanley. *Welcoming but not Affirming*. Louisville: Westminster John Knox, 1998. A notable evangelical theologian engages the issue of the place and role of homosexuals in the church.

Helminiak, Daniel. *What the Bible Really Says about Homosexuality*. San Francisco: Alamo Square, 1994. An in-depth analysis of the particular biblical passages on homosexual sex that contextualizes the reasons behind the condemnations.

McNeill, John J. *Sex as God Intended*. Maple Shade, N.J.: Lethe, 2008. A former Roman Catholic Priest argues for a biblically based understanding of sex that includes gay sex.

Nissinen, Martti. *Homoeroticism in the Biblical World.* Minneapolis: Fortress Press, 1998. An examination of the understanding of same-sex sexual relations in the larger cultural context from which the Bible comes.

Rogers, Jack. *Jesus, the Bible, and Homosexuality: Explode the Myths, Heal the Church.* Rev. and expanded ed. Louisville: Westminster John Knox, 2009. A Reformed theologian examines the issue of homosexuality for the church focusing especially on approaches to biblical interpretation.

Seow, Choon-Leong, ed. *Homosexuality and Christian Community.* Louisville: Westminster John Knox, 1996. An examination of the issue of homosexuality and the church that includes a variety of theologians and biblical scholars on both sides of the issue.

Siker, Jeffrey, ed. *Homosexuality in the Church: Both Sides of the Debate.* Louisville: Westminster John Knox, 1994. An excellent introduction to the issue presenting arguments for each side by a variety of thinkers and engaging all of the sources of authority.

Via, Dan, and Robert Gagnon. *Homosexuality and the Bible: Two Views.* Minneapolis: Fortress Press, 2003. Two biblical scholars who are also theologians engage the issue of homosexuality in the Bible and church.

Chapter 9—Christianity and the Natural Environment

DISCUSSION QUESTIONS

1. Has the health and well-being of the natural environment become a significant priority in U.S. social and political life and personal decision-making? Has religion helped make concern for the natural environment more of a priority, or has it diminished the prioritization of the natural environment as a compelling concern?

2. Is Christianity inherently an anthropocentric religion?

3. Is the idea of stewardship of creation comprehensive and effective enough to serve as the foundational model for the Christian understanding of the relation between God, humans, and the natural world?

4. Does the incarnation of God in Jesus Christ occur only as a result of human sin, or was it God's plan for creation from the start? Does the Divine restoration of all creation provide sufficient motivation for environmental activism, or is it too future oriented, potentially overlooking what needs to be done for environmental restoration in the present?

5. Is it possible for traditional Christian monotheism to affirm that God is present in all things without sacrificing God's transcendence or becoming

idolatrous? Can all of creation and the becoming of the new within creation be regarded as sacred without falling prey to idolatry?

FURTHER READING

DeWitt, Calvin B. *Caring for Creation: Responsible Stewardship of God's Handiwork*. Grand Rapids: Baker, 1998. A succinct argument for stewardship from an evangelical Protestant perspective.

Edwards, Denis. *Ecology at the Heart of Faith*. Maryknoll, N.Y.: Orbis, 2006. A clearly written, accessible, and comprehensive examination of a variety of Christian responses to environmental issues from a Roman Catholic perspective.

Foltz, Richard, ed. *Worldviews, Religion, and the Environment: A Global Anthology*. Belmont: Wadsworth, 2002. A significant anthology in the area of religion and the environment that includes but is not limited to Christian theology.

Fox, Matthew. *Original Blessing*. Santa Fe: Bear and Co., 1983; and *The Coming of the Cosmic Christ*. San Francisco: Harper and Row, 1988. Two works of creation spirituality that creatively promote an understanding of the presence of God in all things.

Gottlieb, Roger, ed. *This Sacred Earth: Religion, Nature, Environment*. New York: Routledge, 1996; and *The Oxford Handbook of Religion and Ecology*. New York: Oxford University Press, 2010. Two significant anthologies in the area of religion and the environment. Neither is limited to Christianity and the environment, although developments in western theology addressing environmental concerns are prominent in each work.

Santmire, Paul H. *The Travail of Nature*. Minneapolis: Fortress Press, 1985; and *Nature Reborn*. Minneapolis: Fortress Press, 2000. The first work argues there is an ambiguity in Christian theology between those elements and thinkers in the tradition that support environmental care and those that do not. The second work argues in favor of a Christian message of environmental care that would overcome the ambiguity in the tradition.

Swimme, Brian, and Thomas Berry. *The Universe Story*. New York: HarperCollins, 1992. A narrative of the unfolding of the universe from the big bang to the present day focusing on the emergence of the new through time.

VanDyke, Fred, et al. *Redeeming Creation: The Biblical Basis for Environmental Stewardship*. Downers Grove, Ill.: InterVarsity, 1996. A call for environmental stewardship from an evangelical perspective written by four biologists.

Notes

CHAPTER 1: SETTING THE STAGE

1. In *The Enlightenment: A Comprehensive Anthology*, ed. Peter Gay (New York: Simon & Schuster, 1973), 384.

2. Two important Enlightenment thinkers from different countries and different generations who broadly affirmed limiting Christian truth to what can be shown to accord with reason were John Locke and Immanuel Kant. Their stress on the importance of reason in religion is seen in the titles of their respective books on religion. Locke's book is called *The Reasonableness of Christianity* (Washington, D.C.: Regnery Gateway, 1965), originally published anonymously in 1695, and Kant's is *Religion within the Limits of Reason Alone* (New York: Harper & Brothers, 1960), originally published in 1793.

3. This is a common theme, for example, in Thomas Paine's *The Age of Reason*, part 1 (New York: Macmillan, 1989), originally published in 1794.

4. Classic deist works include Matthew Tindal, *Christianity as Old as the Creation* (originally published in 1730), and Thomas Paine, *The Age of Reason*.

5. This is not to deny the influence of what could be called "background religious beliefs," or a religious worldview of a certain kind, on scientific discoveries. An analysis of the history of science shows that certain religious worldviews have opened up or made possible an approach to reality that led to certain scientific discoveries.

This is also not to claim that science is purely objective or that it looks at the world in a purely rational, unbiased way. Theoreticians working in the philosophy of science today are, on the whole, sensitive to the way in which science is determined by paradigms that, on some level, rest on nonrational factors. The point is not that science is purely rational, but that it is autonomously self-critical. It seeks critical refinement of its paradigms or new paradigms that more adequately account for problematic elements in old paradigms. It does not, nor should it, submit to revealed authorities to solve scientific problems.

For a sophisticated and systematic discussion of a multitude of issues and perspectives in the fascinating field of religion and science, see Ian Barbour, *Religion and Science: Historical and Contemporary Issues*, rev. ed. (San Francisco: HarperCollins, 1997).

6. Barbour, *Religion and Science*, 9–17.

7. One of the best ways to understand historical criticism is to see how it operates by examining a contemporary academic textbook on the Old Testament/Hebrew Bible or New Testament. Good textbooks summarize major scholarly findings and debates about the biblical texts. A useful example for the Old Testament is Bernhard Anderson, Steven Bishop, and Judith Newman, *Understanding the Old Testament*, 5th ed. (Upper Saddle River, N.J.: Prentice Hall, 2006). Useful examples for the New Testament are Raymond Brown, *An Introduction to the New Testament* (New Haven: Yale University Press, 1997); and Bart Ehrman, *The New Testament: A Historical Introduction to the Early Christian Writings*, 4th ed. (Oxford: Oxford University Press, 2007).

8. As historical critics know, it is actually more complex than this. The biblical authors did not assume a sharp natural/supernatural distinction that contemporary people assume as a heritage of the Enlightenment. In Old Testament times, for example, people did not think that the universe ran by autonomous natural laws, and that now and then, God chose to act in history and break those laws. Instead, they thought the universe's orderly operation was due to the fact that God covenanted with the natural world to make things run in an orderly way. At times, God acted in peculiar ways within this covenant, producing signs and wonders to display God's power and glory. In other words, in the Old Testament view, God was involved with the universe's operation all the time, and sometimes God's involvement took the peculiar and more spectacular form of special signs and wonders. Still, there was a claim of direct involvement by God in natural events like droughts or floods that people today would chalk up to natural causes.

9. As early as the second century, we see this argument in the famous Christian apologist Justin. See "The First Apology of Justin, the Martyr" in *Early Christian Fathers*, ed. Cyril Richardson (New York: Macmillan, 1970), 260–77.

10. These arguments are developed in chapter 4.

CHAPTER 2: SURVEYING THE FIELD

1. Good examples of major theological works that represent biblical literalism and present sophisticated understandings of inerrancy are Wayne Grudem, *Systematic Theology* (Grand Rapids: Zondervan, 1994), 90–104; and Millard Erickson, *Christian Theology*, 2nd ed. (Grand Rapids: Baker Academic, 1998), 246–65.

2. Douglas O. Linder, "*State v. John Scopes*," found at University of Missouri–Kansas City, n.d., http://www.law.umkc.edu/faculty/projects/ftrials/scopes/evolut.htm.

3. David Masci, "The Social and Legal Dimensions of the Evolution Debate in the U.S.," *Pew Forum*, February 4, 2009, http://pewforum.org/docs/?DocID=396.

4. Ibid.

5. Pew Research Center for the People and the Press, "Reading the Polls on Evolution and Creationism," Pew Research Center Pollwatch, *Commentary*, September 28, 2005, http://people-press.org/commentary/?analysisid=118.

6. Epistemology is a theory of how we know something. In this case, it refers to a theory of how we know certain theological truths.

7. This is according to a major poll conducted by the Pew Forum on Religion and Public Life in 2008. See "U.S. Religious Landscape Survey: Affiliations," *Pew Forum*, n.d., http://religions.pewforum.org/affiliations.

8. Ibid.

9. Barth's major theological work, *Church Dogmatics*, contains multiple volumes and thousands of pages. Good summaries of his work are found in Geoffrey Bromiley, ed., *A Karl Barth Reader* (Edinburgh: T & T Clark, 1986); and Clifford Green, ed., *Karl Barth: Theologian of Freedom* (Minneapolis: Augsburg Fortress, 1991).

10. Pannenberg's argument for the historicity of the resurrection of Jesus can be found in *Jesus—God and Man*, 2nd ed., trans. Lewis Wilkins and Duane Priebe (Philadelphia: Westminster, 1977). A more general introduction to his theology is in Pannenberg, *Introduction to Systematic Theology* (Grand Rapids: Eerdmans, 1991).

11. Pew Forum, "U.S. Religious Landscape Survey."

12. The mid-twentieth-century theologian and biblical scholar most responsible for this kind of analysis of myth is Rudolph Bultmann. See his famous essay, "New Testament and Mythology," in *New Testament and Mythology and Other Basic Writings*, ed. and trans. Schubert Ogden (Philadelphia: Fortress Press, 1984).

13. An influential thinker notable for articulating the criteria of knowledge in a way that excludes direct divine intervention is Ernst Troeltsch. See his famous essay from 1898, "Historical and Dogmatic Method in Theology," in *Religion in History*, trans. James Luther Adams and Walter F. Bense (Minneapolis: Fortress Press, 1991).

14. Both of these themes pervade the work of the mid-twentieth-century theologian Paul Tillich, who broadly represents this type. See, for example, his *Dynamics of Faith* (New York: Harper & Row, 1957). A contemporary theologian who echoes these themes and the importance of reinterpreting Christianity in light of them is the retired Anglican bishop John Shelby Spong. See his *A New Christianity for a New World* (San Francisco: HarperCollins, 2001). Yet another contemporary theologian and biblical scholar who restates these themes and argues for reinterpreting Christianity is Marcus Borg. See his *The Heart of Christianity* (San Francisco: HarperCollins, 2003).

15. This issue is examined in greater depth in chapter 6.

16. Bultmann spent the majority of his career as a biblical scholar and never wrote a systematic theology. Tillich did. See *Systematic Theology*, 3 vols. (Chicago: University of Chicago Press, 1951, 1957, 1963).

17. Schleiermacher's renowned systematic theology is *The Christian Faith* (Edinburgh: T & T Clark, 1999), originally published in 1821–1822 and revised in 1830–1831.

CHAPTER 3: GOD AND COSMOLOGY

1. See, for example, the 2008 survey at Pew Forum on Religion and Public Life, "U.S. Religious Landscape Survey," *Pew Forum*, n.d., http://religions.pewforum.org/portraits.

2. Many educated Jews were already exploring the connection between biblical and Greek thought at the time of the beginning of the Christian movement. This is most evident in the work of the Jewish thinker Philo (20 B.C.E.–50 C.E.). See C. D. Yonge, trans., *The Works of Philo*, rev. ed. (Peabody: Hendrickson, 1993).

3. See Francis MacDonald Cornford, trans., *The Republic of Plato* (London: Oxford University Press, 1979), books V–VII.

4. From "The Soliloquies," in *Augustine: Earlier Writings* (Philadelphia: Westminster, 1953), 26–27.

5. An introduction to Thomas's thought is in *A Shorter "Summa": The Essential Philosophical Passages of St Thomas Aquinas' "Summa Theologica"* (San Francisco: Ignatius, 1993).

6. As stated in the first chapter (see note 4 on page 263), classic works of Deism include Matthew Tindal, *Christianity as Old as Creation*; and Thomas Paine, *The Age of Reason*.

7. See John Locke, *The Reasonableness of Christianity* (Washington, D.C.: Regnery Gateway, 1965).

8. The classic argument from design is given by William Paley, *Natural Theology* (Oxford: Oxford University Press, 2006), originally published in 1802.

9. The critiques are in Hume's *Dialogues Concerning Natural Religion* (Indianapolis: Hackett, 1980), originally published in 1779; and Kant's *Critique of Pure Reason*, trans. Norman Kemp Smith (New York: St. Martin's, 1965), originally published in 1781, revised in 1787.

10. Anselm, *Proslogion*, in *Monologion and Proslogion*, trans. Thomas Williams (Indianapolis: Hackett, 1996), 99–100.

11. Thomas Aquinas, *Summa Theologica*, first part, question 2. This work is in the public domain and is available at many Web sites, including *The Internet Sacred Text Archive*, http://www.sacred-texts.com/chr/aquinas/summa/index.htm.

12. William Paley, *Natural Theology* (Oxford: Oxford University Press, 2006).

13. See Ian Barbour, *Religion and Science* (San Francisco: HarperCollins, 1997), chapters 8–9.

14. Barth's rejection of a point of contact between humans and God is in "No! Answer to Emil Brunner," in *Karl Barth: Theologian of Freedom*, ed. Clifford Green (Minneapolis: Augsburg Fortress, 1991), 151–67.

15. *Dynamics of Faith* (New York: Harper & Row, 1957); see especially chapter 1.

16. Tillich makes this argument in *The Courage to Be* (New Haven: Yale University Press, 1952), ch. 6.

17. Tillich's idea of God is presented most clearly in *Systematic Theology* 1, part 2 (Chicago: University of Chicago Press, 1951).

18. See *The "Summa Theologica" of St. Thomas Aquinas* 1 (Westminster, Md.: Christian Classics, 1981), question 13, 59–71.

19. Sallie McFague, *Models of God* (Philadelphia: Fortress Press, 1987).

20. Two contemporary theologians attempting to show the contributions of deconstruction to theology are John Caputo and Mark Taylor. See John Caputo, *The Prayers and Tears of Jacques Derrida: Religion without Religion* (Bloomington: Indiana University Press, 1997); and the more radical Mark C. Taylor, *Erring: A Postmodern A/theology* (Chicago: University of Chicago Press, 1987).

CHAPTER 4: CHRIST AND HISTORY

1. Raymond Brown, *An Introduction to the New Testament* (New York: Doubleday, 1997), 111.

2. Ibid.

3. Works examining these gospels include two books by Bart Ehrman: a reader of primary texts called *Lost Scriptures: Books That Did Not Make It into the New Testament* (Oxford: Oxford University Press, 2003); and a historical analysis called *Lost Christianities: The Battles for Scripture and the Faiths We Never Knew* (Oxford: Oxford University Press, 2005). A classic work on the noncanonical gospels is Elaine Pagels, *The Gnostic Gospels* (New York: Vintage, 1979).

4. Ehrman, *Lost Scriptures*, 19–20. For an English translation of the Nag Hammadi Library texts and more information about the history of the discovery of these texts, see Gnostic Society Library, "The Nag Hammadi Library," n.d., http://www.gnosis.org/naghamm/nhl.html.

5. Ehrman, *Lost Scriptures*, 20.

6. Ibid., 23.

7. Ibid.

8. Ibid.

9. Raymond Brown, *An Introduction to the New Testament* (New York: Doubleday, 1997), 15. For a discussion of the complications and perceived need for forming a canon, see also L. Michael White, *From Jesus to Christianity: How Four Generations of Visionaries and Storytellers Created the New Testament and Christian Faith* (San Francisco: HarperCollins, 2004), chs. 16–17.

10. For information on these important developments of the second century, see one of the classic works on Christian thought: Justo Gonzalez, *A*

History of Christian Thought: From the Beginnings to the Council of Chalcedon
1, rev. ed. (Nashville: Abingdon, 1987), ch. 5.

11. Karen King, *The Gospel of Mary of Magdala* (Santa Rosa: Polebridge, 2003), 3–12.

12. Bart Ehrman, *The Lost Gospel of Judas Iscariot* (Oxford: Oxford University Press, 2006), 67–83.

13. Ibid., 85–98.

14. A discussion about different interpretations of Arius's theology is in Gonzalez, *History of Christian Thought*, 262–65.

15. Henri Leclercq, "The First Council of Nicaea," in *Catholic Encyclopedia* 11 (New York: Robert Appleton, 1911), retrieved from *New Advent*, http://www.newadvent.org/cathen/11044a.htm (Greek insertions deleted).

16. Dennis Bratcher, "Ecumenical Christian Creeds," retrieved from *The Voice*, http://www.crivoice.org/creedsearly.html.

17. See Athanasius, *On the Incarnation* (Crestwood, N.Y.: St Vladimir's Seminary Press, 1993).

18. The question of Jesus' consciousness has always been a complex one for orthodox Christian belief. The creeds of Nicaea and Chalcedon say Jesus was fully human and fully divine. What does this mean when it comes to thinking about Jesus' mind? To be fully human means to have a limited mind that does not know everything. To be fully divine means to have an unlimited mind that knows everything. One historically significant way of resolving this problem is called kenotic Christology, which affirms that the Word of God gave up some divine attributes, including complete knowledge, in becoming incarnate in Jesus. This would imply Jesus' consciousness was limited.

While kenotic Christology is not a universally accepted interpretation of Jesus by Christian theologians, it does show it is possible to affirm that Jesus had a limited consciousness and to affirm an orthodox Christology. If Jesus had a limited consciousness, it is likely the case that his message varied in some degree from the interpretation the church had of him over the decades and centuries after his death. This validates the approach taken in the quest for the historical Jesus and implies that it is possible to engage in the quest for the historical Jesus and still claim, theologically, that the church's post-resurrection interpretation of Jesus was correct.

19. See Thomas Jefferson, *The Jefferson Bible: The Life and Morals of Jesus of Nazareth* (Boston: Beacon, 2001).

20. Albert Schweitzer, *The Quest of the Historical Jesus* (New York: Macmillan, 1968), originally published in German under the title *From Reimarus to Wrede: A History of Investigation into the Life of Jesus* (my translation of the title).

21. See, for example, E. P. Sanders, *The Historical Figure of Jesus* (New York: Penguin, 1996); and Bart Ehrman, *Jesus: Apocalyptic Prophet of the New Millennium* (Oxford: Oxford University Press, 2001).

22. See, for example, Luke Timothy Johnson, *The Real Jesus: The Misguided Quest for the Historical Jesus and the Truth of the Traditional Gospels* (San Francisco: HarperCollins, 1997).

23. The most significant individual text broadly representing this way of thinking about the historical Jesus is John Dominic Crossan, *Jesus: The Life of a Mediterranean Jewish Peasant* (New York: HarperCollins, 1991). Led by Robert Funk, the Jesus Seminar published its findings on Jesus' sayings and deeds that broadly affirm this understanding of Jesus. The findings of the Jesus Seminar are in *The Five Gospels: What Did Jesus Really Say?* (New York: Polebridge, 1993); and *The Acts of Jesus: What Did Jesus Really Do?* (New York: Polebridge, 1998).

24. The classic and widely read work summarizing liberation theology is Gustavo Gutierrez, *A Theology of Liberation* (New York: Orbis, 1973). Another excellent and more accessible summary is Leonardo Boff and Clodovis Boff, *Introducing Liberation Theology* (New York: Orbis, 2002).

25. Leonardo Boff's book on Christology is *Jesus Christ Liberator: A Critical Christology for Our Times* (New York: Orbis, 1978).

26. While Bultmann never wrote a systematic theology, important works are his *New Testament and Mythology and Other Basic Writings*, ed. and trans. Schubert Ogden (Philadelphia: Fortress Press, 1984); and *Jesus Christ and Mythology* (New York: Charles Scribner's Sons, 1958).

27. Jürgen Moltmann, *Theology of Hope* (New York: Harper & Row, 1967).

28. Jürgen Moltmann, *The Crucified God* (New York: Harper & Row, 1974).

CHAPTER 5: HEAVEN, HELL, AND ANTHROPOLOGY

1. See Deuteronomy 28 as a classical expression of this theology.

2. See the dialogue "Phaedo," in *Great Dialogues of Plato* (New York: Mentor, 1956).

3. This was always a subtheme in apocalypticism. The main focus of apocalypticism is God's action in history against the evil powers, with a dramatic sense of expectation for such action to occur immediately. However, there is a subtheme suggesting that while the evil powers may rule history as a whole, some group can at least partially realize the new life that is to come right now. Paul stresses this idea in his letters to his churches, even while he is critical of those who think complete spiritual realization is possible now. As imminent expectation of the end of the world dies down, this subtheme gains prominence. Greater focus is given to realizing the new life or the kingdom right now.

4. F. L. Cross and E. A. Livingstone, eds., *The Oxford Dictionary of the Christian Church*, 2nd ed. (Oxford: Oxford University Press, 1983), 1144.

5. Alister McGrath, *Christian Theology: An Introduction*, 2nd ed. (Malden, Mass.: Blackwell, 1999), 555.

6. A good selection of Augustine's writings on sin and salvation are in Alister McGrath, ed., *The Christian Theology Reader* (Oxford: Blackwell, 1995), 217–23.

7. Two examples of early contemporary philosophical perspectives that work consciously from an evolutionary perspective and stress the interrelationship of all things include process philosophy, which is examined

later in the chapter, and the philosophy of life. The key work in process philosophy is Alfred North Whitehead, *Process and Reality* (New York: Free Press, 1978), based on lectures delivered in 1927–1928. For the philosophy of life, see Henri Bergson, *Creative Evolution* (Mineola, N.Y.: Dover, 1999), originally published in 1907.

8. René Descartes, *Meditations on First Philosophy,* 3rd ed. (Indianapolis: Hackett, 1993), originally published in 1641.

9. Two important feminist theologians who are also ecological theologians, or ecofeminists, and who represent this position are Sallie McFague and Rosemary Ruether. McFague seriously downplays any discussion of the afterlife. See *The Body of God: An Ecological Theology* (Minneapolis: Fortress Press, 1993). Ruether expresses ultimate agnosticism about what the afterlife means. See *Sexism and God-Talk* (Boston: Beacon, 1983), 256–58. Books on feminist theology that avoid discussion of the afterlife include Carol Adams, ed., *Ecofeminism and the Sacred* (New York: Continuum, 1993); and Anne Clifford, *Introducing Feminist Theology* (New York: Orbis, 2001). An exception to this trend is Susan Frank Parsons, ed., *The Cambridge Companion to Feminist Theology* (Cambridge: Cambridge University Press, 2002), which has a chapter on eschatology in which the author bemoans the lack of focus on eschatology in feminist theology (243–60).

10. The extended works relevant for this section are John Hick, *Evil and the God of Love*, rev. ed. (New York: Harper & Row, 1978); and idem, *Death and Eternal Life* (London: Collins, 1976).

11. Alfred North Whitehead, *Process and Reality* (New York: Free, 1978).

12. David Ray Griffin is the process theologian most known for engaging theodicy. This engagement is found particularly in two works, *God, Power, and Evil: A Process Theodicy* (Philadelphia: Westminster, 1976); and *Evil Revisited: Responses and Reconsiderations* (New York: SUNY Press, 1991).

13. A general summary of process theology is in John Cobb and David Ray Griffin, *Process Theology: An Introductory Exposition* (Philadelphia: Westminster, 1976). John Cobb's Christology is most explicitly developed in *Christ in a Pluralistic Age* (Philadelphia: Westminster, 1975).

14. Charles Hartshorne's influential understanding of the process view of the afterlife is in *The Logic of Perfection* (La Salle, Ill.: Open Court, 1962).

15. David Ray Griffin argues for personal immortality in *Evil Revisited: Responses and Reconsiderations* (New York: SUNY Press, 1991).

CHAPTER 6: CHRISTIANITY AND OTHER RELIGIONS

1. Before 1965, U.S. immigration policy was based on country of origin and strongly favored immigration from European countries. From 1965 to the present, immigration policy is based on family reunification (whether a family member is already in the United States) and the ability to contribute to society one's skills and labor.

2. As far as I can determine, the first person to propose this framework was Alan Race in *Christians and Religious Pluralism: Patterns in the Christian Theology of Religions* (Maryknoll, N.Y.: Orbis, 1982).

3. Thomas's method is laid out clearly in *Summa Contra Gentiles, Book One: God* (Notre Dame, Ind.: University of Notre Dame Press, 1975), chs. 1–9.

4. While Thomas drew a clear distinction between truths of reason and truths of revelation, he thought all truth was given in revelation and most people simply need to accept the truths of revelation and do not need to go through the arduous process of discerning the truths of reason.

5. Ibid., ch. 9, p. 77.

6. An excellent summary of Barth's position gleaned from Barth's larger work called *Church Dogmatics* (vol. 1) is found in John Hick and Brian Hebblethwaite, eds., *Christianity and Other Religions*, rev. ed. (Oxford: Oneworld, 2001), 5–18.

7. In the Pew Forum's "Religious Landscape Survey" of 2008, 26.3 percent of Americans identified themselves as Evangelical Protestants. See Pew Forum on Religion and Public Life, "U.S. Religious Landscape Survey," *Pew Forum*, http://religions.pewforum.org/.

8. One notable Evangelical theologian who disagrees with this position and argues for the inclusivist idea that salvation occurs in non-Christian religions is Clark Pinnock. A concise summary of his position is in *Four Views of Salvation in a Pluralistic World*, ed. Dennis L. Okholm and Timothy R. Phillips (Grand Rapids: Zondervan, 1996), 95–123.

9. Douglas Geivett and Gary Phillips in Okholm and T. R. Phillips, *Four Views of Salvation in a Pluralistic World*, 213–45.

10. Ibid., 217.

11. Ibid., 198–99, 270.

12. The lecture is reprinted in Hick and Hebblethwaite, *Christianity and Other Religions*, 19–38.

13. Ibid., 29.

14. An excellent explanation of Rahner on this point is provided by Paul Knitter, *Introducing Theologies of Religions* (Maryknoll, N.Y.: Orbis, 2002), 72–74.

15. *The Metaphor of God Incarnate* (Louisville: Westminster John Knox, 2005), 8; and "The Theological Challenge of Religious Pluralism," in Hick and Hebblethwaite, *Christianity and Other Religions*, 156–71.

16. John Hick, *An Interpretation of Religion* (New Haven: Yale University Press, 1989), 307; and *A Christian Theology of Religions* (Louisville: Westminster John Knox, 1995), 13–15.

17. Hick, *An Interpretation of Religion*, 233–49.

18. Ibid., 236.

19. John Hick, "An Inspiration Christology," in *Disputed Questions in Theology and Philosophy of Religion* (New Haven: Yale University Press, 1993), 35–57.

20. *The Metaphor of God Incarnate*, ch. 11.

21. Ibid., ch. 12.

22. As an example, see Paul Griffiths, *An Apology for Apologetics: A Study in the Logic of Interreligious Dialogue* (Maryknoll, N.Y.: Orbis, 1991).

23. *The Nature of Doctrine* (Philadelphia: Westminster, 1984), 30–45.

24. Ibid., 55–63.

CHAPTER 7: CHRISTIANITY AND FEMINISM

1. Katherine Switzer, "The Real Story of Katherine Switzer's 1967 Boston Marathon—Life Is for Participating," excerpted from Gail Waesche Kislevitz, *Life Is for Participating*, (New York: Breakaway, 2002), accessed at http://www.katherineswitzer.com/life.html.

2. Charlie Lovett, "The Fight to Establish the Women's Race," excerpted from Lovett, *Olympic Marathon* (Westport, Conn.: Praeger, 1997), accessed at MarathonGuide.com, http://www.marathonguide.com/history/olympicmarathons/chapter25.cfm.

3. Institute for Women's Policy Research, "The Gender Wage Gap: 2009," Fact Sheet IWPR C350, September 2010, http://www.iwpr.org/pdf/C350.pdf.

4. Catalyst, "2008 Catalyst Census of Women Board Directors of the *Fortune* 500," 2008, http://www.catalyst.org/file/242/08_census_wbd_jan.pdf.

5. Center for American Women and Politics, "Women in the U.S. Congress 2010," fact sheet, January 2010, http://www.cawp.rutgers.edu/fast_facts/levels_of_office/documents/cong.pdf.

6. Other terms used are *androcentrism* and *kyriarchy*. The first term means "male-centered," and the second means "rule of the Lord." *Kyriarchy* is an intriguing term, since it refers to broader types of oppression than just male-female. This chapter uses the traditional term *patriarchy*, since the main concern is male-female oppression.

7. Elisabeth Schüssler Fiorenza, *Bread Not Stone: The Challenge of Feminist Biblical Interpretation* (Boston: Beacon, 1984), 15–22.

8. Elisabeth Schüssler Fiorenza, "A Critical Feminist Emancipatitive Reading," in *Engaging the Bible* (Minneapolis: Fortress Press, 2006), 81–104.

9. See, for example, Rebecca Merrill Groothuis, *Good News for Women* (Grand Rapids: Baker, 1997).

10. Feminist interpreters do not universally agree that the creation and fall stories of Genesis 2 and 3 are patriarchal. In a widely read and influential essay, the feminist Old Testament scholar Phyllis Trible argues it is not the text of Genesis 2–3 that is patriarchal but its interpretation. See "Eve and Adam: Genesis 2–3 Reread," in *Womenspirit Rising: A Feminist Reader in Religion*, ed. Carol Christ and Judith Plaskow (San Francisco: HarperCollins, 1979), 74–83.

11. A brief summary and critique of the church's historical interpretation of Mary and a proposal for rehabilitating the Christian understanding of Mary based on what can be reasonably inferred about her from the biblical text are

found in Anne Clifford's book *Introducing Feminist Theology* (Maryknoll, N.Y.: Orbis, 2001), 186–94.

12. Karen King, *The Gospel of Mary of Magdala* (Santa Rosa: Polebridge, 2003), 142–44.

13. Robin Griffith-Jones, *Beloved Disciple: The Misunderstood Legacy of Mary Magdalene, the Woman Closest to Jesus* (New York: HarperOne, 2008), 177–79.

14. Ibid., 177 (brackets deleted).

15. Ibid., 178.

16. Lynn Japinga, *Feminism and Christianity: An Essential Guide* (Nashville: Abingdon, 1999), 41.

17. Bonnie B. Thurston, *Women in the New Testament: Questions and Commentary* (New York: Crossroad, 1998), 66–78.

18. Elisabeth Schüssler Fiorenza, *In Memory of Her: A Feminist Theological Reconstruction of Christian Origins* (New York: Crossroad, 1983).

19. Ibid., 162–73.

20. Rosemary Radford Ruether, *Sexism and God-Talk: Toward a Feminist Theology* (Boston: Beacon, 1983), 22–33.

21. Southern Baptist Convention, "The Baptist Faith and Message," *sbc-net*, n.d., http://www.sbc.net/bfm/bfm2000.asp#vi.

22. Rebecca Merrill Groothuis, *Good News for Women* (Grand Rapids: Baker, 1997), 209–230.

23. This journal can be found online at the Web site of the Council on Biblical Manhood and Womanhood, http://www.cbmw.org/Journal.

24. Apostolic Letter *Ordinatio Sacerdotalis* of John Paul II to the Bishops of the Catholic Church on Reserving Priestly Ordination to Men Alone, May 22, 1994, accessed at Vatican Web site, http://www.vatican.va/holy_father/john_paul_ii/apost_letters/documents/hf_jp-ii_apl_22051994_ordinatio-sacerdotalis_en.html.

25. The basis of the claim of the pope to lead the entire church is that Jesus singled out Peter in particular to be the "rock" on which he would build his church (Matt. 16:18-19). It is claimed Peter established the church at Rome and handed on his authority to lead to his successor there.

26. Apostolic Letter *Ordinatio Sacerdotalis* of John Paul II, May 22, 1994.

27. Ibid.

28. Mary Daly, *Beyond God the Father: Toward a Philosophy of Women's Liberation* (Boston: Beacon, 1973), 19.

29. Elizabeth Johnson, *She Who Is: The Mystery of God in Feminist Theological Discourse*, 10th anniv. ed. (New York: Crossroad, 2002), 39–41.

30. Ibid., 39.

31. Ibid., 82–86.

32. Ibid., 86–87.

33. Ibid., 87–100.

34. Ibid., 100–103.

35. Ibid., 104–12.

36. Ibid., 113–17.

37. Ibid., 117–20.

38. *An Inclusive Language Lectionary: Readings for Year B* (New York: National Council of Churches, 1987), 9–10.

39. Ibid., 11–12.

40. Ibid., 12.

41. NRSV Web site (HarperCollins), http://www.nrsv.net/about/faqs/.

42. Committee on Bible Translation, "Preface to the New International Version Bible," June 1978, accessed at *Biblica*, http://www.biblica.com/niv/background.php.

43. NIV Bible Update, "Real Questions and Real Answers," n.d., http://nivbible2011.com/.

44. Valerie Saiving, "The Human Situation: A Feminine View," reprinted in *Womanspirit Rising: A Feminist Reader in Religion* (San Francisco: HarperCollins, 1992; orig. pub. 1979), 26.

45. Ibid., 37.

46. Rosemary Radford Ruether, *Introducing Redemption in Christian Feminism* (Sheffield, U.K.: Sheffield Academic, 1998), 72.

47. Anne Clifford, *Introducing Feminist Theology* (Maryknoll, N.Y.: Orbis, 2001), 25–28.

48. Not only feminist theology, but also liberation theology, has developed this idea of sin.

49. Ruether, *Introducing Redemption in Christian Feminism*, 74.

50. The analysis of critique and reconstruction that follows is heavily indebted to Rosemary Ruether's summary in "Suffering and Redemption: The Cross and Atonement in Feminist Theology," in *Introducing Redemption in Christian Feminism*, 95–107. Ruether names the key feminists involved in critique and reconstruction as Joanne Carlson Brown, Rebecca Parker, Delores Williams, and Dorothee Soelle. She adds her own views as well. Another summary of critique and reconstruction of the feminist view of atonement relied on for this section is Lyn Japinga, "Salvation," in *Feminism and Christianity: An Essential Guide* (Nashville: Abingdon, 1999), 107–26.

CHAPTER 8: CHRISTIANITY AND HOMOSEXUALITY

1. Joseph Cardinal Ratzinger, "Letter to the Bishops of the Catholic Church on the Pastoral Care of Homosexual Persons," Congregation for the Doctrine of the Faith, October 1, 1986, http://www.vatican.va/roman_curia/congregations/cfaith/documents/rc_con_cfaith_doc_19861001_homosexual-persons_en.html.

2. Ibid., point 3.

3. Ibid., points 6 and 7.

4. Ibid., point 7.

5. Ibid., point 17.

6. Many times, "experience" is added as a source of authority. I include it as a form of reason.

7. Southern Baptist Convention, "The Baptist Faith and Message," *sbc-net*, n.d., http://www.sbc.net/bfm/bfm2000.asp#i.

8. Victor Paul Furnish, "The Bible and Homosexuality: Reading the Texts in Context," in *Homosexuality in the Church: Both Sides of the Debate*, ed. Jeffrey Siker (Louisville: Westminster John Knox, 1994), 33 n. 2.

9. Raymond Brown, Joseph Fitzmyer, and Roland Murphy, eds., *The New Jerome Biblical Commentary* (Upper Saddle River, N.J.: Prentice Hall, 1990), 72.

10. Part of the complication lies in the fact that Israel's laws were a mixture of moral, religious, and purity laws given to the whole society in a context in which there was no freedom of religion. The whole society was to embody all these laws, including the religious laws. The contemporary American context affirms freedom of religion while drawing a distinction between universal civil laws, which are not a matter of choice, and religious laws, which are. Christians today would say certain religious laws, like worshipping only one God and not making a cast image of God, are still valid for them but cannot be required of everyone in the culture.

11. Robert Gagnon makes these connections explicit in Dan Via and Robert Gagnon, *Homosexuality and the Bible: Two Views* (Minneapolis: Augsburg Fortress, 2003), 56–68.

12. Examples of arguments for the Levitical prohibitions as purity laws are Dan Via, ibid., 4–9; Furnish, "The Bible and Homosexuality," 18–35; and Daniel Helminiak, *What the Bible Really Says about Homosexuality* (San Francisco: Alamo Square, 1994), 43–54.

13. See, for example, E. P. Sanders, *Paul* (New York: Oxford University Press, 1991), 132; Furnish, "The Bible and Homosexuality," 24; and Herman Waetjen, "Same-Sex Relations in Antiquity and Sexuality and Sexual Identity in Contemporary American Society," in *Biblical Ethics and Homosexuality* (Louisville: Westminster John Knox, 1996), 109–10.

14. John Boswell, *Christianity, Social Tolerance, and Homosexuality* (Chicago: University of Chicago Press, 1980), 109.

15. Richard Hays, "Relations Natural and Unnatural: A Response to John Boswell's Exegesis of Romans 1," *JRE* 14 (1986): 184–215.

16. An important early work examining pederasty as the background for Paul's statements is Robin Scroggs, *The New Testament and Homosexuality* (Philadelphia: Fortress Press, 1983).

17. Furnish, "The Bible and Homosexuality," 26–27.

18. Sanders, *Paul*, 128–32; Furnish, "The Bible and Homosexuality," 27.

19. This way of putting the issue should not be taken to imply that a decision can be made on the basis of one of the sources of authority and completely apart from the influence of the others. While one source may weigh more heavily in relation to the others on some decisions, all sources are involved in all decisions. This means that Christians who accept the

conclusions of human reason supporting the full acceptance of homosexuality do not do so purely on the basis of reason and then turn to the Bible for themes to support their position. Instead, even the openness to the full acceptance of homosexuality based on reason is in some sense already shaped and informed by a biblical perspective.

20. The elements of this paradigm shift are all displayed on the Web site of the American Psychological Association, "Sexual Orientation and Homosexuality," http://www.apa.org/helpcenter/sexual-orientation.aspx.

21. "Being Gay Is Just as Healthy as Being Straight," American Psychological Association, May 28, 2003, http://www.apa.org/research/action/gay.aspx.

22. United Church of Christ, "A Selected Chronology of Relevant Actions and Events," *Justice: Sexuality Education*, n.d., http://www.ucc.org/justice/sexuality-education/a-selected-chronology-of.html.

23. Ibid.

24. Mike Schuenemeyer, "Marriage Equality," United Church of Christ Web site, November 4, 2009, http://www.ucc.org/lgbt/issues/marriage-equality/#Marriage_Equality_and_the_UCC.

25. B. A. Robinson, "The Episcopal Church, USA and Homosexuality: Actions at the Year 2003 General Convention," Ontario Consultants on Religious Tolerance, last updated June 5, 2004, http://www.religioustolerance.org/hom_epis8.htm.

26. B. A. Robinson, "Religious Conflicts: The Episcopal Church, USA and Homosexuality," Ontario Consultants on Religious Tolerance, last updated September 22, 2007, http://www.religioustolerance.org/hom_epis.htm.

27. Anglican Church in North America, "Our Genesis," http://anglicanchurch.net/media/acna_our_genesis_june_2009WITHLINKS.pdf.

28. Anglican Church in North America, "About the Anglican Church in North America," November 16, 2009, http://anglicanchurch.net/?/main/page/about#history.

29. Mitchell Landsberg, "Episcopal Church Approves Ordination of Openly Gay Bishop in Los Angeles," *Los Angeles Times*, March 18, 2010, http://articles.latimes.com/2010/mar/18/local/la-me-episcopal18-2010mar18.

30. Evangelical Lutheran Church in America, "What We Believe: Social Issues," n.d., http://www.elca.org/What-We-Believe/Social-Issues.aspx.

31. Evangelical Lutheran Church in America, "Human Sexuality: Gift and Trust," ELCA Social Statement, adopted August 19, 2009, http://www.elca.org/What-We-Believe/Social-Issues/Social-Statements/JTF-Human-Sexuality.aspx.

32. Ibid.

33. Ibid.

34. Ibid.

35. Mark S. Hanson, "Churchwide Assembly Update," Evangelical Lutheran Church in America, August 22, 2009, http://www.elca.org/Who-We-Are/Our-Three-Expressions/Churchwide-Organization/Office-of-the-Presiding-Bishop/Messages-and-Statements/090822.aspx.

36. Via and Gagnon, *Homosexuality and the Bible*, 17, 29–39.

37. Ibid., 17. Wisdom books in the Old Testament are Proverbs, Ecclesiastes, and Job.

38. Ibid., 39.

CHAPTER 9: CHRISTIANITY AND THE NATURAL ENVIRONMENT

1. U.S. Census Bureau, "Historical Estimates of World Population," International Programs, n.d., http://www.census.gov/ipc/www/worldhis.html.

2. U.S. Census Bureau, "Total Midyear Population for the World," International Data Base, http://www.census.gov/ipc/www/worldpop.php, last updated June 28, 2010.

3. While biblical apocalyptic thought imagined the end of the current world order, including all living things, this was thought to be due to dramatic divine intervention in history, not due to human influence on the natural world.

4. The answer to the question about how many people the earth can sustainably support depends in significant measure on the kind of lifestyle those people maintain. It is clear that the current lifestyle of people in the developed world (primarily the United States and Western Europe) cannot be adopted by everyone on the globe at 2009's population total of 6.7 billion. People in the developed world use far too many resources for everyone on the globe to live in the same way. The Worldwatch Institute estimates that 1.8 billion people could sustainably live the lifestyle maintained by those in the developed world. Worldwatch, *Vital Signs* (New York: Norton, 2006), 93.

While the developed world's lifestyle is unsustainable for the globe, one of the most important global issues today is that vast numbers of peoples in the developing world want to live similarly to those in the developed world, and it appears that significant numbers are poised to do so in the near future. China, India, and Brazil in particular are experiencing tremendous growth in their economies. Together, these nations represent over a third of the world population. With the economic growth of those nations, it is anticipated that over the next several decades, hundreds of millions of Chinese, Indian, and Brazilian people will either achieve or come close to the lifestyle of those in the developed world. This will put unprecedented stress on the natural environment.

One of the major questions arising from this situation is whether there will be technological solutions that will allow people of the developed world to continue to live their current lifestyle in a sustainable way while also allowing those of the developing world to move into and adopt the Western lifestyle. If so, then presumably economic growth and development throughout the world should continue unchecked but should be channeled in the right way. However, if one is more skeptical about discovering sustainable technological solutions, and if one has reasons to question the lifestyle of the developed world in the first place, this can lead to a call for the adoption of alternative lifestyles. For those of the developed world, this includes voluntary simple living embraced not only for the good of the environment but for the sake of global justice under the affirmation that the Western lifestyle is maintained in significant ways at the expense of the poor in the developing world. Significant numbers of Christians and Christian groups take positions on either side of this issue.

5. Lynn White's article originally appeared in *Science* 155 (March 10, 1967): 1203–7.

6. There is ambiguity in the use of the term *anthropocentrism*. At times, it is taken to mean that while everything created has intrinsic value, humans have the highest value of any creature. According to this view, there is a hierarchy of value that runs from God the creator down through humans, animals, plants, and inanimate objects. The fact that humans are regarded as having a higher intrinsic value than other living things, which nevertheless are still regarded as having intrinsic value, is what makes this pattern of thinking anthropocentric. At other times, *anthropocentrism* is taken to mean that only humans have intrinsic value and everything else has instrumental value insofar as it can be put to use for humans and human flourishing. In the context of explaining the critique against Christianity, this chapter uses the term in the latter sense.

7. Many books and articles can be found on Christian stewardship of creation. As a representative sample, see Calvin B. DeWitt, *Caring for Creation: Responsible Stewardship of God's Handiwork* (Grand Rapids: Baker, 1998); Fred Van Dyke, David Mahan, Joseph Sheldon, and Raymond Brand, *Redeeming Creation: The Biblical Basis for Environmental Stewardship* (Downers Grove, Ill.: InterVarsity, 1996); Ken Gnanakan, "Creation, Christians, and Environmental Stewardship," *EvRT* 30, no. 2 (2006): 110–20; and Douglas John Hall, *The Steward: A Biblical Symbol Come of Age* (Grand Rapids: Eerdmans, 1990).

8. Van Dyke et al., *Redeeming Creation*, 97–98; DeWitt, *Caring for Creation*, 32–33; Gnanakan, "Creation, Christians, and Environmental Stewardship," 114–16. There is some tension between the model of stewardship, which is an economic model referring to the care of another's property, and the model of rule or dominion, which is a political model referring to being in charge of other people's lives. While the two models are often distinguished in the literature, those who promote the stewardship model as the controlling or foundational model often subsume the dominion model under the stewardship model.

9. Edwards acknowledges indebtedness to the Jesuit paleontologist and theologian Teilhard de Chardin (1881–1955) as well, but it is Rahner's thought he adopts most thoroughly in developing an ecological theology. Denis Edwards, *Ecology at the Heart of Faith* (Maryknoll, N.Y.: Orbis, 2006), 82–96.

10. Ibid., 87.

11. Ibid., 89.

12. Ibid., 93.

13. Ibid., 96–98.

14. H. Paul Santmire, *The Travail of Nature* (Minneapolis: Fortress Press, 1985), 1–8.

15. Ibid., 8–29.

16. Ibid., 26.

17. Ibid., 200–216.

18. Ibid., 31–53.

19. Ibid., 216–17.

20. Ibid., 217.

21. Santmire does not use the same terminology of motifs and metaphors in the second text, but they are in the background of his constructive work. See, for example, his critique of Matthew Fox and alternative interpretation of Augustine in chapter 2, which restates his interpretation of Augustine according to the ecological motif in *The Travail of Nature*. H. Paul Santmire, *Nature Reborn* (Minneapolis: Fortress Press, 2000), 16–28.

22. Ibid., 29.

23. Ibid., 31.

24. Ibid., 33.

25. Ibid., 56.

26. Ibid., 58.

27. Ibid., 56.

28. Ibid., 56.

29. Ibid., 66–73. In this section, Santmire develops the schematization made famous by Martin Buber: "I-Thou," and "I-It." Santmire adds the relation "I-Ens," or I-existing being. See Martin Buber, *I and Thou*, 2nd ed. (New York: Charles Scribner's Sons, 1958).

30. Santmire, *Nature Reborn*, 70.

31. Ibid., 72.

32. Matthew Fox, *Original Blessing* (Santa Fe: Bear & Co., 1983), 11, 316–19.

33. Ibid., 48–49.

34. Ibid., 47.

35. Ibid., 49–50.

36. Ibid., 50, 76, 85, 251, 299.

37. Fox calls this the Via Positiva, and it is the first and longest of four main "paths" he articulates. Ibid., 33–125.

38. Fox calls this the Via Creativa. It is his third path. Ibid., 175–244.

39. Ibid., 27.

40. Ibid., 122.

41. Ibid., 122–23, 235, 317.

42. Ibid., 318.

43. Matthew Fox, *The Coming of the Cosmic Christ* (San Francisco: Harper & Row, 1988), 83–128.

44. Ibid., 24–27.

45. Ibid., 145.

46. Ibid., 149.
47. Brian Swimme and Thomas Berry, *The Universe Story* (New York: HarperCollins, 1992), 1–5.
48. Ibid., 2–3, 226, 229, 236–38.
49. Ibid., 237.
50. Ibid., 2–3, 226, 229, 236–38.
51. Ibid., 226, 236.
52. Ibid., 1.
53. Ibid.
54. Ibid., 250.
55. Ibid., 249–51.
56. Ibid., 229.
57. Ibid., 238.
58. Ibid.
59. Ibid., 251–52.
60. Ibid., 265–67.
61. Ibid., 238.
62. Ibid., 241–61.

Glossary

Adoptionism: Interpretation of Jesus' identity that claims Jesus was a human who was selected to be the Messiah either at baptism or the resurrection. Jesus was not the incarnation of the pre-existent word of God but someone who fulfilled God's plan of salvation and, as a result, was exalted to be with God.

Agnosticism: Worldview that claims it cannot be known whether or not God exists.

Analogy of being: Classical theological position that claims since God is the source of everything in the universe, God must be like what God causes in some sense or by analogy. At the same time, God is not literally like anything in the universe, as this would make God subject to some aspect of the universe.

Androcentrism: Term used by some feminists that means "male-centered."

Animism: Worldview that affirms a divine or sacred presence in non-human forms of life, natural objects, and natural features.

Anonymous Christians: Term used by Karl Rahner to describe people in other religions who receive salvation. They are Christians because they are saved by the same grace of the same God by which Christians are saved, although they do not have this grace consciously and in its fullness.

Anthropocentrism: Term literally means "human-centered." It refers to a worldview that regards humans as the only thing of value in the universe or of such a high value so as to negate the value of other forms of life and the material world.

Apocalypticism: Worldview that claims the world is under the sway of evil powers aligned against God, but anticipates imminent divine intervention on the side of God's righteous people to defeat the evil powers and usher in an age of justice and peace. This worldview has spawned its own kind of literature.

Arianism: Interpretation of Jesus' identity that was named after the fourth-century Christian priest and popular teacher, Arius. Arius believed Jesus was the incarnation of the Word of God, but the Word of God was a creature and not fully God.

Aseity: Theological term that literally means "not derived." In classical theology, it refers to the being of God and expresses the idea that God is not derived from or dependent upon anything in the universe.

Atheism: Worldview that claims no God or Gods exist.

Autonomy: Term literally means "self-law." It describes an emphasis of much Enlightenment thinking that affirms the power of human reason to know what is good and true on its own and to regulate itself, independent of submission to authorities that are deemed arbitrary.

Biblical literalism: Theological position that refutes modernity and elevates the literal truth of the Bible and with it, a traditional understanding of many Christian doctrines.

Bodily assumption of Mary: Roman Catholic teaching that Mary, the mother of Jesus, was bodily taken into heaven at the end of her life. It was officially declared infallible in 1950.

Born-again or conversion experience: For evangelical Christians, this is a defining experience involving the heart-felt conviction that, despite being a sinner, one receives God's grace made possible through the atoning death of Jesus Christ.

Christian gnosticism: Movement in early Christianity that affirmed an anti-Jewish interpretation of Christianity. Gnostics denied the material world or the Jewish God who made the world was good. They affirmed that Jesus came to give knowledge so the immaterial and divine part of the self can return to God at death.

Christ: Greek word meaning "Anointed One"; the same term in Hebrew is "Messiah." In its Jewish context, it refers to one specially chosen by God to establish God's rule or Kingdom.

Christology: What Christians believe and what the church teaches about the claim that Jesus is the Christ or Messiah. Traditionally, it involves two parts: reflection on the meaning of what Jesus did and reflection on the meaning of who Jesus is.

Church authority: Doctrine that church leaders have the power to lead because they stand in the line of the succession from Jesus' apostles, who were chosen to lead by Jesus himself.

Clan god: Deity worshipped by a particular group of people whose relationship is solely with this particular group.

Complementarian view of gender: View that men and women are to have different roles, with men leading and women being supportive, and the assumption that those different roles imply different natures.

Congregation for the Doctrine of the Faith: Official teaching arm of the Roman Catholic Church that works with the Pope to make official statements about controversial issues and regulate the teaching of Catholic theologians.

Consciousness-raising: Act of becoming aware of one's situation as oppression and rejecting the situation as a true worldview.

Cosmogenesis: Worldview that stresses the temporal becoming of unique material, organic, and self-conscious forms of being through the self-shaping principles of the universe.

Council: Meeting of important church leaders to make decisions about a pressing issue or issues.

Covenant: Term literally means "contract" or "agreement." It refers to the special relationship believed by the Jewish people to exist between them and God.

Creation spirituality: Eclectic theological movement that focuses on the goodness of creation and God's presence in creation.

Creed: Succinct statement of belief.

Critical Feminist Emancipative Hermeneutics: Phrase coined by Elisabeth Schüssler Fiorenza that defines her method of biblical interpretation combining the critique of patriarchy and the appropriation of a liberating message.

Critical reason: Human reason's power to critique religious authorities or sacred objects rather than simply submit to them. It is characteristic of much Enlightenment thought.

Critical-thematic biblical interpretation: Approach to biblical interpretation that gives due weight to contemporary reason, recognizes the way tradition forms and informs all approaches to the Bible, and seeks a word from God deeply in the themes of the Bible rather than in everything the culturally bound authors affirm.

Deconstruction: Post-modern movement that involves severe skepticism and critique of the ability of language to grasp reality.

Deification: Theological affirmation that human beings and the entire universe will become God-like or participate in God's eternality and perfection as the result of the incarnation, death, and resurrection of Jesus.

Deism: Rival religion to Christianity that emerged in the Enlightenment. Deists believe God created a rational and orderly universe but does not intervene in it. Generally, they were optimistic about human moral progress.

Enlightenment: Movement of thought among the intelligentsia in Western Europe and the American colonies that began in the seventeenth century and reached its zenith in the eighteenth. It stressed the capacity of the human mind to know what is good and true on its own, independent of authorities.

Epistemology: Theory of how humans know things.

Eschatology: Doctrine of the end times, traditionally involving the end of the current world, final judgment, and coming of a new heaven and earth.

Evangelical Protestantism: Significant Christian movement in American culture that stresses the importance of a born-again experience and tends to interpret the Bible literally.

Ex cathedra: Term literally means "from the chair." It refers to the Roman Catholic teaching that when the Pope speaks uniquely from his position as supreme head of the church, what he teaches is infallible.

Exclusivism: Christian position toward other religions that claims there is no salvation except that which is explicitly known and experienced in Jesus Christ.

Existentialist theology: Theological approach generally associated with Rudolph Bultmann and his school that denies the significance of the historical Jesus for faith and is concerned with the individual's realization of authentic existence through hearing and responding to the message of the gospel.

Feeling of absolute dependence: Idea developed by Friedrich Schleiermacher, who analyzed universal human experience and claimed to uncover a religious element expressed in the sense of absolute dependence of self and world on a source or whence.

God-language: Human language used to refer to God. Feminist theology in particular has analyzed and questioned why this language is typically male, especially the popular terms "Father, "Lord," and "King," and whether this language should remain male.

Greek anthropology: Understanding of the human person, especially as promoted by the Greek philosopher Plato, who affirms humans have an immortal soul trapped in a material body.

Hermeneutics of suspicion: Approach to the biblical text that seeks to expose and critique patriarchy within it.

Historical contingency problem: Problem caused by the fact that one must be in a certain historical position to hear the Christian message. Whether one is in that position rests on the contingent conditions of the time and place of one's birth.

Historical or higher criticism: Summary term for a view of the Bible that affirms the cultural conditioning and limitations, as well as the individual creativity, of the biblical authors.

Holiness Code: Series of laws in Leviticus 17–26 that consists of a compilation of several legal traditions that developed over a long period of time in ancient Israel and were put into their present form in the sixth century B.C.E.

Homosexual orientation: Idea that a relatively small percentage of the population is oriented in their sexual attraction to members of the same sex rather than members of the opposite sex.

Ideology: Promotion of a worldview that justifies the oppression of one group over another, arguing that this is the way reality is and should be.

Immaculate Conception: Roman Catholic teaching that Mary, the mother of Jesus, was conceived without original sin. This doctrine was declared infallible in 1854.

Immanence: Theological term used to refer to God's presence in and to the universe.

Impassible: Term literally means "incapable of suffering or pain." In classical theology, this idea was applied to God, although a number of contemporary theologians have questioned this application.

Incarnation: In traditional Christian teaching, the doctrine that God became fully human in the person Jesus.

Inclusivism: Christian position toward other religions that affirms members of non-Christian religions can find salvation in their own religions outside the explicit knowledge and acceptance of Jesus Christ; however, it also affirms that Christianity is special in relation to all other religions because the salvation in Jesus Christ is the goal or ideal of salvation, a goal that all other religions have in an inferior way.

Inerrant: Without error.

Infallible: Incapable of failure or error.

Interventionist theism: Form of theism that affirms God is separate or independent from the universe in God's being, but claims God uses God's power to intervene in the universe periodically.

Inspiration or degree Christology: Christology that affirms Jesus was a human in whom the spirit of God was present in an extraordinary degree.

II Isaiah: In contemporary critical scholarship of the Bible, there is a consensus that the Old Testament book of Isaiah was written by more than one author. II Isaiah is the designation of the anonymous author of Isaiah 40–55, who lived in the sixth century B.C.E.

Kenotic Christology: Theological explanation for how Jesus could be both divine and human. It affirms God gave up some divine attributes in becoming incarnate in Jesus.

Liberation theology: Theology that originated in Latin America whose focus is elevating the condition of the oppressed lower classes in the developing world.

Mainline Protestantism: Significant group of Protestant churches in America, many of whom originated with the sixteenth-century Protestant Reformation. These groups tend to be open to culture and contemporary developments of culture.

Metaphysic: Articulation of the most fundamental elements that characterize reality.

Middle knowledge: Doctrine claiming that part of God's omniscience is that God knows what everyone would have done if they were presented with situations different from the ones with which they were presented in their lifetimes. Thus, God knows what people who never had the chance to hear the Christian gospel would have done if they had the chance to hear it.

Monotheism: Worldview that claims a single God exists.

Mujerista theology: Branch of liberation/feminist theology done from the perspective of Latina women.

Natural theology: Tradition that is especially valued in Roman Catholic thought, which affirms the power of human reason to discover some theological truths independent of revelation.

Negative theology: Theology that stresses the lack of correspondence between human ideas or human language and God. It affirms God's otherness, claiming all that can be known or experienced about God is what God is not.

Nicene Creed: Most important creed in Christianity. It was formulated in 325 C.E. and revised in 381 C.E. It stresses that the Word of God that became incarnate in Jesus was fully God.

Oral tradition: Transmitted memory of an event by word of mouth; told and re-told by people in the past in order to keep the memory of their history alive.

Original blessing: Emphasis in Matthew Fox's theology on humans emerging into a bounteous creation, loved by a God they can trust whose being overflows into creation.

Original Sin: Doctrine that was given theological shape in the West by Augustine. It stresses that all humans are born with a twisted nature and inherited guilt because of the primal disobedience of the first human parents.

Orthodoxy: Right belief.

Othropraxy: Right action. Contemporary liberation theologians in particular have stressed the importance of right action in taking a stand against oppression.

Panentheism: Term literally means "God is in everything." It is a worldview that claims God both pervades and transcends all finite reality.

Pantheism: Term literally means "God is everything." It is a worldview that claims God pervades all finite reality but does not transcend it.

Paradigm shift: Major change in the pattern of thinking with respect to a particular issue.

Patriarchy: Term literally means "rule of the father." It refers both to the concrete authority of men over women and the ideas used to justify it.

Pharisees: Respected Jewish leaders before and during the time of Jesus who were experts in applying the Jewish law to new situations. They affirmed the idea of resurrection of the dead, although they did not necessarily agree about what it involved.

Pluralism: Christian position toward other religions that affirms salvation occurs in a relatively equal manner in all religions, thereby denying the claim that any religion is the exclusive locus of salvation or the pinnacle of salvation.

Polytheism: Worldview that affirms the existence of many deities.

Postmodern: Contemporary intellectual movement that critiques Enlightenment thinkers, pointing to the limitations of human reason and stressing the embedded nature of the thinking subject in a particular time and place with presuppositions the subject cannot escape.

Process theology: Contemporary theological movement that synthesizes the philosophy of Alfred North Whitehead and traditional Christian ideas. It understands both the universe and God as being dynamic rather than static.

Prophetic principle: Common theme of the Old Testament, according to Rosemary Radford Ruether, wherein Prophets denounce the oppressive abuse of power in the name of the God of justice. Ruether thinks this theme should be appropriated to critique patriarchy today.

Purity law: Law determining contact with things or processes that make one clean or unclean.

Quest for the historical Jesus: Scholarly attempt to reconstruct the life and teaching of Jesus of Nazareth. It proceeds from the assumption that the New Testament text contains a fusion of historical memory and creative, theological, post-resurrection interpretation of who Jesus was.

Real: Term used by John Hick in his pluralist hypothesis instead of the term "God," because the term "God" can be limited to a Christian or monotheistic interpretation.

Real as variously experienced and thought by different human communities: To John Hick, the idea of ultimate reality grasped in and through human mental categories and in and through a cultural and historical tradition, or one of the world religions.

Real in itself: To John Hick, the universal Divine presence that remains unknown and transcends all mental categories and historical formations.

Revealed theology or special revelation: Set of truths known only through God's self-revelation in history.

Revelation acceptance problem: Problem caused by the fact that revealed truths are traditionally understood as unprovable, yet it is expected that members of other religions should accept them to find salvation.

Sacramental system: Concrete way in which grace is mediated to believers. In traditional Roman Catholic thought, the church is established by God to mediate grace to believers. This occurs through the seven sacraments of baptism, confirmation, penance, eucharist, marriage, orders, and anointing of the sick.

Sadducees: Jews of Jesus' time who denied the resurrection and embraced the sheol idea of the afterlife. They controlled the Jerusalem temple.

Salvation history: Story of God's temporal plan of salvation from creation to final consummation. The center of the story in Christianity is the incarnation of God in Jesus of Nazareth.

Sanctifying grace: Grace that makes one holy or religiously and morally transformed and improved.

Sectarian Protestantism: Protestant groups that stress a sharp line of demarcation between themselves and the world. With the latter, this includes other forms of Christianity, often being regarded as under the sway of evil powers.

Sheol: In ancient Jewish belief, the abode of the dead where everyone goes when they die. It is a place of quietness and rest where people are in a sleeplike state, though not completely obliterated.

Soul-making: Term coined by John Hick that explains the purpose of human life, whereby human beings overcome their selfish nature in the development of moral and religious character.

Sources of authority: Source to which the church turns for guidance about a belief or practice. The classic sources of authority are scripture, tradition, and reason, although all Christian groups do not agree about what the sources are or how they should be used.

Symbol: Finite object or image that mediates the transcendent Divine presence to the religious believer.

Synoptic Gospels: First three books of the New Testament: Matthew, Mark, and Luke. Called the "Synoptics," which means "seen together," because they follow the same structure and can be placed in side-by-side columns.

Synoptic problem: Scholarly question about the literary relationship between Matthew, Mark, and Luke, and the sources each author used to construct their Gospels.

Systematic theology: Orderly exposition of the content of the Christian faith in a particular time.

Substitutionary theory of the atonement: Idea that God is said to take on human flesh to serve as a substitute for human sin, which is understood to be a violation of God's law and entailing a penalty that humans themselves cannot pay.

Theism: Term literally means "Godism." It is a description of reality developed since the Enlightenment that understands God as existing alongside the world and intervening in it from time to time.

Theodicy: Attempt to explain the compatibility between an all-good and all-powerful God and the existence of evil.

Theological literalism: Theological position that accepts historical criticism and yet, overall, remains theologically conservative in affirming direct divine intervention in history according to the main pattern of the biblical story and articulated creedally by the church.

Theological reinterpreters: Theological position that affirms the need to make a serious reformulation of traditional Christian ideas to make Christianity relevant to modern people. They deny direct divine intervention in history, regarding it as a type of religious experience.

Theology of hope: Theology often associated with the early work of Jürgen Moltmann, which focuses on the eschatological meaning for the world of the saving events of Jesus' crucifixion and resurrection.

Third wave feminism: Emergence of a variety of voices testifying to interlocking layers of oppression in feminist theology.

Transcendence: In classical theology, this refers to God's exceeding of the world, including all categories of the human intellect.

Trinity: In classical Christian theology, this refers to the idea that God is one being and three persons: Father, Son, and Spirit. The Trinity presupposes that God became incarnate in the human person Jesus and God is present in the church through the Spirit.

Truths of reason: Truths discovered through natural theology.

Truths of revelation: Truths discovered through revealed theology.

Two-fold method of biblical interpretation: In feminist theology, the approach to the biblical text that involves the critique of patriarchy and appropriation of liberating themes.

Underdevelopment or negation of the self: Idea originally promoted by feminist Valerie Saiving that the unique problem of women is not pride but the denial or suppression of one's capacities and abilities.

Unfalsifiable: Position that is closed to the influence of critical reflection.

Universal forms: In Platonic thought, these are eternal, unchanging, and perfected essences of things that are separate from the finite and changing things of the universe, which are imperfect copies.

Universal moral laws: Laws of a binding character that transcend any particular culture and determine right or wrong actions.

Universalism: Position in Christian theology that all humanity will eventually be saved.

Vatican II: Church council that met from 1962 to 1965 and took decisive steps in opening the Roman Catholic Church to the modern world.

Wisdom tradition: Part of biblical tradition that affirms the capacity of humans to see evidence of God and God's purposes in creation apart from God's special revelation in history.

Word or wisdom of God: In ancient Jewish thought, this is the aspect of God that is the source of the order in the universe.

Works-righteousness: People vainly trying to make themselves right before God by their own efforts.

Worldview: Set of background presuppositions about reality that is held by the people of a particular era.

Womanist theology: Branch of feminist theology from the perspective of African American women.

Yahweh: Personal name of God in the Old Testament.

Index